Australian Politics and Government
The Commonwealth, the States and the Territ

Australian Politics and Government is the first comprehensive comparative study of Australian state and Commonwealth governments and their politics for over forty years. In addition to major chapters on each state in the Australian federation, the book includes chapters on the Commonwealth government and the two self-governing territories, the Australian Capital Territory and the Northern Territory. These are supplemented by a chapter summarizing the distinctive characteristics of Australian government and its various components.

The chapters are written by leading scholars in the field, and use a common analytical framework to chart the evolution of each political system over the last century and to provide an understanding of their current operation. The book is supplemented by charts, an extensive bibliography and a comprehensive index. It is ideal as a reference on Australian government today, and as a textbook on Australian politics.

Australian Politics and Government has been written to link with the Australian Government and Politics website (http://elections. uwa.edu.au). This website is based on a searchable database which contains a wealth of information on Australian government and politics since 1890.

Jeremy Moon is Professor of Corporate Social Responsibility at the Nottingham University Business School. Previously he taught in the Department of Political Science at the University of Western Australia for fifteen years.

Campbell Sharman has been an Associate Professor in the Department of Political Science at the University of Western Australia for many years, and is currently at the University of British Columbia, Canada.

AUSTRALIAN POLITICS AND GOVERNMENT

THE COMMONWEALTH, THE STATES AND THE TERRITORIES

Edited by

Jeremy Moon
Nottingham University
and
Campbell Sharman
University of British Columbia

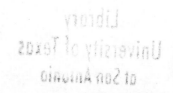

PUBLISHED BY THE PRESS SYNDICATE OF THE UNIVERSITY OF CAMBRIDGE
The Pitt Building, Trumpington Street, Cambridge, United Kingdom

CAMBRIDGE UNIVERSITY PRESS
The Edinburgh Building, Cambridge CB2 2RU, UK
40 West 20th Street, New York, NY 10011–4211, USA
477 Williamstown Road, Port Melbourne, VIC 3207, Australia
Ruiz de Alarcón 13, 28014 Madrid, Spain
Dock House, The Waterfront, Cape Town 8001, South Africa

http://www.cambridge.org

First published 2003

Printed in Australia by Ligare Pty Ltd

Typeface – (*Sabon*) 10/12 pt. *System* QuarkXPress® [MK]

A catalogue record for this book is available from the British Library

National Library of Australia Cataloguing in Publication data
Australian politics and government: the Commonwealth, the
states and the territories.

  Bibliography
  Includes index.
  ISBN 0 521 82507 5
  ISBN 0 521 53205 1 (pbk.).

  1. Federal government – Australia. 2. Australia – Politics
  and government. I. Moon, Jeremy. II. Sharman, Campbell.

320.994

ISBN 0 521 82507 5 hardback
ISBN 0 521 53205 1 paperback

Contents

Contributors

BRIAN COSTAR is Associate Professor in the School of Political and Social Inquiry at Monash University in Melbourne. His research and teaching interests are in the field of Australian politics, and especially the politics of regional Australia and the state of Victoria on which he has published extensively over the last twenty years. Books which he has co-authored or edited include *The Kennett Revolution: Victorian Politics in the 1990s* (1999), *For Better or for Worse: The Federal Coalition* (1994), *Trials in Power: Cain, Kirner and Victoria 1982–1992* (1992), and *Country to National: Australian Rural Politics and Beyond* (1985).

NICK ECONOMOU is Senior Lecturer in the School of Political and Social Inquiry at Monash University in Melbourne. He has published on Australian politics with particular emphasis on state politics and state elections. He is co-author with Brian Costar of *The Kennett Revolution: Victorian Politics in the 1990s* (1999) and has published articles on environmental politics, federal elections, and the changing role of by-elections. He is also an occasional commentator on Victorian politics for the Australian Broadcasting Corporation and commercial radio stations in Melbourne

JENNY FLEMING lectures in the School of Industrial Relations at Griffith University in Brisbane where she has been a Research Fellow in the Key Centre for Ethics, Law, Justice and Governance. Her research and publishing interests include public policy, the politics of criminal justice, police unionism and governance. She is co-editor of *Motivating Ministers to Morality* (2001) and *Government Reformed: Values and New Political Institutions* (2002).

DEAN JAENSCH is Adjunct Professor in the School of Political and International Studies at Flinders University. In his long and distinguished academic career, he has been author and co-author of more than twenty books on Australian politics, and has written widely on Northern Territory politics. His research interests are Australian politics, political parties and electoral behaviour. He is also a leading media commentator on Australian public affairs.

AYNSLEY KELLOW is Professor of Government at the University of Tasmania. A graduate of Otago University, his research interests include public policy, environmental politics and policy, and interest groups. After a period at the University of Tasmania, he taught at Deakin and Griffith universities, before returning to the University of

Tasmania in 1999. He is co-editor of *Globalization and the Environment* (2001) and author of *Transforming Power: The Politics of Electricity Planning* (1996).

JEREMY MOON worked in the Political Science Department, University of Western Australia from 1985 to 2000 holding positions from Lecturer to Associate Professor and Head. His research interests in Australian politics focus on partisanship, the determinants of public policy and new forms of governance. He is currently Professor and Director, International Centre for Corporate Social Responsibility, Nottingham University.

ANDREW PARKIN is Professor of Political and International Studies at Flinders University, and editor of the *Australian Journal of Political Science*. Among his works on South Australian politics are his editorship of *South Australia, Federalism and Public Policy* (1996), *The Bannon Decade* (1992), and *The Dunstan Decade* (1981), and contributions to *The Wakefield Companion to South Australian History* (2001) and *Flinders History of South Australia* (1986). He has also published widely on urban politics and party politics in Australia and is the co-editor of the most successful introductory textbook on Australian politics.

CAMPBELL SHARMAN is a former member of the Political Science Department at the University of Western Australia and is now a Senior Honorary Research Fellow with the School of Social and Cultural Studies. He also holds an honorary position with the Political Science Department of the University of British Columbia in Vancouver where he continues work on the Australian Government and Politics Database, and research on Australian and comparative politics.

RODNEY SMITH is Senior Lecturer in the Discipline of Government and International Relations at the University of Sydney. He is author of *Australian Political Culture* (2001) and *The New South Wales State Election 1999* (2000) and editor of *Politics in Australia* (1997). His journal articles and chapters in edited books include studies of the New South Wales parliament during the Greiner–Fahey era, the New South Wales branch of the Australian Democrats and New South Wales political ethics and corruption. Among other things, he is currently working on a study of Bob Carr for a book on the New South Wales premiers.

PAUL STRANGIO is a lecturer in the National Centre of Australian Studies of Monash University. His most recent book is *Keeper of the*

Faith: A Biography of Jim Cairns (2002). Dr Strangio is a frequent media commentator on Australian and Victorian state politics.

JOHN WANNA is Professor in the School of Politics and Public Policy at Griffith University. His research interests include government budgeting and expenditure management, public policy, government–business relations and parliamentary scrutiny. He has co-authored a number of books and articles on Australian politics including *From Accounting to Accountability* (2001), *Public Expenditure Management in Australia* (2000), and *Public Policy In Australia* (1993). He has also published widely on aspects of Queensland politics and government and co-edited *The Goss Government: Promise And Performance of Labor in Queensland* (1993).

JOHN WARHURST is Professor of Political Science at the Australian National University and was previously Professor of Politics at the University of New England. He writes about Australian politics, particularly elections, political parties and constitutional politics. His two most recent publications are *2001: The Centenary Election* (edited with Marian Simms, 2003) and *Constitutional Politics: The Republic Referendum and the Future* (edited with Malcolm Mackerras, 2003).

PATRICK WELLER AO has been Professor of Politics and Public Policy at Griffith University since 1984. He has degrees from Oxford University, the Australian National University and Griffith University. He is the author of a number of books on Australian and comparative politics, including *Don't tell the Prime Minister* (2002), *Australia's Mandarins: The Frank and the Fearless?* (2001), *Malcolm Fraser PM* (1989), *First Among Equals: Prime Ministers in Westminster Systems* (1985), and (with Michelle Grattan) *Can Ministers Cope?* (1981).

Figures and Tables

Figures

Tables

Acknowledgements

The idea for this book grew out of a research project started by the editors in 1995, when both of us were members of the Political Science Department at the University of Western Australia. The goal was to make a comparative analysis of the politics and government of the Australian states, and the project managed to gain funding from an Australian Research Council Large Grant in 1995. A component of the research was to set up a computer database which would permit systematic comparison of parties, representation and government in the states, based on the invaluable collection of information amassed by Colin Hughes and his associates at the Australian National University in the 1960s and published in *A Handbook of Australian Government and Politics 1890–1964* (Hughes and Graham 1968) and its supplements (see Note on Sources and Links to the Web, page 263). As with most such projects, it proved to be more complicated and time consuming than we first thought. We were fortunate enough to gain further funding for the project from a National Council for the Centenary of Federation grant in 1999, through the History and Education Program. This enabled us to redesign what is now the Australian Government and Politics Project database and to produce the Australian Government and Politics website (http://elections.uwa.edu.au). The grant also prompted the planning of this volume and assisted in funding much of the research on which the book is based.

While we are happy to acknowledge the vital role played by the Australian Research Council and the National Council for the Centenary of Federation in funding the research on which this book is based, we would also like to acknowledge the continuing support of the University of Western Australia, and what is now the School of Social and Cultural Studies in the Faculty of Arts, Humanities and Social Sciences. The University's administrative and financial support over the life of the project has been an essential component for its success and for the completion of this volume. In this respect, we would like to thank Linley Hill, the administrative officer for Political Science, for her unstinting helpfulness in all matters involving the administration of the project.

We would like to acknowledge the patience of the contributors as well as thanking them for their contributions; there must have been times when they doubted whether the volume would ever be brought to a conclusion. This might also be said of Peter Debus and Paul Watt at Cambridge University Press and we thank them and their colleagues for accommodating the delays to which this undertaking has been prone, and the complications of having authors and editors spread over three continents.

While the great bulk of the research for this volume has been under-taken at the University of Western Australia, most of the final editing and indexing has been undertaken in the Political Science Department at the University of British Columbia. We would like to thank the Department and its head, Richard Johnston, for their assistance. And we thank David Clune of the New South Wales Parliamentary Library, and Bruce Stone in Political Science at the University of Western Australia for providing some elusive references at short notice for the completion of the appendix and bibliography.

Jeremy Moon
Campbell Sharman

Chapter

Introduction

Campbell Sharman and Jeremy Moon

The centenary of federation marks the growth of the Commonwealth government from a single public servant on 1 January 1901 to its current role as a national government with involvement, direct or indirect, in almost every area of public policy. This growth has taken place in the context of a federal system whose other components, the states, have also seen a massive expansion of their role over the last hundred years. If there was a major theme to the history of democratic politics in the twentieth century it was the extension of government in response to the ever-expanding expectations of citizens and voters.

In the Australian context, this enlargement of the role of government has been inextricably linked to the evolution of the federal system. The states, now joined by the Northern Territory and the Australian Capital Territory, continue to deliver the great bulk of the day-to-day services expected of government – health, education, transport, the maintenance of public order, land use and the host of regulations affecting social and economic transactions of all kinds. But, in addition to its stated constitutional responsibilities for international relations and commercially related issues extending across the federation, the central government is now involved to some degree in most areas of public policy making. This has been achieved in large part through the leverage that the Commonwealth's superior access to taxation revenue has given it in making conditional grants to the states; in several important areas, the constitutional interpretations of the High Court have also been of major importance in extending the influence of the national government.

The result has been a system of government with seven major players – nine since the addition of the self-governing territories in the 1980s – all of whom are critical components for the delivery of public services and the regulation of social and economic life. The system appears complex because of its goal of incorporating representative government and popular involvement at both the national and regional levels but, by any measure, it has been extremely successful. It has coped, without substantial structural change, with world wars, depression, unprecedented social, economic and technological change, and the expectation that government will provide or regulate a range of services and activities undreamt of in 1901. And this has been done in the context of a system of representative democracy and the preservation of a high level of personal and political freedom.

Institutional themes

In celebrating the centenary of federation it is natural to focus initially on those institutions which originated in 1901. But in the hundred years since federation there have been equally dramatic changes in the institutions which had their origins in the nineteenth century. Nor is it always easy to draw a clear line between the new and the continuing. Take the Commonwealth itself. The governmental institutions of the Commonwealth grew out of debates and constitutional conferences that spanned the 1890s. These, in turn, sprang from intercolonial co-operation and competition that had begun almost as soon the Australian colonies achieved self-government in the 1850s. Most important of all, the ideas about parliamentary government on which the Commonwealth is based grew out of the previous experience of colonial self-government.

This experience had substantially modified the operation of British-style parliamentary government by the time of the federation debates in the 1890s. To begin with, all the self-governing Australian colonies had constitutional documents setting out the broad details and legislative powers of their popular assemblies. In addition, key sections of these documents had a special status indicated by procedural restraints on the process of amendment. Such arrangements made some areas of government activity open to challenge in the courts, a form of constitutional limitation and judicial review that was outside the British tradition of so-called parliamentary sovereignty. Of greater political significance, all six colonies had a tradition of strong bicameralism with a powerful upper house designed to check the excesses of a popular assembly. With the exception of New South Wales and Queensland, these upper houses were elected and had enough political legitimacy to make vigorous use of their constitutional powers, to the annoyance of many colonial governments. While there was some similarity with the House of Lords before 1911, this body was a feudal remnant which, unlike colonial upper houses, was not part of a nineteenth-century design for limited representative government.

There were many characteristics the new national government of the Commonwealth shared with the colonial experience of self-government and which gave it a form which differed substantially from the British parliamentary tradition: the importance of the Commonwealth Constitution as a document setting out the operation and powers of the legislature; the existence of a constitutional document that had special status as a higher law, with the possibility of constitutional challenge in some areas through judicial review; and a powerful upper house with popular legitimacy. Nor should this borrowing be at all surprising since it was from among some of the most able and experienced colonial politicians that the framers of the Commonwealth Constitution can be found. They wanted to replicate at the national level of the new federation a system of parliamentary government which was familiar to them and accommodated their aspirations for a broadly based representative democracy acceptable to the six political communities that were to comprise the new federation.

It is also true that the new Commonwealth modified and strengthened these colonial traditions. The Commonwealth Constitution was a comprehensive statement of the powers of the national government and specified its key components, with the notable exception of the office of prime minister and the operation of a parliamentary executive. The Constitution was not only entrenched in its entirety but its status as a higher law was reflected in an amending procedure that required the endorsement of a popular referendum, an innovation which grew from the popularity of direct democracy and the Progressive movement of the 1890s. The Senate as the upper chamber of a bicameral federal parliament had all the features of the most powerful of the state legislative councils in 1901 except that its franchise was as wide as that of the lower house, and its constituencies were the six state political communities rather than wealthy and conservative interests.

It can be argued that directly elected, powerful upper houses in a parliamentary system are Australia's contribution to the repertoire of representative democracy; they are currently a distinctive feature of six of the nine parliamentary systems in the Australian federation. While the composition of the Senate is closely tied to the federal system, its place in the parliamentary process is very much in the tradition established by elective colonial legislative councils. The changing role that these chambers have played in both state and federal politics is one of the issues considered in the chapters which follow.

Federalism and the states

There is no question that the federation of the six Australian self-governing colonies, their transformation into the six component states of the new Commonwealth of Australia, and the creation of a national government with substantial areas of responsibility, represented a radical change to the system of government for the Australian colonies. Yet, even here, federation reflected the pre-existing realities of Australian society and government rather than the imposition of something completely new. By the end of the nineteenth century, the growth of European settlement had come to be characterised by expansion from a few large urban centres spread widely across the southern part of the continent. These had become the capitals of six largely autonomous political communities. While linked by a common political origin and attachment to British traditions and style of government, each was shaped by a distinctive set of economic and political concerns. One of the claims for colonial self-government and the creation of new colonies had been the demand for both the ability to deal with the issues that were peculiar to each political community, and the freedom to deal with common problems in ways which suited the preferences of local citizens – the same justifications which underpin the adoption of a federal system.

By the end of the 1890s all the Australian colonies were justly proud of their achievements in both the economic and social spheres, especially Western Australia for whom self-government had been delayed until 1890 because of its small European population and large geographic size. Even though the commercial benefits of some form of union were clear, it could not be at the cost of limiting local autonomy in the great bulk of government activities. For this reason alone, federation was the only acceptable form of union. This made the United States model of federal union attractive because the political autonomy of the state political communities could be better protected. Following this model, a narrow list of specified powers was granted to the new central government with the remainder left to the jurisdiction of the states. It is something of a paradox that, by the end of the first century of federation, the Commonwealth Constitution has not prevented the central government from intervening in almost every sphere of state policy making, and yet the centre of gravity for political and government activity remains with the states. In 2001 as in 1901, federation reflected the geographical dispersal and different political preferences of the political communities which make up the Commonwealth.

The importance of federalism for this study is not so much the network of financial transfers and intergovernmental arrangements which have come to characterize the operation of parliamentary federations, but the fact that the states have persisted as the dominant agencies for the delivery of most public services. Over the last forty years, policy in an increasing array of subjects has been shaped by the preferences of the Commonwealth but its involvement in most fields has been indirect. It is state and territory public servants who staff hospitals and schools, provide fire and police services, and regulate traffic, urban growth and local government. This means that, notwithstanding the financial dependence of the states on Commonwealth transfers for much of their revenue, the states still play a critical role in the formation, execution and administration of public policy. The states remain as major components of the federal system whose governmental systems and politics deserve as much interest and celebration as the Commonwealth government with which they are inextricably linked. The centenary of federation is a centenary for all its constituent parts.

Representation

While federalism was a new governmental form for Australia, other aspects of the new national government built on pre-existing assumptions about representative democracy. In addition to the institutions of colonial parliamentary government, the Commonwealth government went even further than the states in extending the scope of popular representation and involvement in the governmental process. The Australian colonies had been adventurous in extending the franchise for their popular assemblies and in pioneering such electoral innovations as the secret ballot. Women had gained the vote in South Australia in 1894 and most states had universal franchise for their lower houses by 1901. Although the right to vote was not specified in the Constitution, there was a presumption that the new Commonwealth should operate in a context of broadly based popular representation.

The Commonwealth Constitution extended popular involvement in two ways which were new to the Australian context. The first was to adopt a broad popular franchise for the choice of members of the federal upper house, the Senate, even though the method of elections meant that each state elected an equal number of senators irrespective of the state's population. This feature was seen as undemocratic by many of the residents of the two most populous states, particularly New South Wales, because it was based on equal representation of political communities rather than individual citizens. Apart from the political reality that equality of state representation in the Senate was insisted upon by the smaller states as a condition for joining the federal union, the move to universal franchise for the selection of members of an upper house in a parliamentary system was itself a major extension of popular representation.

The other feature was the use of the referendum both as a means of gaining initial popular approval of the Commonwealth Constitution and as a requirement for any subsequent amendment. While used in the Swiss federation, such a measure was alien to the British parliamentary tradition and had not been used to provide popular legitimacy or an amendment procedure for either the United States or the Canadian federations. The inclusion of the referendum procedure for Australia grew out of a political need to demonstrate widespread support for union as well as a contemporary concern with the encouragement of popular involvement in government expressed. The experience of the Commonwealth and subsequent use of the constitutional referendum in Australian state politics has, until very recently, been seen less as a way of encouraging popular involvement than making constitutional change difficult for one's partisan opponents. If the Progressives in the 1890s saw the referendum as an opportunity for innovation, the experience of both Commonwealth and state politics over the last 100 years has been that the constitutional referendum has been a conservative device, an issue which is touched on in several of the chapters which follow.

To these two novel aspects of representation could almost have been added a third. Proportional representation was raised in the 1890s as an electoral system suitable for the choice of members of the Commonwealth Senate, but this was not adopted either as part of the chamber's constitutional design or by successive Commonwealth governments for the first half-century of federation. Its adoption for the choice of senators from 1949 has helped to transform the operation of the Senate by working to reduce the ability of the two largest parties to control majorities in the chamber. It is tempting to speculate about what would have been the effect of proportional representation on the Commonwealth government had it been adopted from 1901.

The propensity for electoral innovation – some would say manipulation for partisan advantage – did not end with federation. In both national and state spheres, there has been continuing experimentation with every aspect of the rules affecting elections, campaigning and representation. Preferential voting (the alternative vote) has been tried in all jurisdictions since the 1920s, as has compulsory voting (attendance). A variety of forms of proportional representation have been tried for both lower and upper houses in a number of states, and there have been many schemes for ballot design, campaign finance rules and, more recently, the public funding of elections. Above all, there has been a longstanding debate over the definition, extent and justification of malapportionment – the extent to which the number of voters varies between electoral districts. The political effects of malapportionment may not have been as extensive as its fiercest critics have argued but it has been a factor in shaping the composition of state and Commonwealth lower houses for much of the last century. The willingness of Australian governments to experiment with the system of representation, usually for partisan gain, has ensured that every chapter in this collection deals with changes to some aspect of the electoral rules that have had a significant effect on the political process.

Party

Talking about representation without bringing in political parties is like the sound of one hand clapping – something that is impossible to imagine. Yet the political parties we know today did not emerge in their current form until well into the 1900s. If federation led to a profound structural change in government, the emergence of the modern mass political party has had an equally powerful effect on the nature of politics in Australia.

There had been political parties in the Australian colonies as long as there had been self-government but these had been groupings of likeminded members of parliament clustered around particular policies or leaders, or held together by the benefits of being in office. These groupings were often unstable and few had any organizational structure which extended outside parliament or lasted longer than an election campaign. The engine of change was the rise of the Australian Labor Party (ALP). Based on a coalition of labour unions, groups favouring social and economic change and a few with radical socialist ideas, the ALP emerged in the 1890s and steadily acquired the characteristics that made it both organizationally distinctive and electorally successful. Of greatest importance, it was a party based on an organization outside parliament – its basic premiss was that parliamentarians who were elected under its banner were the servants of the party and not its masters. Candidates had to pledge their loyalty to the party and, if elected to parliament, were expected to vote according to party decisions. The enforcement of strict party discipline transformed the parliamentary process and the relationship between parliament and the government.

The electoral implications were equally far-reaching. Growing out of its commitment to control by its membership, the ALP was a programmatic party in the sense that it campaigned less on the virtues of its candidates, local concerns and single issues, and more on a comprehensive set of policies it would carry out if it won government. This style of politics was endorsed by an increasing proportion of the voters until, in 1910, the ALP won a majority of seats in the House of Representatives. This event was equally significant for other parties. The success of the ALP prompted the fusion of the major anti-ALP parties to form the Liberal Party, a party which, in spite of several changes of name and significant organizational evolution, has continued to be the major rival of the ALP ever since. The success of the ALP also ensured that its style of party politics was adopted by its opponents and continues to characterise the party system today.

Within a year or two of 1910, similar developments had occurred in state politics and a pattern of political rivalry between the ALP and the Liberal Party was established across Australia. This pattern was, however, neither uniform nor stable for the first half of the century. Not only did the emergence of the Country Party (now National Party) around 1918 change the shape of non-ALP politics in most states and in the federal sphere, but war, depression and social change led to major upheavals in all parties and turmoil in the party system until the 1940s.

In spite of a largely stable pattern of competition between the ALP and non-ALP parties after the second world war, it would be wrong to suggest that there have been no significant changes since 1945 or that there are no major differences between the party systems of the states – much of the chapters that follow analyses the idiosyncrasies of state and federal party politics, the insurgence of new parties and the pattern of success and failure of old ones. But, in spite of the fluctuating importance of minor parties, the pattern of a largely dichotomous party system has persisted in all states except Queensland, partly encouraged by the nature of parliamentary government and opposition, and partly induced by the continuing importance of the ALP as, more often than not, the party gaining the most votes at general elections.

This has meant that the major source of variation between political systems in the federation has been on the non-Labor side of politics, and in the variety and importance of minor party and independent candidates represented in parliaments. Such variation has provided many of the distinctive features of politics and government in each system and the rise of new parties continues to be a way in which new groups and issues are incorporated into the political process.

Government and policy

Parties play a critical role in winning office but there are many other factors that are important in the running of government and the framing of public policy. A host of groups ranging from rural, commercial and industrial interests to lobby groups of all kinds want an equally diverse range of government action – legislation, planning permission, exemptions, and government subsidies and public expenditure for an equally diverse set of projects and good causes. Harmonizing all these claims and incorporating some idea of the public interest is a major task of government. The chapters in this collection show how each government has been shaped by the differing sets of demands put upon it and how each has responded in its own way.

While framing policy is clearly a political activity, the implementation of policy can also be important in shaping the final outcome. The administrative agencies of government are themselves participants in the governmental process and the way in which the structure of government is arranged can have a major effect on the style of government. Australian governments have shown great ingenuity in creating structures for delivering public services and there has been considerable variation in the way they have responded to changes in the scope and range of government activity. The number and designations of ministerial portfolios, for example, have varied considerably over the last hundred years, indicating both the modification of the scope of government and the changing pattern of political concerns.

Identifying a style of politics and government can be difficult, but the idea that a system has a distinctive way of coping with political issues is an attractive one. It is a way of combining persistent historical and institutional factors with those that spring from the social and economic profile of the political community, all of which can be blended with political traditions and more immediate political issues of importance to the community. One of the purposes of the chapters which follow is to give a feel for the differing styles of politics that have characterized the components of the Australian federation. Australians may think that their system of government is relatively new but, in comparison with the histories of present-day representative democracies, a hundred years of continuous operation is a long time and certainly long enough to develop a rich and varied tradition. Revealing and exploring this richness is the purpose of this collection.

Contents of this book

The chapters in this collection pursue the themes of representation, party and style of government for the Commonwealth, the six states and two self-governing territories which comprise the Australian federation. While these themes run through all the chapters, there are variations in stress to accommodate the idiosyncrasies of each political system. For the Commonwealth (chapter 2), the distinguishing issues are the growth since 1901 in political influence of a newly created national government, its accommodation of the complexities of partisan change over the century, and the way its governmental structure has been shaped by its involvement in an ever-increasing range of policy areas.

With a political history that long predates federation, a component of all the state chapters is the recognition of the influence of the period of self-government before 1901. This constitutional inheritance is important for all states in affecting both the operation of parliamentary institutions and the style of government over the last hundred years. Another common theme is the importance of the Australian Labor Party as the largest party in terms of vote share for most general elections. But the extent to which this has been reflected in the control of government has varied widely between the states, from extensive periods of Labor government in New South Wales, Queensland and Tasmania, to much more modest success in Victoria. The theme of partisan dominance is a major component of the chapters on New South Wales (chapter 3) and Victoria (chapter 7), and is an important part of the analysis of other states.

Social and economic changes have presented state governments with persistent challenges. For the smaller states in particular, this has presented problems that have dominated the political agenda. Slow economic growth and rival approaches to fostering state development have been major issues in Tasmanian politics (chapter 6), and have coloured much of the political debate in South Australia (chapter 5). But, even in those states which have grown most rapidly, economic development has posed political difficulties. For Queensland, the issue of harmonizing the political interests of the burgeoning south-east of the state around Brisbane with the resource-rich hinterland of the state has long coloured the state's politics and continues to present conflicting demands on the state government (chapter 4). In a similar fashion, successive West Australian governments have had to cope with the rival claims of suburban Perth and the demands of regional areas across a vast and diverse area (chapter 8).

The latest additions to the Australian federal system – the self-governing territories of the Australian Capital Territory (chapter 9) and the Northern Territory (chapter 10) – present strong contrasts across almost every dimension of political activity. Their patterns of partisanship, systems of representation, parliamentary operation and style of government are at opposite ends of the range to be found across Australia. As such, they are useful correctives to the view that the Australian political experience is uniform. And, as the territories differ in both socio-economic and demographic characteristics as well as in their electoral systems, their experience raises questions about the relative effect of social factors and institutional design on the shape of political activity.

This issue might be seen as the central theme of the whole collection; the way in which institutional design interacts with social context to create the politics of any given community. Almost all Australia's governmental institutions were based on a narrow repertoire taken from nineteenth-century British imperial and colonial experience. Yet, once established, each political system produced its own distinctive politics and, over time, modified the institutions to suit local preferences. This process began with the self-government of the Australian colonies in the 1850s and has accelerated since federation. The result is an array of lively variations on the theme of parliamentary representative democracy, matched with an equally competitive set of partisan rivalries and varied governmental regimes, the nature of which are explored in the concluding chapter.

The bottom line is that the Australian federation remains a vigorous set of political communities – national, state, and territory – each with its own governmental institutions and political style. The goal of a federal union which would preserve a measure of local autonomy and distinctiveness with the benefits of national regulation of common problems has proved to be as attractive in 2001 as it was in 1901.

Chapter

The Commonwealth

Patrick Weller and Jenny Fleming

The Commonwealth government was born of compromise and reared on opportunism. The centenarian of 2001 is unlike the infant conceived by its progenitors in 1901. Its powers are greater, its influence more extensive. The number of departments has fluctuated. Seven departments in 1901 grew to a maximum of twenty-eight in 1985 and more recently was reduced to eighteen but with no reduction in the scope of Commonwealth government action. The programs and budgets of the federal government have become dominant in regulating the level of government activity and the direction of the economy in Australia. Federal politics is the big game, the one that is perceived as making the greatest difference. Yet the changes to the Constitution created in 1901 have been incremental and minimal; successful moves to expand the formal authority of the federal government have been few.

Changes to the provisions of the Constitution were to be determined by referendums, with support from a majority of states and a majority of voters. But such proposals for constitutional change have a record of failure. Since 1901 Australians have voted on forty-four proposals to alter the Constitution, the most recent being the proposal to make Australia a republic, a proposal that failed. Constitutional referendums have been successful on only eight occasions, demonstrating a general reluctance on the part of Australians to allow the government in Canberra any greater control.[1] But this reluctance to accept formal constitutional change has not prevented a transfer of power from the states to the federal government.

There seems now to be little in common with the small country of 1901 and the larger more complex society today. In 1911 the population was just over 4.5 million; fewer than 120 000 (under 4 per cent) were born in countries other than Australia and the other parts of what was then the British Empire. By 2001 the total population had grown to 19 million with 13 per cent born in places other than the old commonwealth.

The same holds for the economy. In 1901 Australia was, in comparative terms, wealthy and stable. Gradually, other countries have caught up and passed its standing in terms of per capita income. In the first fourteen years of its history, the new Commonwealth government appeared as though it would follow a radical path as the Australian Labor Party gained in strength in both federal and state politics. The new protectionism of the Deakin government was followed by a reforming Labor government under Andrew Fisher, who had felt able to say that 'we are all socialists now'. But it was followed by thirty years of hardship: two world wars and a great depression scarred the society, with few families escaping the twin torment of casualty lists and unemployment. After 1945 there were new ideas available to government. Encouraged by the ideas of Keynes, the government set out a manifesto for full employment and a greater involvement in the economic life of the society. Immigration from a wide range of European nations, especially those people displaced by war, provided a mix of cultures. Australia too began to play a more significant and positive role in international affairs. Threats of invasion had made it less a British outpost tied by strings of heritage and more conscious of regional interests after 1945. In the cold war that dominated international relations from 1945 to 1989, the perceived threat of communism drove the Australian government into alliance with the United States, an alliance that was to commit it to sending troops to the wars in Korea and Vietnam in the 1950s and 1960s.

If fear of communism and perceptions of class were the dividing chasms of Australian politics, gradually both subsided, to be largely eliminated by the time of the fall of the Soviet empire in 1989. By then, Australia's engagement with the world was complete. Better transportation, an international economy, trade with the regional countries, particularly Japan, and the growth of international capital all meant that Australia's peripheral status was over. It now had to compete on the international economic stage. Divisions between the Labor and Liberal–National parties declined as both adopted a similar approach to economic management, born of necessity and the adoption of a more limited view of the role of the state in providing services. Whether governments delivered programs, or used others to deliver them, has become a matter of convenience rather than ideology. The age of big government might be over, but there is little sign that governments are doing less or have fewer responsibilities. The world in which the government must live and work is now very different but it is the style that has changed rather than the aims of government. This has had major implications for the operation of the federal system and the balance between national and state government.

In this chapter we trace developments in four areas: the electoral rules that the federal government introduced, which in turn shape the political battle between the parties and determine the shape of parliamentary representation; the patterns of partisanship over the century, both in terms of electoral support and parliamentary strength; the growth in federal ministerial portfolios and the distribution of responsibilities; and the management of government. It provides an explanation for the growth of Commonwealth power and the way that it has been used to create a national political culture.

The Constitution and system of government

The founders of the Commonwealth Constitution accepted, almost without dispute, the British system of parliamentary government for the new Commonwealth, a system which had already been adapted to the needs of Australians as the Australian colonies gained self-government after 1850. The Commonwealth government would have to maintain a majority in the House of Representatives, from which most ministers would be drawn. The prime minister would be the leader of the largest party and would need to maintain its support. None of these conventions were written into the Constitution of 1901 which made no mention of the prime minister or cabinet. According to the Constitution, the executive power of the Commonwealth was vested in the governor-general, as the agent of the monarch. But everyone knew that these words were perfunctory, reflecting British practice. As it did in Britain, political power lay with the parliament, and by virtue of parliament's authority, within the cabinet (see generally, Galligan 1995; Reid and Forrest 1989).

But there were several questions that had to be determined. One was state representation in the Senate. The smaller states, concerned that New South Wales and Victoria would dominate the parliament, insisted that the Senate, like its United States counterpart, have an equal number of senators from each state; in 1901 the number was six. There was also a nexus between the two houses, with the House of Representatives to be, 'as near as practicable', twice the size of the upper house. As a consequence, if the numbers in the House of Representatives were to be increased as the population grew, so too was it necessary to increase the number of senators elected by each state. An attempt to break that nexus was put to the people in a referendum in 1967, but although it had the support of both major parties it was defeated by a campaign that argued against more politicians. Perversely, the defeat ensured there were to be more. As the House of Representatives has been expanded from seventy-five seats in 1901 to around 150 in 2000, so the Senate had to grow from thirty-six to seventy-six.[2]

The Constitution gave to the Senate almost equal power to the lower house. Even if it could not initiate money bills, it could make suggestions for change, and was not obliged at any stage to accept the proposals from the more popularly elected house. Elected and powerful, the Senate could threaten the existence of the government. At the constitutional conventions which framed the Constitution in the 1890s, only one delegate prophesied that the Senate would immediately become a party house and not a states' house (see Bolton 2000).

The founders of the Constitution also had to determine what powers would be given to the new national parliament. There were two models that could be followed. One was the Canadian model which gave specified powers to both the central government and the provinces and left some residual powers to the national government; the other was that of the United States of America which prescribed the powers of the national government and left all the remainder to the states or to the citizenry. The Australian Constitution followed the American model, listing the powers that were to be exercised by the national parliament, with a High Court to be responsible for determining whether the federal legislation was within the allocated powers whenever there was a challenge to its constitutionality. The intention was that the great majority of powers were to be left to the state governments (La Nauze 1972), particularly the responsibility to deliver the regular services of government to its citizens, for example, health, law and order and education.

Initially, the national government's financial discretion was restricted: it could collect customs and excise duties and other taxes, but was required to return three-quarters of the revenue to the states. The founders had a clear concept of a limited national government, a view that reflected assumptions about the constrained role and capacity of national governments at the turn of the century and pride in the accomplishments of state governments. Had federation come a decade or so later it might have been different. As it was, the Constitution inevitably reflected contemporary attitudes and interests, that is, the interests of the middle-class lawyers and merchants who drew it up.

There was no one from the working class at the constitutional conventions; most of those who wrote the Constitution were themselves state politicians, some of whom hoped to pursue their careers in the parliament of the newly formed nation.

The Constitution contained a number of contradictions, combining British and American experience to such a degree that some observers speak of a 'Washminster' model. It incorporated Britain's parliamentary system and the concepts of responsible government without question. But it was also a federal government, with an upper house with greater power and authority than the British model. Federalism and strong elective bicameralism did not sit easily with the principle of parliamentary and responsible government. The powers of the federal government were spelt out, but there were within the Constitution a number of clauses that gave precedence to the decisions of the federal government and allowed it, after a period of time, to make its own decision about the best methods of funding, consistent with the other parts of the Constitution (Galligan 1995).

The picture of a national government with limited powers and small expenditure is not one that is readily recognisable today. From the beginning, federal politicians began to exercise their wits to develop and expand their powers. Over the century, the gradual accretion of authority greatly modified the balance of power.

What are the driving forces for change in the federal balance and for the expansion of federal power? In part, as we have suggested, they were circumstantial. War helped create a sense of nationhood. Communications improved to tame some of the problems of distance. Economic thought developed so that the government could play a more constructive role in shaping the fortunes of the nation. As Asia became more significant trade patterns changed. The British Empire crumbled and decayed as Australia became more independent and confident. Perhaps it was inevitable that Australia's national government would begin to be seen as the epitome of the nation, its leaders the national symbols.

In part the forces were constitutional. The Constitution had to be agreed between the delegates of the states but in several places the final wording was the result of a last minute compromise designed to allow the federal government to become established even if the wording was ambiguous. Many of the crucial arrangements of a political system were left to the new parliament to sort out; it had to establish a High Court, decide what the electoral system would be, determine whether the parliament should be increased in size. And it had the power to determine by what system its finances would be arranged after 1910.

Such an opportunity to enhance the power and influence of the new government was a temptation for any politician.

Often the decision was political, a deliberate exercise of power, pushing to a limit the rights that the Constitution allowed. Within a few years, for instance, the federal government had managed to circumvent the clause that required it to return any unexpended funds to the states. It put them into a trust fund which, the High Court agreed, meant that they had duly been expended. That careful exploitation of the wording of the Constitution continued throughout the century. The federal government always had the right under section 96 to make grants to the states for any purpose that parliament might define. It was therefore able to put conditions on its grants, requiring perhaps matching grants from the states or the provision of information to ensure that the funds had been spent on the prescribed programs (Mathews and Jay 1972).

The High Court was established in 1903 to give effect to section 71 of the Constitution, which required the 'judicial power of the Commonwealth [to be] vested in a Federal Supreme Court'. Now with seven appointed justices, the High Court is the highest court of appeal in Australia and most of its work entails listening to appeals from other federal and state courts. The High Court's role in interpreting the Constitution is potentially its most controversial function as it seeks to interpret and determine the constitutional validity of legislation. Many of its findings have shaped political debate and some, like the Mabo case concerning native title, have prompted major changes to public policy (Patapan 2000; Galligan 1987).

At times the High Court assisted the government by its broad interpretation of the clauses in the Constitution that gave authority to the Commonwealth. Section 51 prescribes the powers that the federal government can exercise. The question for the Court is whether any piece of legislation can fall within these clauses; if it can then the legislation is constitutional. The wider the interpretation, the greater the powers of the federal government. Over the century that interpretation has allowed greater power, not always consistently nor in a constant stream, but gradually. The federal government could, for example, use its foreign affairs power to insist on the implementation of the clauses of international treaties, unheard of at the time that the Constitution was developed, to move into areas that had initially been seen as the sole responsibility of the states.

Sometimes these steps were essential; new developments, such as civil aviation, that had not existed in the 1890s required national regulation in the interests of both safety and the orderly growth of the industry. But other moves were opportunistic, a means of putting into effect a policy preference which the federal government regarded as important. An example of this was the decision of the Hawke government in 1983 to use the foreign affairs power, among others, to stop the Tasmanian government building a dam across the Franklin River (Coper 1983). This action was upheld by the High Court and was seen as a precedent for more extensive use of the foreign affairs power by the federal government. Anti-discrimination legislation was another policy area in which the federal government relied on the foreign affairs power to give it authority to act. The possibility that international agreements and conventions could be used in this way to increase the scope of the national government's power had not been envisaged when the Constitution was forged.

Defence powers in the two world wars ensured extensive regulation was permitted and allowed the federal government to extend its taxing powers. What was intended by the framers of the Constitution and how the terms were interpreted by the judiciary may be very different things, depending on the approach and assumptions about the Constitution held by the members of the High Court at any one time.

The Commonwealth has benefited from its superior access to tax revenue. Although the level of dependence has varied widely since federation, the states have had to rely on financial transfers from the central government for a large component of their expenditure. This has particularly been the case since the Commonwealth secured a monopoly of the collection of income tax after 1942. This dependence was accentuated in 2000 by the imposition of a goods and services tax (GST). While the revenue from this tax has been assigned to the states, it is a Commonwealth tax and its future will be determined by federal and not state political priorities.

Growth in the influence of the federal government was also a consequence of the different role that government was expected to play after the traumas of the great depression. The advent of Keynesian economics brought the government into areas of demand management and the regulation of new policy areas. The second world war and the 1945 White Paper on Unemployment signalled a new role for an activist federal government. In the last decades of the twentieth century, the scope for direct government action may have diminished, but the expectation of government to solve all manner of problems remained high.

To cope with the joint involvement of both spheres of government in many areas of public policy, federal and state leaders meet at premiers conferences. Sometimes regarded as a forum for the federal government to advise the states what they could expect to receive in financial transfers from the Commonwealth, these conferences have seldom been regarded by the press as more than bad theatre for grand-standing heads of government. The agenda has usually been limited to financial matters. By the 1990s, the dependence of the Commonwealth for state cooperation in furthering a national reform agenda led to the creation of the Council of Australian Governments. This body has sought to bring a common approach to issues of reform that run across state borders but its success has been limited and the inherent tension between the interests of state and national political interests continues to persist (Painter 1998).

All these developments illustrate the fate of constitutions. Their provisions can be reinterpreted by successive governments who may take advantage of ambiguities in the document or changing conditions to bend constitutional rules to their advantage. Constitutions reflect the balance of political influence at the time of their creation; they provide a snapshot of political ideas and contemporary views on the role of government. As circumstances change, so too does the way that governments are perceived and responsibilities allocated. The operation of the federal government of 2001 may not look much like its 1901 ancestor, but the changes have largely been a matter of choice and calculation and can be seen as variations on themes set up by the framers a century earlier.

The electoral system

A basic tenet of democracy is the direct participation by the people in the political process. In practical terms this concept has come to be represented by the rights of individual members of society to vote for parliamentary representatives. Determining this representation is critically dependent on the electoral system.

Australia had already had experience of a variety of electoral systems used in the Australian colonies since self-government in 1856 (Sawer 2001). The colonies had been adventurous in electoral administration, and the early use of the secret ballot in Victoria, for example, gave the name 'Australian ballot' to this alternative to voting on the hustings. But voting in the nineteenth century was predominantly for men only and, while the franchise was broad in comparison with most European nations of the time, property qualifications were important for much of the period. Women were granted voting rights in the colonies of South Australia and Western Australia in 1894 and 1899 respectively.

When it came time to design an electoral system for the new Commonwealth government, there was strong pressure for universal franchise which was achieved by the 1903 election (Sawer 2001). The right for all Aborigines to vote at Commonwealth elections, however, was not granted until 1962. The franchise for Commonwealth elections applied to both the House of Representatives and the Senate, the only upper house in Australia with close to a universal franchise from the early 1900s.

Australia adopted a system of single-member electoral districts for the House of Representatives, with a first-past-the-post method of election. But, with the emergence of the Labor Party, the non-Labor parties saw this system as a disadvantage. The Labor Party stressed the importance of organization and usually ensured that only one Labor candidate stood in each electoral district. By contrast, more than one anti-Labor candidate was often nominated in each electoral district, splitting the anti-Labor vote and permitting a Labor candidate to gain election with well short of majority support. Consequently, the Nationalists introduced preferential voting (the alternative vote) for the 1919 general election so that the preferences of the anti-Labor candidates could be exchanged, forcing Labor candidates to gain 50 per cent of the vote in order to win the seat. This system allowed voters to cast their first preference vote for small parties and still have their votes count in the final decision. It is a good example of changes to the electoral system designed for partisan advantage (note Sharman et al. 2002).

In any country, the design of an electoral system requires a trade-off between the representation of the diversity of political opinion, and a system where parties representing majority groupings control legislatures with only modest accommodation of minority opinions. The Commonwealth parliament has an unusual combination of the two.

The first part of this dilemma was solved by the system of proportional representation, adopted for Senate elections since 1949. Over the years, this has led to an increase in the representation of minor parties and independents. Since 1980 these groups have held the balance of power in the Senate and denied governments with majority support in the House of Representatives the ability to force their legislative programs through the Senate. This has had a dramatic effect on the legislative process in Canberra and has increased the potential for parliamentary scrutiny of the executive (Young 1999).

By way of contrast, the preferential system adopted for the House of Representatives from 1919 operates on the basis of single-member electoral districts where electors are required to rank all candidates in order of the voter's preference. Although this system favours the largest party groupings and tends to produce governments with partisan majorities in the House, it can create distortions in the representation of the vote. Parties can win a majority of seats with well short of a majority of votes. And in 1954 Labor won 50 per cent of the primary vote but did not win the election, much of its vote being tied up in large majorities in safe electoral districts. By contrast, in 1989 the Labor Party won less than 40 per cent of the primary vote but won a majority of seats by being the beneficiary of the second preferences of minor party voters.

Compulsory voting, introduced in 1923, also works to favour the two major party groupings in Australia. Designed in large part as a way of addressing the issue of declining voter turnout, compulsory voting reduces the need for parties to ensure that their supporters go to the polls on election day, curtailing both financial and administrative costs for parties. In spite of recent arguments from some quarters for the abolition of compulsory voting on the grounds of freedom of choice, it has broad public support and the strong endorsement of political parties. In addition, compulsory voting has been favoured as a mechanism for increasing political awareness and interest within the community. It has been argued that if forced to vote, electors will pay closer attention to issues and thereby become more informed on political matters generally. Whether or not this is true is open to conjecture. Voter apathy has long been an issue in Australian politics, and indications that change is occurring in this area may not be a result of compulsory voting so much as a response to the rapid social and economic change.

The political parties

The federal parliament inherited the party systems which had developed over forty years of parliamentary self-government in the colonies. These loose party groupings divided mainly on the issue of tariff policy. From Victoria came the Protectionists led by Alfred Deakin, from New South Wales the Free Traders with its former premier, George Reid, as leader. In the 1901 election Reid and Deakin campaigned across the country to gain support for their candidates, as did Edmund Barton, leader of the Federalist movement, a leader of the Protectionists in New South Wales, and Australia's first prime minister. Members of the Labor Party were elected from all states except Tasmania, but the campaigns were strictly local and, although there was a common platform, there was no recognised leader.

In the first parliament, no party had a majority; Barton headed a

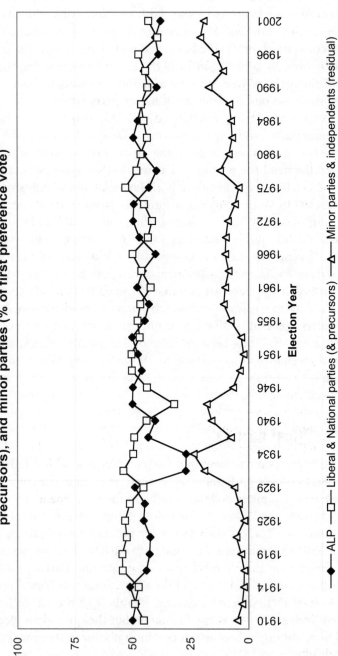

Figure 2.1 Commonwealth House of Representatives, general elections 1910–2001: vote share of ALP, Liberal and National parties (and their precursors), and minor parties (% of first preference vote)

Source: calculated from the Australian Government and Politics Project database, University of Western Australia.

Protectionist government, supported by Deakin. Labor agreed that it would not take a stand on the tariff debate and left its members to make their own decisions when voting on the issue. But it agreed to give support to the government in exchange for legislation it wanted enacted. Under this three-party arrangement, there was the potential for frequent changes of government (Marsh 1995, ch.10; see also Reid and Forrest 1989). In 1903–04 there were three governments, Deakin's Protectionists, Labor briefly under Chris Watson, and then a Free Trade government under Reid. When Labor decided to return to its strategy of 'support in return for concessions', Deakin returned to office until 1909. Then Labor withdrew its support, and formed a second, albeit short lived minority government. Deakin combined his party with the remnants of the Free Traders in anti-Labor Fusion and brought the minority Labor government down. The party system that has characterized Australian federal politics ever since (see figure 2.1) had been formed (Jaensch 1989).

Anti-Labor parties have appeared under a number of guises: Liberal 1909–17, Nationalist 1917–31, United Australia Party (UAP) 1931–44, and thereafter Liberal again (Nethercote 2001). The extent of party organisation varied; in the earlier forms the party was a classic cadre party, primarily organized from the top by parliamentarians and their supporting élites to ensure their re-election. The UAP in particular was seen as a vehicle for business to have its views heard in government and its policy was strongly influenced by a small group of Melbourne business notables.

Under Robert Menzies, the Liberal Party was reformed in 1944 as a modern mass party with a large membership and a branch structure which could maintain an independent existence from those who funded it. The party has maintained a strongly federal structure whose state branches provide the basis for party organization and have retained considerable independence (Hancock 2000).

The one principal newcomer to the political scene after the formation of the Liberal Party in 1909 was the Country Party (renamed the National Party for federal elections from 1983). The party grew out of rural discontent around 1920 and, at the federal level, was able to enter a coalition with the Nationalists in 1923 (Graham 1966). Its price for joining a coalition with the Nationalists was the head of the prime minister, Billy Hughes. The Country Party has been a vital component of anti-Labor governments since then and has used its numbers to extract substantial concessions from its larger coalition partner in terms of cabinet positions and key policies affecting rural interests. On three occasions, the UAP/Liberal Party has had sufficient seats in the lower

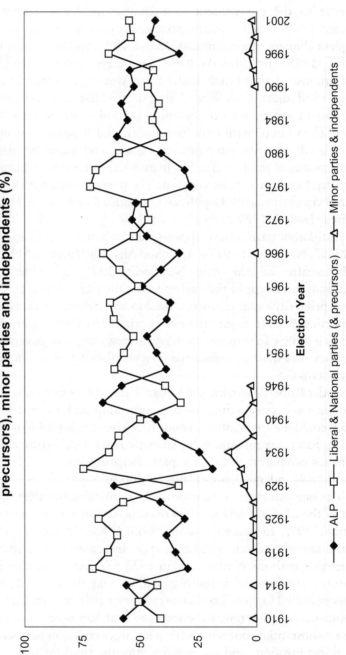

Figure 2.2 Commonwealth House of Representatives, general elections 1910–2001: seat share of ALP, Liberal and National parties (and their precursors), minor parties and independents (%)

Source: calculated from the Australian Government and Politics Project database, University of Western Australia.

house to form a government on its own. In 1931 it chose to do so, only to be forced back into coalition after the election of 1934. In 1975 and 1977 the prime minister, Malcolm Fraser, chose to retain the coalition. The result has been that the Australian party system in the House of Representatives has been divided between two blocs (see figure 2.2), which is why they are so often defined as Labor and non-Labor.

The Australian Labor Party

The Australian Labor Party is the oldest of Australia's political parties. It has had a continuous existence since 1891, but has a history of divisions and splits. In the early years many of those elected under the Labor platform found it hard to accept the discipline that required the members of parliament to abide by decisions of the parliamentary caucus (Faulkner and Macintyre 2001). A few left; others were expelled. In 1917 came the first great split. Despite party opposition, Prime Minister Hughes wanted to introduce conscription for war service. Unable to get his proposals through government, he ran a plebiscite asking the people to approve. When the first one failed in 1916, he tried again in 1917. That too failed but, by then, Hughes was so out of sympathy with the party organization that he anticipated his expulsion by walking out of caucus and inviting 'all those who thought like him' to come with him. He initially formed a National Labor minority government, after winning an election with the conservatives. Labor itself was kept out of office until it won just as the great depression struck in 1929. Policy indecision and scandal ensured the disintegration of the Scullin government and its defeat in 1932. This period saw a major split in the Labor Party and the creation of a Federal Labor Party which contested the 1931 and 1934 federal elections in the face of rival Labor groupings, particularly in New South Wales (Hogan and Clune 2001, vol. 2).

From 1941 to 1949 Labor was able to hold office in Canberra, drawing the war to a conclusion and establishing the post-war order but, as economic conditions improved, the country once again turned to the Liberals. Labor split again in 1955, this time over the question of how strongly it should oppose communist influence in trade unions and the party's own organization and, more generally, how it should frame its attitude to the cold war (Murray 1972). The right of the party split off in Victoria and Queensland, destroying the state governments in those two states and leading to the formation of the Democratic Labor Party. This party pursued a determinedly negative objective: to use its preferences and later its numbers in the Senate to ensure that the Labor Party never won office in Canberra. For nearly twenty years it succeeded until the Labor victory in 1972.

It can be argued that Labor has largely been the cause of its own misfortunes. Not until the 1970s did it develop the cohesion and organization that allowed it to determine internal disputes without splintering. It is not an accident that, since the party reforms of the late 1960s, it has been far more successful as a political party in federal politics (Parkin and Warhurst 1983; Warhurst and Parkin 2000).

The Whitlam period of government from 1972 to 1975 has been the source of legend; it was activist and often creative, but lacked the discipline and economic wisdom to survive for long. In 1975 the Senate, controlled by the opposition, blocked its supply bills. After three weeks of brinkmanship, the governor-general intervened, arguing that a government without supply could not govern. He sacked the government, installed the leader of the opposition and, acting on his advice, called an election that the Liberals won easily (Kelly 1995).

In the 1980s a more pragmatic Labor Party emerged. It had learnt the lessons of earlier times, was better disciplined and less ideological. Working with the unions through an economic accord, the Hawke and Keating governments managed to win five elections in a row, the only time in the century that Labor had managed to win more than two. It was assisted by the divisions in anti-Labor ranks, particularly by an ill-fated attempt by the Queensland premier, Bjelke-Petersen, to move to Canberra at the head of a National Party putsch. In addition, the end of the cold war narrowed the ideological the gap between the two major party blocs and enabled the Labor Party to pursue pragmatic policies which had broad electoral appeal (Kelly 1992).

The party system

How then can the federal party system be characterized? Until 1910 all governments were minority governments. There were seven changes of prime minister and six changes of government in nine years. For most of that time, Labor supported the government dominated by Alfred Deakin and it was only when that arrangement broke down that minority Labor and Free Trade governments were formed. The process appears to have worked smoothly, but the range of government was still limited and the scope for change minimal.

From 1909 to 1983 Australian national politics appears as a predominantly conservative fiefdom. Labor governed at times: 1910–13, 1914–16, 1929–31, 1941–49 and 1972–75: in all a total of eighteen years out of seventy-three, less than 25 per cent of the time. It could be argued that Labor was unlucky. At one stage it appeared to be the dominant party, with wins in both houses of federal parliament, in 1910 and in 1914. Then it became a party of opposition. Controversy generated from war and depression destroyed two governments, a third lasted for nearly a decade, a fourth fell to an obstructive Senate and a governor-general's ambush, before a decisive blow was administered in the ensuing election. In only two cases did the government survive for longer than the nominal three-year term of a parliament. If success for Labor at state level was common, in the federal arena it was a rare commodity.

It is possible to overstate this case. The Liberal hegemony from 1949 to 1972 was not unchallenged. In 1954 Labor got more than half the vote after the distribution of preferences, and in 1961 Menzies was returned by one seat when, in the last constituency to be declared, ninety-three communist voters chose to give their preferences to a Liberal candidate rather than to Labor; they were enough to give the candidate victory and Menzies a majority.

Since the 1980s circumstances have changed and the political system is far more competitive. Labor won five elections and the coalition two. No longer is it assumed that the result is a foregone conclusion. The system has become competitive, with the vote often split evenly between the major blocs after the distribution of preferences. But the primary vote of the major parties has been in decline in the last decades. In all but one of the elections between 1910 and 1987 (and that was in 1943 when non-Labor disintegrated) Labor and the two non-Labor coalition parties together got at least 88 per cent of the vote. In the 1990s each of the two main blocs have at times slipped to below 40 per cent of the primary vote and they are dependent on the distribution of minor party preferences to win (figure 2.3).

The causes of this decline in support for the major parties is not clear: the lack of distinction between the parties, the dislocation caused by economic reform, the distrust of politicians, and close media scrutiny are all given as causes. But there is no doubt that although the discontent is deep, it is not reflected in the composition of parliament and especially in the House of Representatives where the major parties have retained complete control.

But the decline in the support for the major parties has changed the dynamic of party politics. The major parties need to negotiate with minor parties and independents: the Australian Democrats, the Greens, the gun lobby and One Nation (Simms and Warhurst 2000). These parties may rarely win seats in the House of Representatives, but they attract support which enables them to bargain over policy with the major parties (Sharman et al. 2002). The party system is a long way

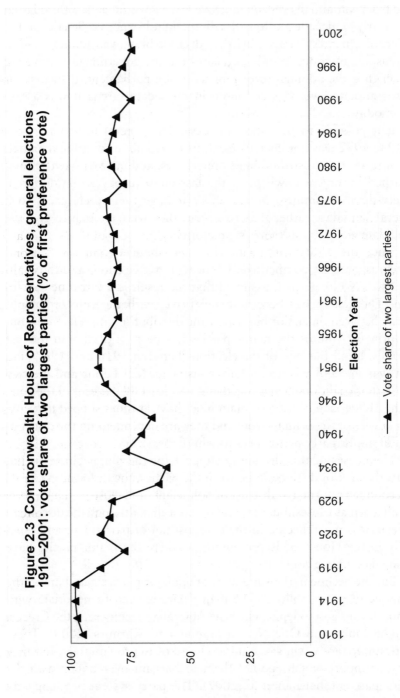

Figure 2.3 Commonwealth House of Representatives, general elections 1910–2001: vote share of two largest parties (% of first preference vote)

Source: calculated from the Australian Government and Politics Project database, University of Western Australia.

from a major realignment, but its operation has become much less predictable than it has been.

The major parties will seek to protect their position. For a long time the existence of parties was not recognised in the Constitution. They were seen as private organisations with the right to determine their own procedures without state intervention. But this view of parties is being challenged. First, a constitutional amendment was adopted in 1977 which ensured that occasional Senate vacancies were filled by a member of the same party as the retiring senator. Parties are thus now recognised in the Constitution. In 1984 federal parliament provided for the public funding of parties, the level of support being determined by the vote a party won at the previous federal election. The argument was that if all parties received support from the public purse, there would be less reliance on fund-raising, money would not buy influence and all parties could compete on an equal footing. But it also ensured that those parties that currently got most of the votes would gain most of the benefit, and it would be harder for new entrants to break into parliament. The long-term consequence has been that parties are seen as semi-public organizations in the body politic (Johns 1999) and are now far more liable to court action and public regulation of their operation.

Minority governments

Minority governments are now uncommon. They existed in the past as much because of the fragmentation of parties as because of the election of independents. Defeats on the floor of the House of Representatives are rare. In 1916 Hughes headed a minority National Labor government for three months after he split the Labor government over conscription, but he had the support of the official opposition for that period and then combined with them to fight and win an election. The Bruce–Page government lost a vote in the House of Representatives in 1929 when a small number of their supporters crossed the floor; forcing an election, which the government lost. In 1931 the Scullin government was forced into minority status when one group deserted to the opposition and another, supporters of NSW premier Jack Lang, broke away on the left. Although the government survived for another ten months, it was always liable to defeat and was eventually brought down by Lang's supporters. The Scullin government, too, lost the ensuing election.

After the 1940 election the Menzies–Fadden coalition depended on the support of a country independent. When Menzies was thrown out as prime minister by his own party in August 1941 and supplanted by the Country Party leader, Fadden, another UAP member deserted in disgust and became a second independent. The two decided to support Labor when a vote of no confidence was moved against Fadden in October 1941. They too then maintained Curtin in wartime office for nearly two years until the Labor Party's election victory in 1943.

Since 1941 no government has been brought down by an adverse vote in the House of Representatives. Party discipline has been tight and even a majority of one is sufficient. Indeed the smaller the nominal majority, the tighter the discipline may be. Nor has there been an occasion since 1943 when independents have been crucial for the survival of a government. The House of Representatives has been a forum for theatrical debate between the main political blocs, with the outcome on all issues following party lines. In terms of party predominance, there have been five occasions when the coalition parties have won three or more consecutive elections; there is only one Labor example.

The Senate

In the Senate outcomes are much more uncertain. The federal upper house has equal representation from each state and senators will often push the interests of their constituents. In that sense the equal numbers allow states to be represented as bodies. The Senate has rarely divided on state lines, nor have the senators from smaller states combined to thwart the interests of the main centres of population, but the Senate has often been a significant political force (see figure 2.4).

Until 1946 the voting systems adopted for the Senate allowed a party with 51 per cent of the vote in a state to win every seat in that state. This led to very one-sided outcomes. In 1922, for example, one Labor senator faced thirty-five Nationalists. Between 1947 and 1949, three Liberals opposed thirty-three Labor senators (see figure 2.5).

Fearing the loss of a large number of their senators in the 1949 election, the Chifley Labor government decided to introduce proportional representation for the Senate at the same time as increasing the number of members of both the Senate and the House of Representatives to 60 senators and about 120 members in the House of Representatives. As a calculation of long-term political advantage for the Labor Party, the move to proportional representation in the Senate failed badly. Since the double dissolution election of 1951 Labor has never controlled a partisan majority in the Senate. For a time, between 1964 and 1974, the Liberal–Country Party coalition relied on independent and Democratic Labor Party senators to maintain its control. After 1972 and the election of a Labor government, the Liberal and Country parties twice used

Figure 2.4 Commonwealth Senate, general elections 1910–2001: vote share of ALP, Liberal and National parties (and their precursors), and minor parties (% of first preference vote)

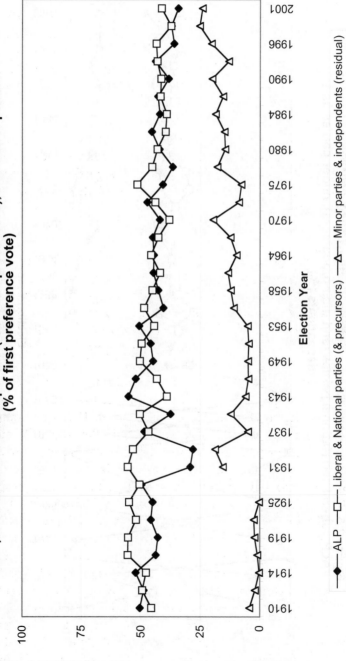

Source: calculated from the Australian Government and Politics Project database, University of Western Australia.

Figure 2.5 Commonwealth Senate, general elections 1910–2001: seat share of ALP, Liberal and National parties (and their precursors), minor parties and independents (%)

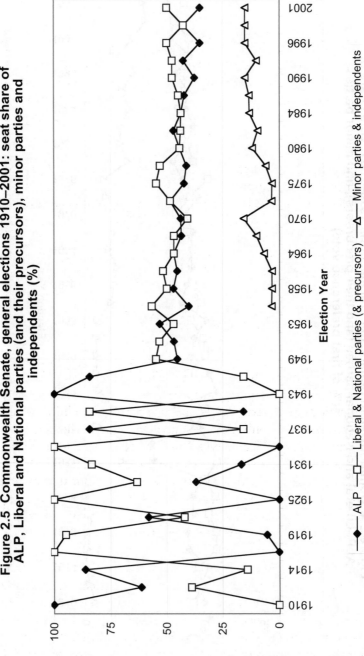

Source: calculated from the Australian Government and Politics Project database, University of Western Australia.

their numbers in the Senate to reject the government's supply bills to force an election.

For five years after the double dissolution election of 1975, the Liberal and National Country Party government of Malcolm Fraser controlled both houses. After 1980 the Australian Democrats held the balance of power in the Senate and, since then, no government has been able to guarantee that its legislation will be passed unamended. A medley of Democrats, Greens and other minor parties and independents has been elected. Governments must now compromise their way through the Senate. The Howard government had to negotiate the passing of its GST through the Senate, even though it had just won an election with the GST as a major plank in its manifesto. At first the government hoped to gain the crucial support of a strategically placed independent; when he refused to support the legislation, the government had to compromise with the Australian Democrats.

The Senate may not be a states house in a federal system but it has become a highly effective house of review that neither major party can control (Mulgan 1995). Nor is it likely that such a party will control the Senate in the foreseeable future, as the primary vote of the major parties declines and as voters differentiate between the two houses and vote more readily for minor parties in the Senate. The Senate is not only powerful because of its constitutional position but because of its party make-up (Sharman 1999). It will remain politically influential only as long as a government does not hold a Senate majority.

Over the century, the Commonwealth's political system can be described as moderately competitive. There have been eleven major changes of governing party, but these are interspersed with some lengthy periods of government by a single party or coalition. Since the Labor split of 1916, only two periods of party government, those of Labor prime ministers Scullin and Whitlam, have lasted for less than six years. Once elected, Australians seem to give governments at least two chances to perform before they withdraw support. But that assumes a neat split between the main political forces. This might not continue if the electoral support for the major parties continues to fragment. However, the decline in the major parties is not so great, and the dynamics of parliamentary politics are so strong, that it seems unlikely that minor parties and independents will win more than the occasional seat. Major parties are likely to continue to dominate the parliament, even if not the electorate. Since the 1920s the party system in the House of Representatives has been frozen and no new party players have been able to break through the system of single-member electoral districts, preferential and compulsory voting. The experience of the Senate demonstrates what could happen if there is a major realignment in the party system, and as the traditional divisions of economy and class decline as the principal determinant of voting behaviour.

Government and public policy

In 1901 the range of the federal government's functions was limited. The first prime minister, Edmund Barton, had a ministry with only nine members, two of whom had no portfolio responsibilities. The prime minister took responsibility for external affairs. There was an attorney-general, a treasurer, a postmaster-general, a defence minister, a minister for trade and customs and a home affairs minister who took on the other responsibilities. These were functions that are almost entirely interpreted as defining activities. They were concerned with regulation rather than delivering any services or providing infrastructure development. They were the functions of post, defence, trade and customs, and law, that were required to run across the borders of the states. All the other detail was left to the state governments.

This has changed over the years. There were seven departments in 1901, twenty-four in 1946, twenty-eight in 1985 but sixteen in 1990. Why the changes? Where several functions could once be gathered in a single department, for instance home affairs in 1901, they became separated as political requirements dictated. Sometimes they reflected new initiatives; the department of prime minister and cabinet became the incubator for developing functions of political importance to the leader of the government. The Commonwealth departments of education, the environment and Aboriginal affairs originated from sections in the department of the prime minister and cabinet.

There was also change in the kinds of activity undertaken by the Commonwealth. Of the nine portfolios identified for the 1901–09 period, eight are categorized as providing basic functions of government and only one as providing physical infrastructure. In the first 40 years the balance of these characteristics changed only slowly. By 1939 there were eleven defining portfolios, six physical infrastructure portfolios and a single portfolio concerned with social issues. Commonwealth activity in 1939 reflected, in large part, the assumptions of the limited role which the national government had been expected to play by the founders. Substantial change came in the 1940s. Defining portfolios rose to eighteen, a level at which they have stayed since, but portfolios concerned with physical infrastructure almost doubled to eleven. And, following the successful passage of a constitutional referendum in 1946 that permitted the federal government to pay a range of social welfare benefits, portfolios began to emerge which were concerned with social issues. Three existed by the end of the 1940s and thereafter six in the 1960s, ten in the 1970s and over twenty in the 1980s. Portfolios concerned with the physical infrastructure grew to around seventeen over the same period. There was a consolidation of administrative arrangements in the 1990s but the growth of portfolios until the 1980s illustrates the changing activities of the federal government.

A second reason for the growth in portfolios grew out of the way the Constitution has been interpreted. Section 64 of the Constitution states that the governor-general may appoint officers to 'administer such departments of state of the Commonwealth as the Governor-General in Council may provide'. Interpretation of that clause in the 1950s held that every minister should have a separate department to administer. If two ministers were joint appointments to the same department (as, for instance, as senior and junior minister) the actions of one might be unconstitutional. As a consequence, an increase in the number of ministers meant that there had to be a number of departments equal to or greater than the number of ministers. This was rarely a problem as there were usually more departments than ministers, with some ministers having responsibility for two or more departments, but in some cases, departments were created more to provide a minister with a job than to fulfil an administrative need. Once created, such departments set out to carve a role for themselves.

If it was seen as necessary that a second minister assist a senior minister in administration, two strategies were possible. A minister heading a junior department could be made 'minister assisting', or a skeleton department could be created with a staff of only one or two. The Department of Special Trade Representations was one such entity; it was an awkward attempt to satisfy the demands of a narrow reading of the Constitution.

But administrative logic is by itself not a reason for changing the machinery of government. There are several other reasons. One is ministerial overload; a minister finds the burden too great and the functions are removed to another department or the department is split into two with the work divided between two ministers. A second reason is the existence of a political crisis caused by ministerial or administrative failure which can sometimes be remedied by changing the administrative structure. A third reason is the need for symbolic change. Governments created new agencies to indicate that they were interested in new areas of activity, or to distance themselves from administrative failure or policy areas that were too closely identified with previous governments. A final reason for change can be to alter the nature of the

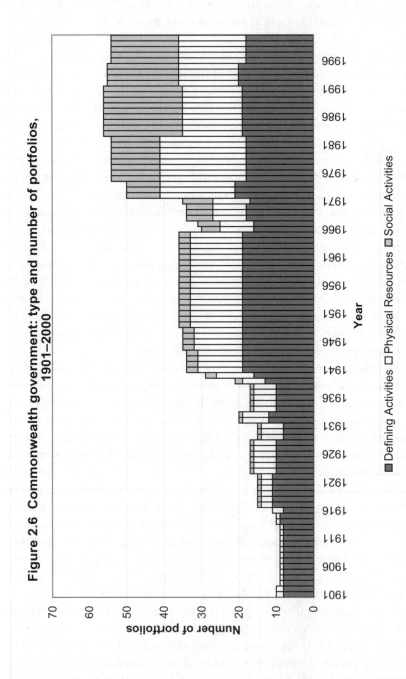

Figure 2.6 Commonwealth government: type and number of portfolios, 1901–2000

■ Defining Activities □ Physical Resources ■ Social Activities

Source: calculated from the Australian Government and Politics Project database, University of Western Australia.

advice that is being provided to the government. The split of the treasury in 1976, for instance, was a reaction to the dissatisfaction Prime Minister Fraser felt about the economic advice he was getting and he sought to diversify the sources of advice on economic policy.

In 1987 there was a major change in the way Commonwealth ministries were constructed. A re-interpretation of section 64 of the Constitution by the solicitor-general advised that there was no bar to more than one minister administering the same department as long as both were formally appointed to administer it. A consequence was that the prime minister could increase the number of ministers while reducing the number of departments substantially (from thirty to sixteen). A senior minister could represent every department in cabinet, while there were more junior ministerial positions to satisfy the aspirations of members of the parliamentary party. This led to greater departmental stability because there was less need to solve problems of ministerial incompetence by changing the administrative structures.

Departmental structures have always been determined by a combination of administrative and political factors. It should be noted that it is far easier to change the administrative arrangements that establish departments and allocate functions in Australia than in other similar countries. All that is required is a decision of the prime minister. Cabinet need not be involved and rarely is. Even after the re-interpretation of the Constitution in 1987 there is volatility in administrative arrangements that is unique to Australian Commonwealth government.

Cabinet and the Public Service

The federal government adopted the principles of parliamentary cabinet government from the colonies; all the members of the first cabinet had experience in colonial governments and they took for granted that similar practices would apply. Cabinet was selected by the prime minister or, in the case of Labor after 1908, elected by caucus (the parliamentary party). The Constitution provided that ministers had to be (or become) members of parliament. Once the party system in the House of Representatives settled into a contest between two major party groupings in 1910, each of which had strong party discipline, the executive became dominant within the parliament.

Cabinet was collectively responsible for all the decisions of government, so that ministers were obliged to support in public even those decisions that they had opposed in cabinet. Prime ministers might interpret the rules in various ways, but the basic elements of collective cabinet responsibility have remained. As the prime ministers hold their position because they are party leaders, they retain office only as long as they maintain the confidence of their party. If they are too dictatorial, too ineffective, or too much of a political liability, the party can remove them. In 1941 Menzies lost the confidence of his party and resigned. In 1971 Gorton voted himself out of office after the Liberal Party in parliament split evenly on a vote of confidence. In 1991 the Labor caucus deposed Hawke in favour of Keating. Prime ministers may be powerful, and are often dominant, but they are never all-powerful. They are made, and maintained, by the confidence of their colleagues (Davis 1997).

Cabinet gradually grew in size as the role of government expanded. By the 1950s Menzies felt it had become too large and he split the ministry into two: the senior ministers who were members of cabinet, and a 'second eleven' of more junior ministers who held the less significant portfolios. This division has been retained since with the exception of the Whitlam government. Then, all twenty-seven ministers were members of cabinet with no formal division between them. It proved unwieldy, too large for effective debate and the making of timely decisions. Later Labor governments resumed the practice of dividing the cabinet into senior and junior teams. In 1987 the changes to the machinery of government allowed the prime minister to appoint senior ministers for all portfolios, and thus ensure that all parts of government were represented in the cabinet. The assistant ministers stayed in the outer ministry.

Cabinet has also become more bureaucratized. In the early days, ministers kept their own records of what was decided in cabinet. Not until the 1940s was a secretariat appointed to maintain an official record of decisions. As the pressure on governments grew, more formal processes were required to ensure that what the government determined was accurately recorded and properly circulated to those responsible for implementing the decisions.

Ministers must answer to the parliament for the actions of their departments but it has not been the practice in Australia that ministers will take responsibility for the actions of their departments in the sense that they resign when serious mistakes are shown to have occurred. Demands that a minister resign for such reasons are part of the repertoire of opposition rhetoric designed to embarrass the government rather than prompt a resignation. But ministers are required to maintain control over the administration and fix errant practices where they are identified. If it is shown that a minister failed to act, misled parliament or committed some other significant error, the question of resignation is one of a political assessment by the prime minister as to whether the minister's resignation is required for the greater good of the government (Weller 2001a).

Ministers are supported by a career, non-partisan public service. For a long time that service was based on seniority and early recruitment. It provided continuity, expertise and advice which was not tied to partisan advancement. The Commonwealth public service was seen as powerful, even dominant, and the real determiner of policy with ministers as its puppets. This was never true. Good ministers always had a major effect in shaping government decisions affecting their departments and policy responsibilities. But not all ministers were good or capable and some have clearly been strongly influenced by their senior public service advisers.

The traditional picture of the public service is now in need of serious revision. Lateral recruitment is now a major feature and has been since a plan for graduate entry was set up in the 1960s. Tenure became less certain in the 1990s. The heads of department lost the title of permanent head and became departmental secretaries on contract. These changes have reflected the changing nature of the wider job market where notions of lifetime employment are felt to be no longer appropriate. There has also been a demand for the provision of a public service that is more directly responsive to ministers and the public. Administrative changes which have forced heads of department to be more responsive to the political preferences of ministers were a conse-quence of a belief among some ministers that they had ceded too much power to officials. Ministers with an urgent political agenda did not want to be contradicted by officials whose advice was based on many years of experience and security of tenure. It also reflected a more general questioning of the ability of government to solve national prob-lems and an acceptance that advice in framing policy should be drawn from a range of sources. By the end of the century, there was much less reliance on the public service as the principal source of advice to minis-ters than there had been fifty years earlier (Weller 2001b).

The Future

In general, the Commonwealth government has expanded its functions and activities throughout the century, not consistently but in spurts. The two world wars and the advent of an activist Whitlam government were perhaps the most obvious catalysts for change. The first periods of rapid growth were driven by necessity of mobilizing the nation for war and, in the case of the second world war, by Keynesian economics which gave to a reforming government the justification for wide involvement in social change and the regulation of the economy. The

Whitlam government from 1972 to 1975 was built on a view of greatly extended Commonwealth government activity without nationalization, using the Constitution to direct spending through tied grants in areas where the Commonwealth had never been involved before.

Whether the Commonwealth chooses to exert its financial muscle for political ends is now a matter of choice. Through the Council of Australian Governments the federal government has been able to persuade the states to accept national competition policy and reform transport, water and electricity. It introduced the goods and services tax (GST) and passed on the income to the states, supposedly in place of other grants and state taxes, thereby making the states dependent on federal legislation for their funds. But the political costs of such intervention can be high, as the fate of the Whitlam government shows. And it is no accident that Canberra is often blamed for many of the problems which emerge in state politics, particularly at election times.

The federal compact has been irrevocably altered. The federal governments have often talked of returning power to the states, rather more often than they have done so. The Commonwealth is now the major player in the federal system. The Constitution allows it, the central government likes it, and the battle is, and will remain, about the exercise of power and the never-ending calculus of political costs and benefits.

Chapter

New South Wales

Rodney Smith

After the Liberal Party–National Party coalition's 2001 federal election victory, much Labor blame for the result centred on the party's poor performance in New South Wales. Premier Bob Carr claimed that Labor's federal policies had not appealed to his economically buoyant state and argued that New South Wales Labor urgently needed to improve the quality of its federal representatives. His former state cabinet colleague, Rodney Cavalier, lamented that after supplying much of the ALP's federal leadership for ninety-six years, New South Wales Labor was no longer producing leadership contenders (*Sydney Morning Herald*, 13, 19 November 2001).

The twin themes in these comments were anxious variations of the two major traditions for understanding twentieth-century New South Wales politics. The first tradition is what Hirst (1998, 464) has called 'the pre-eminence of NSW'. The second is that New South Wales is a Labor state. What concerned Carr and Cavalier was that the 2001 federal election might indicate an undermining of both traditions.

The premier state

The claim that New South Wales is pre-eminent in Australian state politics has a number of related dimensions. One rests on the state's foundational status. By some interpretations, the foundation of New South Wales as a convict settlement in 1788 began its role in setting the 'defining moments and symbols' of the wider nation. This process continued in the myths of the selectors, the great strikes of the 1890s, the formation of the Labor Party and Sydney's rise as 'the quintessential Australian city, raffish, hedonistic, where old wealth means nothing and new wealth is admired and ostentatiously displayed' (Hirst 1998, 464–5; see also Holmes and Sharman 1977, 55–6).

A second dimension is size. Although New South Wales is not the largest state physically, it has the highest population and the greatest wealth. In 2000 it had 6.4 million people (1.7 million more than Victoria) and generated 35.8 per cent of Australia's gross domestic product (compared with Victoria's 25.5 per cent). Its sheer size makes New South Wales politics important to the rest of Australia (Evatt Research Centre 1989, 159; ABS 2000b; ABS 2001a).

A third dimension is its place in the federation. New South Wales is often seen as the state politically closest to the national centre. The evidence seems mixed. On the one hand, the state's citizens do seem to identify more closely with the centre and have weaker state loyalties than do citizens of other states. The state's political institutions and party competition arguably fit more closely with the Commonwealth than those of other states. New South Wales sends fifty of the 150 members of the House of Representatives to Canberra, connecting it strongly with national politics. On the other hand, New South Wales political leaders have often made mileage from clashing with Commonwealth governments, particularly over taxes and finances. The so-called 'battle of the plans' between Premier Jack Lang and the Commonwealth (and other states) in the depression crisis of the early 1930s provided the most dramatic example. Many others have followed, however, including conflicts between Premier Robert Askin and both John Gorton and Gough Whitlam, Neville Wran and Malcolm Fraser, and Bob Carr and John Howard (Holmes and Sharman 1977, 34–59; Parker 1978, 347–53; Steketee and Cockburn 1986, 182; Hagan and Turner 1991, 133–4; Robinson 2001, 56–60; R. Smith 2001a, 281–2; Harwin 2001, 43–5).

The final dimension is institutional and policy pre-eminence. Near the start of his extensive survey of New South Wales politics, Parker claims that:

> The seniority, size, and relative sophistication of the state are reflected in a more elaborately shaped apparatus of government than those of *most other* states, for example in matters like cabinet organization, departmental structure, public service control and training, and professionalized political party organizations (Parker 1978, 9–10; emphasis added).

Hughes' (1984) comparison of state ministerial portfolio proliferation found that most developments originated in Victoria or New South Wales. Similarly, in Nelson's (1985) comparative study of policy innovation from 1900 to 1985, New South Wales was one of the innovative states, along with Victoria and South Australia. In each case, New South Wales sits among the leading states, rather than as outright political leader. Nonetheless, combined with the other dimensions, the claim of New South Wales to be 'the premier state' remains strong, particularly for the residents of the state.

A Labor state

Labor's post-1941 dominance of state politics has encouraged the view that New South Wales is a natural Labor state. Labor has governed longer than its rival anti-Labor coalition[1] and has gained vote and seat shares that its opponents have never matched (Turner 1985a; Green 2001, 299). One consequence of Labor's dominance has been a lack of academic and wider critical interest in the New South Wales non-Labor parties and leaders. There are, for example, two book-length histories of the state Labor Party but none of the state Liberals; three books on Premier Wran and his decade of government but none on Askin and his decade (Dale 1985; Chaples et al. 1985; Steketee and Cockburn 1986; Hagan and Turner 1991; Freudenberg 1991).

Labor's success has rested partly on the state's geographic and social patterns. Labor draws heavy support from the state's populous industrial heartland, the Hunter–Sydney–Illawarra region, which provides it with a large number of safe and winnable seats. The National Party's natural vote is limited to the far larger, but much more sparsely peopled, rural and regional areas. Much of the Liberal Party's vote is locked up in safe northern Sydney 'dress circle' seats, while Labor holds most of the seats in the 'stalls', south of the Harbour and out to the western suburbs. Apart from these advantages in the distribution of classes, Labor has benefited from the historically higher than average proportion of Catholics living in New South Wales (Spearritt 1978, 191–219; Turner 1985a).

Constitutional development

The early constitutional politics of New South Wales were marked by a series of shifts from authoritarian penal settlement rule to representative and responsible parliamentary government. These shifts began with various Acts passed by the Imperial Parliament from 1823 to 1850. The 1850 *Australian Constitutions Act (No. 2)* gave the colony the opportunity to devise its own constitution. The New South Wales Legislative Council proposed a constitution which, after the Imperial Parliament had made some amendments, received assent as the 1855 *New South Wales Constitution Act*. The 1855 Act established a constitutional framework in which the executive was responsible to a bicameral parliament comprised of an elected Legislative Assembly and an appointed Legislative Council (Lumb 1977, 3–24).

Against the intentions of colonial conservatives like W. C. Wentworth, a provision of the 1855 Act inserted by the Imperial Parliament ensured that all sections of the Constitution could be amended by legislation passed by simple majorities in the New South Wales Parliament (Hirst 1988, 41–5). The straightforward procedure for constitutional amendment later produced dramatic tensions between governments and members of the Legislative Council and between governments and governors. The Constitution has developed through parliamentary amendments to the Constitution Act, changes brought about by other constitutional legislation, particularly the *Commonwealth of Australia Constitution Act 1900*, and referendums. Since 1929 governments have periodically passed Acts to entrench sections of the Constitution by requiring popular assent at a referendum before they can be altered. The Legislative Council was entrenched in this way in 1929, for example, as were various changes to electoral arrangements in 1978 (Hawker 1971, 244; Turner 1985b, 82–3).

The entrenchment of some constitutional provisions has not prevented governments from seeking constitutional change. The referendums resulting from these initiatives have almost all been successful. They include three important changes to the Legislative Council (51.5 percent 'Yes' vote in 1933, 82.6 per cent in 1978 and 57.7 per cent in 1991), a four-year term for the Legislative Assembly (69 per cent in 1981), a fixed term for the Legislative Assembly (75.5 per cent in 1995) and independence for the judiciary (65.9 per cent in 1995). The major failure was the 1961 referendum to abolish the Legislative Council (42.4 per cent 'Yes'; see Turner 1969, 2–3; Hawker 1971, 244; Mackerras 1985, 191; Turner 1985b, 79–83; Steketee 1993, 29; R. Smith 1995, 26; Green 2001, 316; T. Smith 2001, 363). In contrast to Commonwealth constitutional development, reform to the New South Wales Constitution has not usually been impeded by the unwillingness of electors to vote for change.

The governor

From the early days of white settlement, distance and the policy of the Imperial authorities meant that government came from within the colony rather than London. Although authority ultimately rested with the Imperial government, governors were empowered to make regulations and ordinances for the colony. Pressures to reduce the governor's wide-ranging powers grew with the increased numbers of free settlers and emancipists. These pressures resulted initially in the establishment of a Legislative Council and judicial review of the governor's proposed legislation in 1823. From 1856 the bicameral parliament represented a much more significant shift from the rule of governors to representative and responsible parliamentary government (Hawker 1971, 10; Foster 1976; Lumb 1977, 3–10).

Governors still faced important political decisions, particularly in determining who would form ministries, the timing of elections, the composition of the Legislative Council and the resolution of deadlocks between the houses. In the late colonial period of faction politics, these matters required considerable acumen. The development of disciplined parties gradually reduced rather than immediately ended the governor's political role. The most well-known case of post-federation action by a governor occurred in May 1932, when Governor Philip Game dismissed Premier Jack Lang for issuing orders of dubious legality to NSW public servants during Lang's conflict with the Commonwealth over debt repayments. Game installed the United Australia Party's (UAP) Bertram Stevens as premier, parliament was prorogued and the election that followed was won by the UAP–Country Party coalition. Three other cases are worth noting. In 1916 Governor Gerald Strickland refused assent to Premier William Holman's bill for extending the life of the parliament (the Colonial Office later recalled Strickland). On 20 December 1921 Governor Walter Davidson commissioned Nationalist George Fuller as premier but refused him an election after Labor's James Dooley was defeated on the floor of the Assembly. Davidson recommissioned Dooley later the same day after Fuller was defeated in the house. In 1939, faced with rival UAP contenders, Governor Lord Wakehurst commissioned Alexander Mair as premier over E. S. Spooner (Aitkin 1969, 56–60; Hawker 1971, 57–94, 215–16; Parker 1976, 176; Ward 1977; Evatt 1979, 319–21; Nairn 1986, 236–61; Robinson 2001).

The restructuring of the Legislative Council in 1933 ended conflicts between governors and premiers over appointments to the Council and introduced a mechanism for resolving deadlocks between the houses that reduced the governor's role. These changes were sparked by repeated conflicts between Lang and Governors Dudley de Chair and Game over Lang's attempts to have large numbers of new members of the Legislative Council appointed to gain control of the Council (see also below). Finally, the 1995 constitutional entrenchment of fixed election dates removed, in most circumstances, the governor's role in the timing of polls.

While the governor formally retains some political powers, the office has become an overwhelmingly ceremonial and social one. Indeed, the major controversies over the position since the 1940s – such as the appointment of the first Australian-born governor in 1946 and the 1996 decision of Premier Bob Carr to turn over Government House to public use and reduce the formality of the office, which some monarchists viewed as republicanism by stealth – have largely concerned symbolic issues (Parker 1976, 171–2; *Sydney Morning Herald*, 1 March 1996; Cunneen 2000, 174–7).

The Legislative Council

The appointed Legislative Council, established in 1823 with no power to initiate or block legislation, bore no resemblance to the democratically elected chamber with extensive legislative powers which exists today. The transformation of the Council stretched over 160 years, punctuated by crises and conflicts over its role. Between 1823 and the passage of the 1855 *New South Wales Constitution Act* establishing a bicameral legislature, the Legislative Council had gradually won powers from the governor (Hawker 1971, 3–4; Ward 1976; Lumb 1977, 10–15).

The 1855 *Constitution Act* inaugurated a bicameral parliament. Tensions between the two houses were immediate, and have continued in various forms to the present day. The new Legislative Assembly took over and extended the role of popular representation and responsible government developed by the Council over the previous decades. Although Wentworth's proposal for a colonial peerage to stock the new Council was doomed, famously mocked by Daniel Deniehy as an attempt to create a 'bunyip aristocracy', the Council was redesigned as a bulwark against the excesses and defects of mass democracy. It was to have at least twenty-one members, appointed by the governor on the advice of the Executive Council. While it could not initiate money bills, in other respects the Council's powers over legislation matched those of the Assembly. The appointed members of the Legislative Council (MLCs) soon came to view themselves as above the factional loyalties and electoral self-interest which characterized much of the politics of the lower house. This period also saw the upper house acquire its image as a leisurely gentleman's club for part-time legislators, an image it is still struggling to shake off[2] (Hawker 1971, 5–6, 17, 132–7; Parker 1978, 200–2; Hirst 1988, 32–8, 40–5, 174–93).

For democrats and liberals, the conservative-dominated Council needed major reform. The first unsuccessful attempts to reconstitute the Council as an elected or semi-elected body came as early as 1859. Unable to reform the Council and faced with potential deadlocks between the houses, governments resorted to appointing their supporters as additional members to achieve majorities in the upper house. As a result, the number of MLCs increased. Between Henry Parkes' 1872 and 1889 ministries, for example, the Council doubled from thirty-six to seventy-two members (Hawker 1971, 17–20, 131–2, 141–4).

In the first part of the twentieth century, the tensions between the houses shifted from factional to party politics. From 1901 to 1932 the Council demonstrated a greater propensity to reject Labor bills than non-Labor ones. Labor's platform proposed abolition of the Council. Despite this, the early ALP governments of McGowan and Holman did not attempt abolition, or even 'swamping' the Council with Labor MLCs. Instead, much to the frustration of others in their party, they compromised with non-Labor MLCs over legislation (Hawker 1971, 242; Radi 1977, 102; Evatt 1979, 266, 322; Hagan and Turner 1991, 70–1, 98, 103–5).

Lang took a less conciliatory approach. Faced with a hostile Council, in 1925 he negotiated with the governor for the appointment of twenty-five new Labor MLCs. They were intended to act as a 'suicide squad' by passing a bill abolishing the upper house, a strategy the Queensland Labor government had successfully employed in 1920. Lang's abolition bill failed 41 to 47 votes, however, when two Labor MLCs voted against abolition and five others absented themselves (Turner 1969, 6–7, 12–13; Hawker 1971, 204, 242–4; Radi 1977, 109–11; Nairn 1986, 95–118).

Lang's efforts to abolish the Council prompted the Nationalist government of Thomas Bavin to entrench the Council in 1929. UAP Premier Stevens' 1933 reforms resulted in a Council of sixty members with staggered twelve-year terms, elected by the members of the two houses on a proportional basis. The Council's powers to amend money bills were restricted, while a lengthy and complicated procedure for resolving deadlocks, culminating in a referendum, was introduced. These reforms removed the possibility of governments 'swamping' the

Council. The new terms and election methods meant that at least in their early years governments would have to deal with an upper house in which their opponents held the majority. This situation faced Labor from 1941 to 1949 and 1976 to 1978, and the Liberal Party–Country Party coalition between 1965 and 1967 (Turner 1969, 20–7, 41; Aitkin 1969, 156–9; Hawker 1971, 244; Parker 1978, 214; Page 1990, 7).

Dissatisfaction with the composition and performance of the Council continued among Labor and non-Labor politicians and in wider public debate. After its failed 1961 referendum, Labor shifted its goal to establishing a popularly elected Council. In 1978 the Wran government successfully proposed a democratically elected Council of forty-five members. One-third of the MLCs would be elected for three Assembly terms at each state election, using a form of proportional representation (see below). The powers of the Council would remain unchanged. Labor's 1981 move to extend the Assembly term to four years meant MLCs' terms were again stretched to twelve years. In 1985, reflecting their full-time status and increased professionalism, MLCs were granted the same basic salary as MLAs (Turner 1969, 2–3; Turner 1985b, 79–81; Page 1990, 10–13; Page 1991, 25–6).

The main long-term impact of Wran's reforms was precisely what neither he nor the coalition wanted: to place a powerful and rejuvenated Council beyond the control of the major parties. Although Labor won majorities in the new Council from 1978 to 1988, since then minor parties have held the balance of power (see table 3.1). The Greiner government's 1991 reduction of the Council to forty-two members with eight-year terms, half elected at each state poll, ultimately accelerated the major parties' loss of control of the upper house by making it easier for minor parties to win seats (Turner 1985b, 81; Page 1990, 23–4; Page 1991, 30; Green 2001, 316–17).

Governments have been able to get their legislative programs through the Council despite their lack of majorities; however, they have been forced to accept amendments, delays and committee scrutiny of their bills. The post-1988 period has seen the emergence of a system of Legislative Council committees. In addition to select committees, five general purpose standing committees currently cover government portfolio areas and act as estimates committees, while three specific standing committees deal with law and justice, social issues and state development. These initiatives signify a contemporary Council that has developed its legislative role beyond that of its predecessors (Page 1990, 7–9, 26; Page 1991; R. Smith 1995, 30; R. Smith 1997, 215–22; Evans 1997, 47–8).

Table 3.1 New South Wales Legislative Council, general elections 1978–1999: vote share (%) and seats won by party (*n*)

	Election Year												
	1978		1981		1984		1988		1991		1995		1999	
Party	%	*n*	%	*n*	%	*n*	%	*n*	%	*n*	%	*n*	%	*n*
Australian Labor Party	54.9	9	51.8	8	46.9	7	37.5	6	37.3	6	35.3	8	37.3	8
Liberal-National (Country) parties (joint ticket)	36.3	6	33.8	5	42.6	7	46.2	7	45.3	7	38.5	8	27.4	6
Subtotal major parties	91.2	15	85.6	13	89.5	14	83.7	13	82.6	13	73.8	16	64.7	14
Family Action/ Call to Australia/ Christian Democrats			9.1	1	6.1	1	5.7	1	3.6	1	3.0	1	3.2	1
Australian Democrats			4.0	1	3.2	0	2.7	1	6.7	1	3.2	1	4.0	1
Greens											3.8	1	2.9	1
Shooters Party											2.8	1		
A Better Future For Our Children											0.3	1		
Pauline Hanson's One Nation Party													6.3	1
Reform the Legal System													1.0	1
Unity													1.0	1
Outdoor Recreation Party													0.2	1
Other	8.8	0	1.3	0	1.2	0	6.9	0	7.1	0	13.1	0	16.7	0
Total	100	15	100	15	100	15	99	15	100	15	100	21	100	21

Source: Calculated by the author from a variety of official and scholarly sources

Non-government MLCs have also used their recent Council majorities to increase scrutiny of the executive. In 1995, for example, they revived the practice – dormant since 1932 – of moving that government papers be produced. Much to Labor treasurer and MLC Michael Egan's displeasure, they forced him to table a large number of papers relating to Carr cabinet decisions on a range of issues. The frustrations of dealing with the Council, as well as the results of the 1999 election, which took the number of minor party MLCs to thirteen, prompted Egan to suggest a referendum to, among other things, weaken the

Council's power to amend bills. Although the coalition initially supported the idea, it later backed away, leaving the Legislative Council a strong upper house out of the hands of the government of the day (Evans 1997, 48–9; R. Smith 2001b, 375–6, 411).

The Legislative Assembly

From 1856 the Legislative Assembly took on the functions of a popularly elected parliamentary lower house: representing constituents, providing the personnel for executive office, keeping them accountable, initiating, debating and passing legislation, and providing a proving ground for the state's current and potential political leadership.

The predominant basis for lower house representation, constitutionally entrenched in 1978, has been single-member constituencies. Since the late nineteenth century, the number of representatives has fluctuated rather than grown (see table 3.2). In 2002 each member of the

Table 3.2 New South Wales Legislative Assembly: changes to the membership of the Assembly, 1856–2001

Year of increase/decrease in membership	Number of members *n*	Change *n*	%
1856	54		
1858	80	26	48
1859	72	−8	−10
1880	108	36	50
1894*	141	33	31
1895	125	−16	−11
1904	90	−35	−28
1950	94	4	4
1971	96	2	2
1973	99	3	3
1988	109	10	10
1991	99	−10	−9
1999	93	−6	−6

* Between 1880 and 1894, the Assembly grew incrementally to reflect the growth in the number of registered voters.
Sources: Hawker 1971; Hogan and Clune 2001.

Legislative Assembly (MLA) represents over 44 000 electors, nearly six times the number in 1904. As this growing ratio indicates, the causes of the fluctuation in numbers of MLAs have not been related to population growth (but see Stone 1998, 46) and some of the early changes were sparked by alterations to the ambit of NSW government. Queensland's creation as a separate colony in 1859 produced the drop from eighty to seventy-two MLAs and the 1904 reduction took into account representation in the new Commonwealth parliament. This reduction followed a plebiscite at which 90 was the winning figure against the alternatives of 110 or 125 MLAs.

Since 1904 each of the changes to the size of the Assembly have resulted from government attempts to gain electoral advantages by triggering redistributions. Between 1950 and 1988, two coalition and two Labor governments increased the size of the Assembly to achieve this outcome. Drawing on neo-liberal arguments for smaller government and perceptions that (as in 1904) the people preferred fewer members of parliament, the Greiner and Carr governments reduced the Assembly size in 1991 and 1999 respectively to precipitate redistributions. Partisan motives, rather than population size or debates about adequate representation, have driven changes to the size of the Assembly (Goot 1986, 14–31; Dickson 1999, 17; Hogan 2001b, 30).

Since 1856 most ministers have sat in the Legislative Assembly, although governments have always had at least one minister to represent them in the Legislative Council. Consequently, the main task of keeping ministers accountable has fallen to the Assembly. Measured purely by the few ministerial dismissals and resignations forced by the Assembly, this task would seem to have been imperfectly performed. Governments have usually relied on their numbers and ambiguities in the cases against their ministers to weather opposition attacks (Hawker 1971, 234–8; Parker 1978, 202–3).[3]

The capacity of the Assembly to scrutinize the executive has been limited by the reluctance of governments to develop a lower house committee system. Eighty-two select committees were formed between 1901 and 1910 before party politics solidified, compared with three in the 1950s. Assembly committee activity has increased since its nadir in the 1960s, when Premier Askin's coalition government rejected any need for select committees. Wran allowed select committees to investigate several policy areas in the 1970s but resisted the establishment of standing committees until 1982. Despite the potential of this reform, the outcomes have been limited. The current Staysafe Joint Standing Committee on Road Safety was formed in 1982 and the Public Accounts Committee (PAC) in 1983. Both have done valuable work, with the PAC gaining extensive powers to examine government expenditure. The high point of Assembly committee work arguably came in the period 1991 to 1995, when the coalition government's memorandum of understanding with the Independents resulted in a number of legislation committees which examined and made recommendations on draft government bills. Non-government MLAs also chaired several select committees in this period. The resumption of majority Labor government from 1995 saw these developments halted (Hawker 1971, 283–5; Clune 1992, 19–21; Kerr 1993; R. Smith 1995; Collins 2000, 139–40; Clune and Turner 2001, 79, 84; Turner 2001a, 186–7; Turner 2001b, 224–5).

The popular idea that the Legislative Assembly is the toughest chamber of the Australian parliaments – summed up in its longstanding nicknames the 'bear garden' and 'bear pit' (Aitkin 1969, 266; Parker 1978, 223; Clune 1992, 15; Collins 2000) – is doubtful when comparisons are made with, for example, Queensland. Nonetheless, the politics of the Assembly have often been robust. Because governments try so hard to dominate the house, the Assembly has been a proving ground for successful opposition leaders like McKell, Askin, Wran, Greiner and Carr. Poor parliamentary performances have helped to undermine other contenders like Liberal opposition leaders Bruce Macdonald and Peter Collins (Dale 1985, 14; Thompson 1985; Cunneen 2000, 112; Collins 2000, 132; R. Smith 2001b, 374; Turner 2001b, 223–4).

Majoritarian party politics has been the key factor underlying these features of the Assembly. Two other factors have been important. First, as indicated above, the political styles of premiers have some impact on the Assembly culture. The second factor has been the stance of the speaker. In the party era, the nineteenth-century notion of an impartial speaker has been difficult to maintain. The early experiences of the Liberal Henry Willis (speaker 1911–13) and the Nationalist Daniel Levy (initially speaker 1919–21, later 1921–24, 1927–30 and 1932–37) pointed to the major parties' desires to use the speakership to their advantage. Both took the speakership when the party numbers in the Assembly were evenly balanced, giving their Labor opponents government. Both were heavily criticized and Willis, having fallen out of his party's favour, lost his seat at the 1913 election. Governing parties have consistently used their majorities to impose speakers from their parties on the Legislative Assembly.[4] Proposals, like those of Levy and Liberal Kevin Rozzoli (speaker 1988–95), to establish an independent speakership have been rejected by the major parties (Hawker 1971, 249–57; Clune 1992, 20; Hogan 2001e, 122–3, 147).

The executive

Once the political role of governors diminished, the key figures in the state executive have undoubtedly been the premiers. Unlike some other states, no single individual dominates the ranks as the longest serving premier. Current record holders Neville Wran (Labor, 1976–86) and Robert Askin (Liberal, 1965–75) each held the office for just a little over a decade. Six other leaders – Joe Cahill (Labor, 1952–59), Bertram Stevens (United Australia Party, 1932–39), Bob Carr (Labor, 1995–), William Holman (Labor and Nationalist, 1913–20), William McKell (Labor, 1941–47) and James McGirr (Labor, 1947–52) – served for at least five years. Wran, Askin, Stevens, Carr, Holman and McKell each set a strong stamp on government by winning elections that took their parties from opposition to government, setting government policy directions and strategy, and defining public perceptions of their administrations. The same features marked the briefer premierships of figures like Jack Lang (Labor, 1925–27, 1930–32) and Nick Greiner (1988–92).

There is evidence for a recent trend towards more presidential-style premiers. Elections have centred more closely on the leadership contenders since Labor's successful 1978 'Wran's Our Man' and 1981 'It's Got to Be Wran' campaigns. Day-to-day media coverage centres on the leaders, while published public opinion polls often highlight the leaders' standings ahead of those of their parties. Within government, the machinery available to the premier for policy coordination and direction has increased in recent decades. Wran's building of a policy role for the premier's department and his creation of policy bodies like the Ministerial Advisory Unit and Greiner's creation of a Cabinet Office to take over these policy roles indicate this trend.

The extra-parliamentary party constraints on non-Labor premiers have always been tenuous and recent Labor premiers appear to have faced fewer party-related constraints than their predecessors. It is worth remembering, however, that the Labor premier who probably exercised greatest personal power over his party was Jack Lang in the 1920s and that Premier Carr was forced by the threat of defeat by Labor's State Conference to abandon his electricity privatization policy as recently as 1997 (Parker 1978, 345–6; Chaples et al. 1985; Dale 1985; Nairn 1986, 70–209; Steketee and Cockburn 1986, 144–53; Painter 1987, 44, 97–105, 113–15, 185–9; Laffin 1995, 74–81; T. Smith 2001, 378–9).

The number of other government ministers has doubled over the past century, from around ten in the first decade to about twenty from the 1980s. The number of portfolios held by ministers has increased around fourfold over the same period, from eleven or twelve to over forty. The rate of both increases has been fairly steady across the century. As these trends imply, not only have recent governments covered more ground than their earlier counterparts, individual ministers have increasingly held multiple portfolio responsibilities. The introduction of a cabinet standing committee system in the mid-1970s was one important response to these increases in ministerial numbers, scope and workload (Parker 1978, 250–8; Painter 1987, 61, 94–6; Moon and Sayers 1999, 155–6).

Most alterations to the structure and scope of ministries have not occurred immediately after a change in the party of government. The initial portfolio shape of most incoming governments has been remarkably similar to that of their immediate predecessors. Portfolio changes have been incremental, made as administrations have settled into the tasks of government (Parker 1978, 252–3).

The public sector

The development of the New South Wales public sector can be broadly divided into three phases: expansion of public sector in the colonial period to meet basic governance and physical infrastructure needs, further expansion until the 1980s primarily to meet an increasing range of social needs, and contraction across the board since the 1980s.

The colonial period established high public sector employment and activity in New South Wales. The requirements of the penal colony meant that almost all employees were initially on the public purse, while later colonial governments met the demands of settler capital and society for services such as railways through a growing number of statutory corporations. Until the late 1980s state public sector employment grew fairly steadily, rising from 107 000 in 1939, for example, to 374 000 in 1987–88. For long periods, this growth outstripped those of the state's total population and workforce. Coalition and Labor governments from 1988 to 2001–02 have reversed these trends. The absolute number of state public sector employees is down to 352 000, the same level as in the early 1980s. The proportion of the workforce in state public sector employment has dropped from 20 per cent to 14 per cent (Parker 1978, 338–9; Painter 1987, 56; Young 1987; Evatt Research Centre 1989, 163; ABS 2002).

The priorities of state public sector activity have shifted over the past century, broadly reflecting the changes in ministerial portfolio coverage. Areas like law and order have retained a reasonably fixed share of government expenditure. The share of expenditure on physical infrastructure has declined, while the social activity areas of education, health and social welfare have grown from around one-fifth of state expenditure to over one-half. Agencies delivering education, health and social welfare services also dominate state public sector employment (Painter 1987, 26; Parker 1978, 274–5; New South Wales Treasury 2001; NSW Premier's Department 2000).

Until the 1970s public sector activity typically developed in an ad hoc way, facilitated by an incremental approach to budget preparation by Treasury and by the power of an independent Public Service Board (PSB) over staffing and resources in all public service departments. Since the 1970s Labor and coalition governments have tried to achieve greater policy coordination and direction. Following recommendations by the Review of New South Wales Government Administration chaired by Peter Wilenski, the Wran government reduced the power of the PSB in 1979. The Greiner government abolished it altogether in 1988. Decisions about staffing, budgets and resource allocation within agencies shifted to the government of the day and agency heads. The Greiner government gave ministers stronger control over agency heads by establishing a performance- and contract-based Senior Executive Service, another idea foreshadowed in Wilenski's Review. Over the same period, governments moved Treasury to redefine its work in more strategic terms linked to the government of the day's explicit policy goals, first through program budgeting and later through medium-term target budgeting (Parker 1978, 277–328; Painter 1987, 39–42, 46–9, 62–4, 103–12; Halligan and Power 1992, 114–60; Alaba 1994; Laffin 1995, 78; NSW Treasury 1999).

In related shifts, the Greiner government applied strategies of corporatization, commercialization and, in cases like Graincorp and the State Bank, privatization to the public sector. Previous areas of public sector monopoly such as railways and electricity became government trading enterprises operating against specific targets and, where possible, in neutral competition with non-government rivals. Under Greiner, New South Wales led the states in these developments. Although reforms slowed under Fahey and Carr, and Victoria took the lead in public sector micro-economic reform, later governments maintained the market, 'post-bureaucratic' directions that Greiner set (Halligan and Power 1992, 146–50; Gellatly 1994; Laffin 1995, 86–7; Painter 1995; Domberger and Hall 1996).

The electoral system

Electoral developments in the different states have followed idiosyncratic paths. New South Wales has not consistently led or followed any other state in electoral reforms. The major changes to electoral arrangements in New South Wales were concentrated in the first three decades and final three decades of the twentieth century. The explanation for this pattern of activity and inactivity seems clear enough. In the first period, the emerging major parties each attempted to consolidate their positions by adding or changing electoral features. Having won the 1941 election under electoral rules established by its opponents in 1928, Labor saw little need for reform during its long post-war rule. Impetus for reform came only when Labor struggled to regain office after losing to the coalition in 1965. The election of the Wran government in 1976 provided the opportunity to implement change.

The main dimensions of enfranchisement in New South Wales were settled in 1902, when almost all women gained the vote. By then, virtually full male franchise for British subjects (including Aboriginal men) had operated for forty-four years and 'one man, one vote' for nine years. In less dramatic changes, people living on charity aid were enfranchised in 1926, the voting age was lowered from 21 to 18 years in 1973 and Australian citizenship became the primary basis of enrolment for state residents in 1984. Compulsory voter enrolment was introduced in 1921, ten years after the Commonwealth, and compulsory voting in 1928, four years after the Commonwealth and fourteen years after Queensland. The Wran government entrenched compulsory voting in 1978. Prior to 1928, voter turnouts had ranged between 56 per cent (1920) and 82 per cent (1927) (Parker 1978, 13–17; Cosgrove 2001, 334; Electoral Council of Australia 2002).

The type of ballot confronting voters changed four times between 1910 and 1928. Each change brought controversy and confusion. Until 1910 elections used first-past-the-post ballots. Between 1910 and 1917 a second run-off ballot between the two most popular candidates was used if no candidate won a majority of votes in the first ballot. Elections between 1918 and 1926 used the single transferable vote system of proportional representation with multimember electoral districts of three or five members, under which voters had to fill out preferences for all candidates. This widely criticized system was replaced by preferential voting (the alternative vote) with optional expression of preferences in single-member electoral districts at the 1927 election, before preferential voting with the compulsory ranking of candidates on the ballot (full preferential voting) became the norm for the next fifty years in 1928.

Each of these changes reflected attempts to gain partisan advantage. Labor favoured the original first-past-the-post system. The Liberals and Nationalists introduced the second ballot and then proportional representation to try to compensate for Labor's large vote and the split of non-Labor votes between competing anti-Labor candidates. The early rural parties favoured proportional representation as a means of ensuring parliamentary representation. When Labor's 1926 attempt to return to a first-past-the-post system was blocked in the Legislative Council, Labor accepted the next-best alternative – optional preferential voting. In 1928 Bavin's Nationalist–Country Party coalition government introduced full preferential voting. This allowed the Nationalist and Country parties to run candidates against each other, and the Country Party to run multiple candidates in individual seats, without delivering seats to Labor (Aitkin 1969, 98–100; Aitkin 1972, 221–36; Parker 1978, 19–21; Hogan 2001d, 99–100; Hogan 2001g, 183–9; Cosgrove 2001, 334–9; Robinson 2001, 6–7).

The Wran Labor government's return to optional preferential voting for the Assembly in 1979 was partly an attempt to reduce informal voting, widely believed to affect Labor more than the anti-Labor parties, and partly an effort to disrupt preference flows between competing coalition candidates in three-cornered contests. The optional preference system has achieved the latter aim more successfully than the former. The Greiner Liberal Party–National Party coalition government's 1990 electoral amendments, which made a single tick or cross on a ballot paper an informal rather than formal vote, increased Labor's problems with informal votes. Informal voting in the 1991 Assembly poll almost tripled, disadvantaging Labor in a close election. Unsurprisingly, after its 1995 election the Carr Labor government made ticks and crosses formal once again. The informal vote fell back to its pre-1991 level (Turner 1985b, 82; Green 1994, 36–42; Green 1999, 68–73; Dickson 1999, 17; Green 2001, 318).

Optional preferential voting has been used for the Legislative Council since elections for MLCs began in 1978. The non-Labor dominated Council rejected the Wran Government's original plan to introduce a state-wide party list system of proportional representation, designed to keep minor parties and independents out of the Council. As a compromise, with fifteen MLCs to be elected at each election, voters had to rank a minimum of ten candidates to complete a valid vote under a single transferable vote system of proportional representation. When the number of vacancies to be filled at each election rose to twenty-one at the 1995 election, the minimum number of candidates to be ranked was raised to fifteen. The optional expression of preferences eased the potential difficulties of voting in state-wide Council elections with many candidates (Turner 1985b, 80–1; Steketee and Cockburn 1986, 132).

Council voting was further simplified in 1988, when an 'above-the-line' group ticket voting option was introduced, and in 1990, when registered party names were included on Council ballot papers. The latter change undoubtedly benefited minor parties without the ability to distribute how-to-vote cards at all polling places. The almost universal choice of above-the-line voting by voters had the effect of transforming the electoral system into a list system of proportional representation and enabled parties to control the flow of preferences in Council elections. In the 1999 election an Outdoor Recreation Party MLC who won just 0.2 per cent of the first preference vote was elected on preferences from other group tickets. The established parties became concerned that the system was allowing tiny and sometimes bogus parties to manipulate Council elections. The Carr government has subsequently legislated to alter above-the-line voting so that restrictions will be put on the ability of parties to transfer preferences to other parties (R. Smith 1997, 226; R. Smith 2001b, 408–9; Green 2002).

Four key factors have affected the sizes of Assembly electoral districts and their fairness in terms of proportionally translating votes into seats. The first three have been decisions of parliament concerning the number of seats (see above), the timing of redistributions and the division of the state into different electoral zones. The fourth factor has been the decisions of the commissioners responsible for drawing boundaries within the constraints of the first three factors.

The legislated gap between 'normal' redistributions has fluctuated from between five and nine years. Since 1979 redistributions have been required after every second election. After 1995 this meant every eight years, given the fixed four-year parliament. A 1990 amendment, not yet invoked, provides for additional redistributions under some circumstances when over one-quarter of electoral districts vary from the average enrolment by over 5 per cent. Normal redistribution cycles within these different periods have been interrupted by changes to the number of electoral districts and to electoral zones. From 1965 to 1999 candidates contested twelve elections on eight sets of boundaries as governments attempted to derive electoral advantage from redistributions (Parker 1978, 29–30; Green 1997, 3–5; R. Smith 2001b, 387–8).

Governments intervened even more directly in electoral boundaries between 1928 and 1978 by dividing the state into electoral zones containing electoral districts with different average numbers of voters. Until 1893 country electoral districts in the colonial period were generally deliberately designed to have fewer voters than city districts. Formal electoral zoning began in 1918, when the new proportional representation system required rural seats to return three members each and metropolitan seats five. These requirements could, however, be achieved without much difference in the quotas needed to elect city and country MLAs (Hogan 2001g, 187–8).

In 1928 the Bavin Nationalist–Country Party coalition government introduced zones specifically designed to over-weight rural votes. Bavin's scheme produced a Sydney Zone of 43 seats, a Newcastle Zone of 5, with the remaining 42 in the Country Zone. In 1949 Labor redrew the zones to its advantage, dividing the state into a Sydney Zone of 48 seats and a Country Zone, now incorporating Newcastle, of 46. In 1969 the coalition shifted Newcastle into a 63-seat Central Zone with Sydney, Wollongong and parts of the Blue Mountains, leaving 33 seats in the Country Zone (Parker 1978, 26–8).

Just before the Wran government abolished zoning, Country seats had around two-thirds the voters of Central seats. Such malapportionment was relatively mild compared with that in Western Australia, South Australia and Queensland. Moreover, unlike some other states, previous Labor administrations had been able to manipulate the zonal system to their favour. By the 1970s, however, the long-term decline in the Labor voting rural workforce and the growth of the greater Sydney population made Wran's abolition of zones in favour of 'one vote, one value' the measure that best advantaged Labor (Rydon 1968; Blewett 1973; Rydon 1976, 412; Parker 1978, 28, 64–5; Green 2001, 300–1).

New South Wales has a long tradition of independent electoral boundary drawing. The law specifying the three Electoral Districts Commissioners is slightly looser than in most other states, allowing the government to choose a judge and a surveyor to sit with the only fixed appointee, the Electoral Commissioner. The appointments of particular commissioners have sometimes been contentious, as have the results of their deliberations. From the 1950s to the 1980s independent commissioners consistently drew boundaries favouring the government of the day. This pattern may have been broken in the 1990s. The 1990–91 redistribution eliminated the then government's electoral disadvantage under the 1988 boundaries but did not penalize the Labor opposition. The 1997–98 redistribution actually favoured the opposition, reducing the swing it needed to win office while making the Carr Labor government's task of retaining office harder (Mackerras 1973, 189–90; Parker 1978, 22, 30–4; Goot 1986, 2–3; Green 1994, 29–35; Green 1997, 5–6; Green 1998; Green 2001, 301–4; R. Smith 2001b, 387–8).

Parties and the party system

The Labor Party

The origins of the party system lie in the success of thirty-five Labor Electoral League candidates, sponsored by the trade union Labor Council, at the 1891 elections. The new Labor Party disrupted the colonial political pattern of factions forming around leaders like Henry Parkes, John Roberston, James Martin and Charles Cowper. Labor's key organizing principles – incorporation of trade unions within its formal organizational structures, policy platforms set by its extra-parliamentary bodies, and parliamentary representatives bound to vote as a bloc – were established within a few years (Loveday and Martin 1966; Loveday et al. 1977a; Hagan and Turner 1991, 3–33).

The New South Wales branch is widely regarded as one of the most successful but more conservative of Labor's state branches. Labor governed for 58.7 per cent of the period from 1910 to 2000, a proportion only bettered by Tasmania's 60.6 per cent (Australian Government and Politics database). The state party suffered two major splits over that period, both in the first half of the century. In the first, Premier William Holman supported conscription in 1916, was expelled from the ALP and became leader of the state's anti-Labor forces. All but one minister followed Holman out of the party, which was reduced from forty-nine to twenty-four of the Assembly's ninety seats. The second major split followed Premier Jack Lang's confrontation with the Commonwealth and the other states over government expenditure and payment of government interest debts to Britain during the depression. The Labor Federal Executive expelled its New South Wales branch in 1931 with the result that, between 1932 and 1936, state and federal elections were contested by two Labor parties, the Federal Labor Party and the State Labor Party. Labor's combined state vote dropped from 55.1 per cent in 1930 to 44.5 per cent in 1932, almost all of it won by expelled State Labor candidates. The Federal Party was forced to re-admit State Labor after a similar election result in 1935. Labor did not regain office until May 1941 but has governed for 70 per cent of the period since (Evatt 1979, 300–24; Nairn 1986, 210–306; Hagan and Turner 1991, 85–94, 106–15; Cunneen 2000, 104–29; Hogan 2001f, 164–79; Robinson 2001, 56–64).

The perception of New South Wales Labor conservatism has been fuelled by the post-war ascendancy of the Right faction, with its strong conservative Catholic element. Even prior to the factional system, the dominant strand within New South Wales Labor was always labourism[5] rather than radical socialism. The earliest Labor platforms, for example, emphasized wage arbitration, pensions, land reform, white Australia and state ownership of selected enterprises (Markey 1988; Hagan and Turner 1991, 15–56; Cumming 1991; Simms 2000; Leigh 2000, 429).

This relative conservatism has several causes. First, New South Wales Labor has always had a strong rural, as well as urban, membership and supporter base. The Australian Workers Union (AWU), primarily representing shearers and other seasonal rural labourers, deeply influenced the party in its formative years. Although its influence declined in the turmoil of the Lang era and with the later shrinking of the rural workforce, the AWU helped establish the party's conservative labourist ethos (Markey 1988; Hagan and Turner 1991, 33–46, 81–94; Hearn and Knowles 1996).

Outside its organization, Labor's electoral dominance in New South Wales has always rested on its capacity to win rural electoral districts. Its historic rural electoral successes, particularly under McKell in the 1940s, are part of the party's mythology. Recent leaders like Wran and Carr have deliberately set out to emulate them. Economic and social policies that might scare off non-metropolitan supporters are thus treated with caution (Hallam 1983; Hagan and Turner 1991, 33–46, 172–6; Cunneen 2000, 127–8; Clune 2001b, 184–9, 199; T. Smith 2001, 405).

Secondly, New South Wales Labor has overwhelmingly seen winning and retaining office as its goal, and the need to appeal to a broad constituency as the key to that goal. It assimilated these lessons as early as 1898, when, after the steady decline in Labor votes that followed its dramatic electoral debut of 1891, the party moderated its ideological position to draw in new groups of voters (see figure 3.1). Labor has since shown a willingness to change policies to capture or recapture sections of the electorate, even when this has produced conflict with the federal party. In the mid-1960s, for example, the branch moved against the wishes of Labor's Federal Executive to appeal to Catholic voters by matching the opposition's promises on state aid for independent schools (Hagan and Turner 1991, 18–32, 189–94; Hogan 2001b, 39; Hogan 2001c, 72–3; Puplick 2001, 446–50; Dempsey 2001, 12–14).

The early Labor governments of McGowen and Holman disappointed many in the labour movement by their legislative caution, setting a pattern to be repeated during Labor's later periods in office. The exception to the pattern – Lang, whose political style was, in fact, much more inflammatory than most of his policies – only proved the merits of cautious gradualism for most in the party. This pragmatic

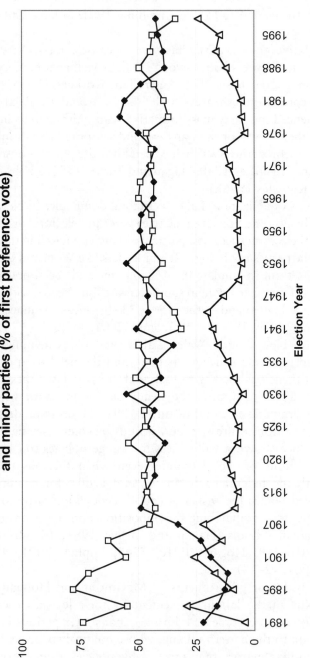

Figure 3.1 New South Wales Legislative Assembly, general elections 1891–1999: vote share of ALP, Liberal and National parties (and their precursors), and minor parties (% of first preference vote)

—□— ALP   —□— Liberal & National parties (& precursors)   —◁— Minor parties & independents (residual)

Source: calculated from the Australian Government and Politics Project database, University of Western Australia.

approach to politics might be seen as characteristic of the Right faction. Importantly, however, it has had strong adherents among the Left (Nelson 1977; Evatt 1979, 266; White 1985; Hagan and Turner 1991, 70–1, 102–6; Simms 2001, 107–8).

The third and most recent factor is the power of the Right faction, otherwise called Centre Unity or the Officers Group. The Right has held long-term majorities on the floor of State Conference, in the State Executive, the parliamentary caucus and Labor ministries. Its leadership organized the rise to the parliamentary leadership of the factionally non-aligned Neville Wran in 1973 and his successors Barrie Unsworth and Bob Carr, both members of the Right, in 1986 and 1988 (Steketee and Cockburn 1986, 73–95; Cumming 1991; Hagan and Clothier 2001, 259; Green 2001, 294).

The Right's dominance originated in the 1950s. Despite the post-war anti-communist activities of the Industrial Groups (Groupers) in the New South Wales labour movement, Labor did not suffer a mid-1950s split like Victoria or Queensland and the creation of a substantial breakaway Democratic Labor Party (DLP) vote. Memories of the disastrous 1931 split proved strong enough to prevent outright warfare destroying the party. Instead, the Groupers remained within the party, winning control of the executive in 1955 and later becoming part of the majority Right faction. The Combined Unions Steering Committee formed to combat the Groupers gradually evolved into a minority Left faction. Conflicts between Right and Left from the late 1960s led to Federal intervention in 1971 and the rewriting of the branch rules under State President John Ducker to regularize conflict between the two factions. These rules guaranteed the Left certain positions while legitimizing the power of the Right. In recent years, the Right and Left factions have both splintered as cold war politics have faded and personality and union based loyalties have emerged more strongly. Nonetheless, the combined sub-factions of the Right remain firmly in control of New South Wales Labor (Wheelwright 1983; Hagan and Turner 1991, 150–71, 209–22; Leigh 2000).

The Liberal Party

As in the other colonies, the establishment and early growth of Labor forced a rethinking of politics. By 1907 in New South Wales, the conflict between Free Traders and Protectionists which had dominated politics for half a century ended in non-Labor forces becoming the Liberal Party to contest the 1901 election. By the 1904 election the Liberals were organizationally and ideologically supported by the

Liberal and Reform Association, a group with strong roots in business and the Protestant churches. The Protectionists drew their primary support from farmers and manufacturers who supported tariffs and contested the 1901 election as Progressives or Ministerialists. They could not match the Liberals' organizational strength. The number of Progressive candidates, votes and seats dropped dramatically in 1904. Premier Joseph Carruthers was unwilling to allow his Liberals to fuse with the weakened Progressives, preferring to let the Progressives wither and then absorb their best representatives in his own party. By the 1907 election these processes were complete, inaugurating the now familiar Labor-versus-Liberal style of party politics (Hogan 2001a, 7–8, 10–12, 23–5; Hogan 2001b, 33–4, 37–8; Hogan 2001c, 59, 64–68).

By the mid-1930s the Liberal Party had undergone two transformations driven by state and federal parliamentary developments. In 1917 the party became the National Association of New South Wales, commonly known as the Nationalists, absorbing Holman and other parliamentary Labor conscription defectors. Suspicion of the ex-Labor parliamentarians and competition between rival Nationalist electoral candidates destabilised the party but did not produce change to its decentralized extra-parliamentary organization. The extra-parliamentary organization remained effective until the late 1920s but was much weakened by 1932, when the Nationalists, spurred mainly by federal parliamentary events, merged with the All for Australia League to form the United Australia Party (UAP). The UAP was organizationally weaker than its predecessors, with less coordination between its parliamentary and extra-parliamentary wings. Some individual UAP candidates were strongly influenced by external finance committees, and others were associated with outside groups like the paramilitary New Guard (Campbell 1965, 140–7; Amos 1976, 76; Watson 1979; Hogan 2001d, 98).

The disintegration of the UAP in 1943 was potentially more damaging than the previous two re-alignments of the major non-Labor party. Following its 1941 New South Wales and 1943 federal election losses, the UAP was challenged by alternative conservative extra-parliamentary organizations like the Commonwealth Party and the Liberal Democratic Party (LDP). The UAP and Commonwealth Party combined in the short-lived Democratic Party in 1943, before the LDP joined them to form the New South Wales Division of the Liberal Party in 1945 (Cunneen 2001, 211–15; Clune 2001a, 247–50).

The new division proved more durable than its predecessors. Its key organizational reform was to reject external control of party funding in favour of control by a strong state executive. Organizational coherence was assisted by the powerful, forward-planning and long-serving General Secretary John Carrick, who held his post from 1948 to 1971. Although tension existed between Carrick and Robert Askin (deputy leader 1954–59, opposition leader 1959–65 and premier 1965–75) over campaign finances, Askin's long parliamentary leadership also helped give the party stability (Clune 2001a, 249; Puplick 2001, 435–6, 462; Harwin 2001, 37–40).

Ironically, the Liberals' post-war organizational stability has not translated into a greater share of government. Non-Labor parties governed for 63 per cent of the period from 1910 to 1945 but only 31 per cent of the time since. One reason is that the post-war Liberals faced a far more stable Labor machine than their predecessors. Secondly, since the mid-1970s the party has been impatient to win office, regularly toppling state parliamentary leaders in the hope of finding an election winner. Thirdly, in contrast to New South Wales Labor's regularization of factional conflict, the Liberals have struggled to accommodate or even acknowledge rising factional divisions between moderates and conservatives since the 1970s. Mostly out of power, the Liberals have turned on each other in the way long-term Labor oppositions have done in other states (Connell and Gould 1967; Turner 1985a, 17; Collins 2000, 100–5, 144–6, 148–9; Harwin 2001, 38).

The National Party

Since 1919 the non-Labor side of party politics in New South Wales has been divided between parties of town and country. The 'country' party, called the National Party since 1982,[6] has been stronger than its counterparts in every other state and territory except Queensland. The traditional bastions of the National Party have been rural communities in the north of the state based on grazing, mixed farming and wheat-growing. The party's strength in northern New South Wales was reflected in its active campaigning until the 1950s for a new state of New England. Like country parties in other states, the National Party has won support by appealing to regional town dwellers as well as people directly involved in agriculture. Although the Nationals toyed with the idea of following their Queensland counterparts and pushing into metropolitan seats in the mid-1980s, resource limitations and Liberal hostility prevented such a move (see Aitkin 1969; Aitkin 1972; Lucy 1985a; Turner 1985c, 202–4).

New South Wales rural political organizations date from the late nineteenth century. The Country Party emerged in 1922 from the

Progressive Party, a group of dissident urban and rural Nationalists supported by the Farmers and Settlers Association and the Graziers Association. At the core of the Country Party were rurally based Progressive MLAs – the True Blues – who had rejected a Progressive–Nationalist coalition in 1921. After pursuing a relatively unsuccessful 'support in return for concessions' strategy with the Nationalists, however, the Country Party accepted four ministries and junior coalition status in Bavin's 1927 administration (Graham 1966, 55–65, 167–75, 269–79; Aitkin 1969, 33–124; Hogan 2001b, 39; Hogan 2001d, 100).

Coalition relations have persisted in government but not always in opposition. They have periodically proved difficult on several fronts. First, the ideology and policies of the coalition partners have not always aligned. Longstanding Country Party Leader Michael Bruxner, for example, thought the UAP too disparate to be a genuine party with sound policies. National Party social conservatism and enthusiasm for state spending on development have caused more recent friction with 'small l' liberals and free marketeers among the Liberals. The second difficulty has been seniority, with the number and nature of portfolios allocated the Nationals in governments a matter of concern to both coalition parties. Sometimes seniority has produced tensions in opposition. In 1981, for example, when the numbers of National Country Party and Liberal MLAs were even, National Leader Leon Punch unsuccessfully sought recognition as opposition leader ahead of Liberal Leader John Dowd. Third, the coalition parties have found it difficult to agree on who should run for which non-metropolitan seats, particularly given the absence of clear Liberal and National heartlands (Aitkin 1969, 133, 143–4, 150, 164–5, 214–5, 250–15; Aitkin 1972, 279–96; Lucy 1985a; Lucy 1985b, 134–5; Turner 1985c, 202–3; Collins 2000, 259–60; Turner 2001b, 229–31).

Despite urban population drift, the Nationals have retained steady parliamentary representation. Apart from a brief heyday in the 1930s when they held about one-quarter of the Assembly seats, the Nationals' seat share has not exceeded 18 per cent. Nor, in the post-war period, has it fallen below 14 per cent (see figure 3.2). The forces against the National Party retaining this seat share have been strong. The party's responses have included its name change from Country to National, leadership change and greater emphasis on regional as against strictly rural concerns. These changes have, in turn, sparked defections from the party and the loss of several safe National seats to conservative independent candidates. The Nationals have, however, proved remarkably resilient and have resisted the periodic calls for amalgamation with

Figure 3.2 New South Wales Legislative Assembly, general elections 1891–1999: seat share of Liberal Party (and precursors), National (Country) Party, minor parties and independents (%)

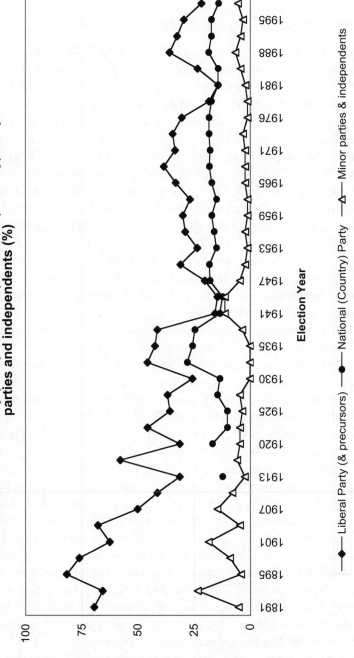

Source: calculated from the Australian Government and Politics Project database, University of Western Australia.

the Liberals which began in the early 1940s (Aitkin 1969, 251; Aitkin 1972, 65; Lucy 1985a; Turner 1985c, 203; Costar 1990, 22–3; Turner 2001b, 241–2; T. Smith 2001, 393–5, 408).

Minor parties and independents

Apart from these major parties, a large number of minor parties and independents have contested political office and some have achieved relevance in New South Wales politics. Since 1910 minor party and independent activity has peaked in three periods (see figure 3.3). The first was the mid-1930s to mid-1940s, when a number of breakaway and alternative parties clustering around the existing Labor and the anti-Labor parties were formed. The second wave built in the late 1960s and early 1970s, peaking at 13 per cent of the first preference Assembly vote in 1973. This peak reflected an increased DLP vote, but also votes for independents and for the new Australia Party (a 'new politics' predecessor of the Australian Democrats). The third period extends from the mid-1980s to the present, during which time the Australian Democrats, the Greens and independents have drawn the largest pools of Assembly votes. In the 1999 election the One Nation vote added to this mix and helped push the non-major party first preference Assembly vote to 24 per cent.

While minor parties and independents have often been important to the electoral fortunes of the major parties, the electoral system has meant that few have achieved parliamentary representation. After 1910 minor parties and independents won hardly any Assembly seats, with small peaks of thirteen seats won by alternative Labor and non-Labor candidates and independents at the 1941 and 1944 elections and seven independent seats after the 1988 election (see figure 3.4). These peaks do not correspond with the periods when lower house minor party and independent representatives could exercise greatest influence, which occurred during the minority Labor governments of 1920 to 1922 and 1950 to 1953 and the minority coalition governments of 1991 to 1995. The Labor minority governments were supported by Labor-leaning independents; however, the coalition minority governments had to cope with, among others, three non-aligned independents to remain in office.

Since the democratization of the Legislative Council, nine minor parties have won seats. Three features of this representation are worth noting. The first is the steady growth in votes and seats won by minor candidates, reaching 35 per cent and seven of twenty-one seats at the 1999 election. The second is diversity – upper house votes and seats are not concentrated on one minor party such as the Democrats, but are

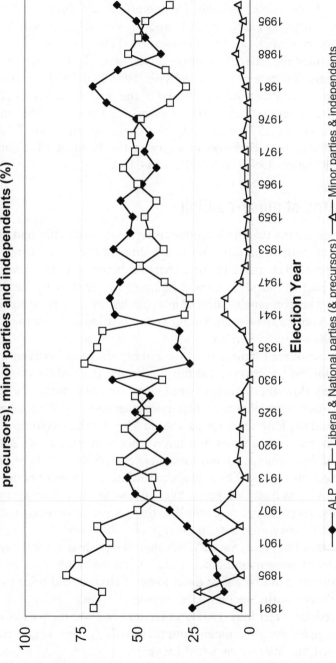

Figure 3.3 New South Wales Legislative Assembly, general elections 1891–1999: seat share of ALP, Liberal and National parties (and their precursors), minor parties and independents (%)

Source: calculated from the Australian Government and Politics Project database, University of Western Australia.

spread across a range of candidates (see tables 3.1 and 3.3). Upper house minor party representation encompasses single issue and interest parties such as the Shooters Party, ideologically based parties such as the fundamentalist Christian Democratic Party (formerly Fred Nile's Call to Australia Party, or CTA) and the Greens, and broad-spectrum issue parties such as the Democrats. Third, no minor party has commanded the balance of power on its own. The Democrats and CTA shared the balance of power between 1988 and 1995. Overwhelming support for coalition bills from two of the three CTA MLCs effectively gave the Democrats the balance of power between 1988 and 1991, while between 1991 and 1995 the coalition plus two CTA MLCs formed the most common majority in the Council (R. Smith 1995, 23–7; R. Smith 1997; Nile 2001, 126–204).

Patterns of office-holding

Throughout the twentieth century, New South Wales has had one of the most competitive patterns of office-holding among the Australian polities. From 1910 government alternated between Labor and the non-Labor parties fourteen times, a figure exceeded only by Victoria with fifteen. The average duration of government by a party or coalition has been a comparatively short 6.02 years, beating only Victoria and the Australian Capital Territory.

These overall figures disguise a sharp division between a volatile party contest for government during the first third of the century and a relatively slow alternation between parties in office during the final two-thirds. Between John See's first post-federation NSW government in 1901 and the UAP's win over Labor in May 1932, government changed party hands eleven times and governments averaged just 2.82 years. Nine of those changes of government occurred after 1910, after Labor's first election victory. The average period of government between 1910 and 1932 was just 2.40 years. Even if George Fuller's first government of only seven hours is excluded, there were still seven substantive changes of government at an average of 2.70 years.

At that rate, New South Wales should have had around twenty-two changes of government since 1932. It has had only five, and parties have survived in office four times longer than they did prior to 1932. If Labor's currently uncompleted period of office under Bob Carr is included, between May 1932 and December 2000 the parties averaged 11.45 years in government once elected. If Carr's government is excluded, the average rises to 12.6 years.

After 1932, then, the pattern of NSW government switched from brisk competition to slowly oscillating hegemony. The coalition governed from 1932 to 1941, Labor from 1941 to 1965, the coalition from 1965 to 1976 and Labor from 1976 to 1988. Of these periods, Labor's eight consecutive election wins and 24-year rule from 1941 represented by far the longest party predominance. It is worth noting, however, that after three elections this predominance was seriously threatened in 1950, when the coalition won as many seats as Labor and the governments of James McGirr and Joe Cahill relied on two pro-Labor independents until 1953. Had Labor lost office in 1950, its period of predominance would have been no longer than that of the UAP-led coalition it succeeded.

Office-holding since 1988 has conformed more closely to the post-1932 than the pre-1932 pattern. The coalition's 1988 electoral triumph looked a likely basis for a new period of party hegemony. The coalition's unexpected loss of its majority at the 1991 election, followed by its narrow 1995 loss to Labor, left this expectation unfulfilled (see Green 2001; T. Smith 2001). Although the coalition failed to achieve party predominance in the 1990s, this did not represent a return to pre-1932 government fluidity. The seven years of coalition government under Nick Greiner and John Fahey exceeded by one year the tenure of the longest-serving government before the 1930s (the Liberal government of 1904 to 1910).

What explains these patterns of office-holding? The NSW pre-1932 pattern is not atypical of the Australian states (Butler 1968, 16–17; Parker 1978, 53). The formation of stable party systems and the building of consistent electoral support did not occur quickly. Only Victoria, Queensland and Tasmania had periods of predominant parties before the 1930s, each dating from between 1915 and 1917, the period of Labor's conscription split. Each helps explain why New South Wales did not have similar early party dominance. In Victoria, unlike New South Wales, the Labor vote simply did not grow enough to challenge the Liberals. In Queensland, the Labor vote was the strongest of any state by 1916 and, uniquely, the state branch was united against conscription. Premier Ryan led Labor through the wartime crisis to initiate Labor's first period of governing hegemony (see Fitzgerald 1984, 8–11). In Tasmania, Labor had built up enough votes to govern from 1914 but it lost support after the party split in 1916 over conscription.

In New South Wales, Labor could have built a similar period of hegemony to that in Queensland. Like Ryan, by 1916 Holman led a Labor Party that had more than doubled its vote over the preceding decade. It had won the previous two elections. After 1916, NSW Labor took a path closer to Tasmania's than Queensland's as the conscription split destroyed its opportunity for early dominance. Equally, the under-lying strength of Labor's NSW vote and instability in the non-Labor parties prevented dominance by non-Labor parties until the 1931 Labor split.

Labor's long post-war hegemony was the last to begin with an opposing party's collapse. The post-war pattern of party dominance occurred less via default than through stable party organization, government manipulation of electoral systems and use of public policy to shore up support in apparently wavering electoral districts. Strong leadership by McKell, Askin and Wran may also have helped. With the exception of McKell, their successors failed to extend significantly their party's hegemony. On the other hand, it is extremely doubtful that Askin and Wran would have won the next elections had they stayed on. The fall of post-war NSW governments has had more to do with policy exhaustion, electoral dissatisfaction over government management and the build-up of perceptions of government corruption than the retire-ment of strong leaders (Hickie 1985; Steketee and Cockburn 1986, 262–91; Reading 1989; Hagan and Turner 1991, 186–95, 243–51; Gleeson et al. 1992; Chaples and Page 1995; Bennett 2001; Hagan and Clothier 2001).

Conclusion

At the start of the twenty-first century, the position of New South Wales as the most populous and wealthy state seems assured. To the extent that it can claim to be the premier state in terms of its political institu-tions and public policies, the evidence of this chapter suggests that such a result has been arrived at by accident as much as by design. Institutions such as the Legislative Council have become important in ways not anticipated by those who sought to reform them. The elec-toral system has developed out of struggles for supremacy between the major parties. The path of public sector micro-economic reform in the 1990s was effected by the accident of three non-aligned independent MLAs holding the balance of power. The other chapters in this book suggest equally contingent patterns of political development in the different states. Sometimes New South Wales is the leader, sometimes the follower, sometimes it is on its own.

The extent to which New South Wales remains a Labor state is also under question. This might seem a surprising thought after the ALP's landslide victory – fifty-five Assembly seats to the coalition's thirty-three – at the 1999 state election. Nonetheless, Labor's share of the first pref-erence Assembly votes in 1999 was just 42.2 per cent and its Council vote just 37.3 per cent. Compared with past Labor victories, these figures are meagre indeed. New South Wales is less straightforwardly a Labor state than it was under McKell or Wran. But the erosion of support for the major parties is not something that is unique to New South Wales. In this, as in other respects, the state continues to be a microcosm of larger, Australia-wide trends.

Chapter

4

Queensland

John Wanna

The fundamentals of Queensland's political system were established in the initial decades of white settlement and colonial self-government. The contentious separation of the colony in 1859 from the already self-governing colony of New South Wales and the challenges of building communities in a largely tropical environment remained important factors shaping the polity. In addition, Queensland became the most decentralized mainland state, with rural populism being an important component of both the Labor and anti-Labor politics (Mullins 1986; P. Smith 1985) complemented by strong party leaders who often became autocratic and intransigent premiers. Elements of this country bias have persisted, especially among the anti-Labor parties, with the rural-based National Party remaining the largest anti-Labor party in terms of parliamentary representation.

More than any other state, Queensland politics has been character-ized by hegemonic party rule. The main parties have enjoyed long periods of rule winning election after election with relatively stable voter support. The Australian Labor Party (ALP) governed from 1915 to 1957 with only one interruption; while the anti-Labor parties, usually in coalition, governed from 1957 until 1989. This winner-take-all hegemony has had a profound influence on the nature of state politics, on the configuration of the political institutions, and on Queensland's insular political culture. Threats to party hegemony have occurred only infrequently and the dominance of the governing party has been chal-lenged only in times of war, depression or internal party crisis. Although Queensland politics has changed since the 1980s, elements of a culture of hegemonic party rule remain.

Foundations

For eighty years after the first European settlement on the east coast of Australia, the territory later to become known as Queensland formed part of New South Wales. Brisbane was initially established as a remote penal colony after the NSW Governor Sir Thomas Brisbane had sent the surveyor-general, John Oxley, in 1823 to find a suitably remote river north of the Clarence on which a penal settlement could be established for hardened convicts. For the first twenty years, convicts were the mainstay of the Moreton Bay and Northern Districts communities. But early reports noted the fertile lands around Brisbane and the abundance of vegetation; the area was considered attractive for free settlement and internal convict transportation was ended in 1842.

Under administration from Sydney, and with nine northern members in the New South Wales parliament, early settlers expressed a strong preference for self-rule and campaigned vigorously for recognition as a separate colony to be called Cooksland. Separation from New South Wales became the dominant topic for local politics (*Pugh's Almanac* 1859), and self-rule as the colony of Queensland was granted in June 1859 when the European population was around 23 500. Self-government was seen as a means of fostering economic development; it was not driven by noble ideals of establishing a new kind of political system or a more humane and tolerant society. Nor was it based on political, religious, or cultural differences or the desire to establish a more liberal political regime (compare Pike 1967). Self-government was based on the need to counter geographic isolation, to reflect territorial identity, and to enhance the representation of local producer groups. Queensland began largely as a business venture to lure settlers and to spur economic development.

Early politics were intensely parochial. The first elections for the lower chamber, the Legislative Assembly, were held over two weeks in April and May 1860. A total of 4790 voters in sixteen electorates returned twenty-six members – a ratio of one representative to each 320 electors. The elected representatives met in temporary accommodation, the Old Convict Barracks, located in Queen Street, on 22 May 1860. Following the model of New South Wales, the upper chamber, the Legislative Council, was composed of fifteen appointed members selected by the governor for five years. Subsequently, all councillors were appointed for life. The non-elected Council was meant to curb any populist enthusiasms of the Assembly.

For the first sixty years of self-rule, Queensland operated as a pastoralist landholders' democracy. At first, only domicile males over

21 years of age who were British subjects with property and residential requirements were entitled to vote; itinerant workers, many labourers, were excluded. The early franchise excluded women but included a small number of Aboriginal and Torres Strait Islander people who met the property qualification used as the basis for the colony's electoral roll. The franchise was steadily extended although all women did not acquire the vote until the 1907 election. Over this period, there was some experimentation with electoral rules, often with partisan gain in mind. These included plural voting, multi-member constituencies, and first-past-the-post (plurality) voting. Compulsory registration of electors and compulsory voting were introduced in 1914 by the Liberal government of Digby Denham.

On the economic front, development centred on the pastoral industries, timber, plantations and mines. By 1870 about half the colony's land mass had been occupied by European settlers (Fitzgerald 1982, 133–8). The decentralized pattern of settlement was a consequence of exploration and the development of regional centres based on coastal ports – transport by land was difficult and time-consuming. Much of the workforce was low paid manual labour which generated opportunities for early unionization among Queensland workers. The labour movement became dominated by powerful trade unions of general labourers, shearers, miners and railway workers, most of which were later combined into the Australian Workers Union. The shortage of cheap labour led to the importation of Chinese and later, Kanaka (South Sea Islanders) labourers to work on sheep stations, plantations and in mines. This created hostility to Asian and islander workers and the employers who hired them. By the 1880s white workers were susceptible to forcefully expressed views of racist and radical industrial unionism. This was an important element in the colony's politics until the 1890s.

Parliamentary politics in the nineteenth century were fluid and marked by the fluctuating fortunes of various business interests. Independents and non-aligned local representatives were initially the most numerous, and governments were often formed by shifting coalitions of ministerialists, a style of parliamentary politics which continued until 1912. Members tended to divide on issues according to the interests of their local supporters. Gradually, factions and loose parties coalesced around issues and personalities. Parties were parliamentary-based labels serving as banners under which aligned candidates stood for election. In the 1880s Sir Thomas McIlwraith formed a northern Nationalist (Conservative) party while Sir Samuel Griffith led a group of southern Liberals based in Brisbane. The Labor Party was formed in 1890, after four endorsed Trades and Labour Council candidates had stood unsuccessfully at the 1888 election. After a shaky start and the defeat of direct action in the strikes of 1890, Labor won 33.3 per cent of the vote in 1893 but secured just sixteen seats in the 72-seat Assembly. As with the other Australian colonies, the entry of organized labour changed the nature of parliamentary politics, obliging the fragmented conservative side of politics to coalesce to combat Labor.

At the beginning of the twentieth century, the role of colonial governments was relatively limited. Even so, government played a significant role in several areas of social and economic policy. Land administration and immigration assistance policies were crucial to development. Queensland governments regulated and then prohibited the importation of islander labourers. Various schemes of Aboriginal and Torres Strait Islander 'protection' were proposed. Given labour shortages, the regulation of industrial relations and the prevention of strikes were considered paramount. Rudimentary primary education was provided but not made compulsory until 1900. Funds were borrowed for the provision of railways and public buildings. Postal services were commenced, public order was maintained by a local constabulary, including a mounted native police force, and a small defence contingent was established. Customs and excise duties formed the main sources of government revenue, and a source of much irritation.

In spite of these measures, a strong anti-Brisbane sentiment emerged throughout the last decades of the nineteenth century reflected in the rise of a separation movement advocating the division of Queensland into three self-governing states. The residents of Northern Queensland strongly supported moves towards federation in the 1890s as a way of countering Brisbane's domination of the colony and because they hoped that the new national government would support the creation of new states, a policy resisted by a series of Queensland governments. The majority of Brisbane, Ipswich and Rockhampton voters, by contrast, had serious reservations about joining the federation. Even though Queensland voted in favour of federation at the 1899 referendum, these communities saw the federal movement as an extension of Sydney-Melbourne dominance. A strong sense of regional identity and a fear of southern dominance became continuing characteristics Queensland politics.

The main contours of Queensland politics were set in the nineteenth century. Queensland had a narrowly based economy and a challenging climate. Brisbane was located close to the southern border with New South Wales while the rest of the colony's population was dispersed among communities centred on provincial towns along the coastline. The colony relied on government inducement for development but the public sector was not yet large or engaged in public enterprise. The structure of the political institutions inherited from British colonial administration and the experience of self-government as part of New South Wales was designed, in part, to keep a check on radical politics. Parties had formed but were embryonic and not yet set up as modern political organizations. And Queenslanders had acquired a strong sense of pride in their achievements and a distrust of the more populous southern capitals.

Political culture

Throughout the twentieth century, Queenslanders accepted the need for extensive government intervention in both social and economic domains – initially state socialism under the Labor Party and later, a kind of developmental statism – in addition to a parochial insularity and an antipathy to Canberra. To this could be added a predilection for strong leadership, a preference for low taxes and an acceptance of a brokerage-style of politics. It was a political culture focused on ends not means. Conventional wisdom held that Queenslanders were practical and utilitarian, and would prefer strong governments getting on with the job and delivering services rather than promises of accountability and integrity. Outside critics often considered Queensland to have an anti-intellectual and illiberal style of politics in which simplistic slogans were used to appeal to the electorate. On occasion, governments were able to get away with the abuse of state power with little electoral back-lash. Until the last decade of the century, little attention was paid to civil or political rights, to the plight of indigenous peoples or minorities, or to the need for opportunities for participatory involvement in politics.

The imperative for government intervention was accepted by both sides of politics; they merely differed on the preferred beneficiaries (Morrison 1960). Labor introduced development programs based on public works, state-owned enterprises, large-scale public employment of unionized labour, farm assistance, public health services and protectionist regulation of local industry. Although Labor was only briefly motivated by socialist ideas (Fitzgerald 1984) it maintained a strong commitment to government solutions to development of the state.

Coalition governments also believed in using state power to advance the interests of the state, rapidly pursuing projects with state assistance and establishing a wide array of state-supported producer agencies and statutory marketing authorities. Favourable leases were granted to stimulate the development of the mining and pastoral industries throughout the state. Queensland maintained an extensive public hospital system in part to attract and hold its labour force but within the general context of a low tax and low expenditure regime (Gerritsen 1988).

Political campaigns were often premised on pork-barrelling and brokerage politics. Both Labor and anti-Labor premiers were known to threaten that, unless the government's candidate was returned in an electoral district, the voters in the district would be deprived of public works. This style of politics was occasionally linked with corruption. Labor Premiers Ted Theodore and Bill McCormack were both discredited in 1929–30 over a scam involving mining shares in Mungana Mines at Chillagoe (Kennedy 1978; Lack 1962). The Labor minister, Tom Foley, was brought down in 1956 over bribes for the renewal of land leases (Parker 1981). In the 1970s the family of Premier Bjelke-Petersen was accused of accepting Comalco mining shares (Lunn 1987).

Academic interpretations of Queensland's political culture have often been advanced to explain the state's distinctiveness. Alan Morrison (1960) considered Queensland represented a set of paradoxes in which the community displayed divergent political allegiances. It had a highly unionized primary-based economy yet produced a non-socialistic Labor Party, and it prized popular sovereignty at the same time as it gave 'extreme deference' and 'veneration' to the executive. The labour historians Denis Murphy and Roger Joyce believed Queensland was dominated by 'agrarianism' and an 'anti-Brisbane sentiment' (Murphy and Joyce 1981). For Ross Fitzgerald, Queensland politics has displayed a Faustian character, consisting of well-meaning but flawed politicians who have been captured by the demon of developmentalism. Colin Hughes has argued that Queensland politics was 'concerned with things and places rather than people or ideas' (Hughes 1980, 5). He also ventured the view that while state politics was adversarial, colourful and with a penchant for bluster and hyperbole, the eventual shifts in voter support for the main parties tended to vary little from election to election (Hughes 1969).

Mullins (1986), Murphy and Joyce (1981), Head (1986a), Bulbeck (1987), and Charlton (1983) have debated the degree to which Queensland politics is dominated by rural populism and different from the politics of other states. While they agree that social and economic differences have produced a distinctive political regime, they question the extent to which the nature of Queensland politics is generically different from other states. While populism has been important in Queensland politics, populism – however it is defined – cannot alone explain the dynamics of the state's politics. Traditional explanations based on the socio-economic structure of the state and the close relationship between party dominance and political institutions are more persuasive. Similarly, such political factors as the electoral system, the structure of the legislature, the long periods of weak parliamentary opposition and the absence of formal avenues to challenge government have all been critically important in shaping Queensland politics.

The system of government

At the time of self-government in 1859, Queensland was established by Letters Patent and administered under an Order in Council issued from New South Wales. Under this authority the governor and a newly established legislature of Queensland were empowered to make laws 'for the peace, welfare and good government of the colony'. Eight years later, in 1867, the Queensland parliament passed its own *Constitution Act*. This Act was in the form of a conventional British colonial constitutional document, based on Westminster notions of responsible government. It reaffirmed the office of governor and the existence of a bicameral legislature comprised of a popularly elected Legislative Assembly and a nominated Legislative Council. The document dealt with such matters as the eligibility to stand for the Assembly, the powers, composition and privileges of the Assembly, and the procedures for the appointment of officials. It also set out the procedural requirements for the appropriation of revenues and the management of crown lands. There were also several clauses dealing with the disqualification and penalties for non-attendance of members of parliament.

As with British-derived colonial constitutions of the day, the principles of parliamentary government were left unspecified, particularly those relating to the exercise of executive power and there was no mention of the office of premier or the relationship which should exist between ministers and parliament. Over time, other Acts have been added to the framework of government so that about twenty-seven statutes can now be considered as part of the constitutional system regulating Queensland government. Unlike some other states, there has been no systematic consolidation of these constitutional provisions. The Electoral and Administrative Review Commission attempted to both update and consolidate the various Acts relating to the state's constitutional system and produced a report and a series of recommendations (EARC 1993). Although this report has been considered by a parliamentary committee and draft bills have been released, consolidation has yet to occur.

One of the most significant and controversial constitutional issues in the state's history occurred in the early 1920s when the Labor government abolished the upper house. The episode did not reflect well on the process of representative government and showed Labor's determination to abolish the Legislative Council even if the rules had to be bent a little. The Labor Party's platform in Queensland, as in most of the other states, was committed to the abolition of the upper house, in Queensland's case, an unelected chamber. When the party came to government in 1915 only four of the thirty-nine councillors were Labor, and the government considered the chamber to be stacked against it and obstructionist. Labor's first premier, T.J. Ryan, called a referendum in 1917 seeking approval to abolish the chamber but the referendum failed to pass.

His successor as leader of the state Labor Party, Premier Theodore, took the opportunity of the absence of the governor to appoint a former Labor parliamentarian and speaker to be lieutenant-governor. The new lieutenant-governor was persuaded to appoint himself as president of the Council and to appoint an additional fourteen Labor councillors. With Labor councillors in the majority Theodore introduced legislation in 1921 seeking to abolish the chamber. Labor's 'suicide club' was supported by seventeen Country Party members who sought to reform the Council by making it an elected chamber. The Council was abolished in March 1922 and, in the absence of agreement about how a reformed Council should be organized, Queensland has remained a unicameral legislature ever since. To prevent the creation of a restructured upper house along the lines adopted in New South Wales in 1934, in the same year, the Queensland Labor government introduced legislation requiring a referendum before the Legislative Council could be reinstated. Neither Labor nor non-Labor governments have campaigned for a return to bicameralism in the state, and the Australian Democrats and Greens are the only significant parties which have argued for a Legislative Council elected by proportional representation.[1]

Much has been made of Queensland's lack of an upper house in terms of both unbridled executive power and a lack of accountability. Executive dominance and a tradition of strong premiers have been enhanced by the absence of any institutional requirement for the government to compromise with its opponents in parliament. The absence of a second chamber is often seen as the reason for the late development of parliamentary committees in Queensland. The lack of a political brake in the upper house was also cited as the major reason for the ease with which the government of the day could achieve electoral malapportionment to its partisan advantage – a tool once solely in the hands of the premier and the ruling party.

The size of the Assembly has increased periodically by statutory amendment. There was a bi-partisan consensus until recent years that increases in the number of parliamentarians ought to be roughly commensurate with increases in the size of the state's population. From twenty-six members in 1860, the Assembly grew rapidly to seventy-two in 1893 and remained at that number until the depression. The number of seats was reduced to sixty-two before the 1932 election as an economy measure and there was no increase until the 1950 election when the numbers rose to seventy-five. In 1960 the number of representatives was again increased this time to seventy-eight, and in 1972 the number went to eighty-two. In 1985 the size of the Assembly was set at eighty-nine at which it has remained despite an additional one million voters joining the electoral roll between 1977 and 2001. While some would argue that the increase in representation has widened the available talent pool, the main institutional issue has been the accommodation of members in Parliament House itself. During the 1960s and 1970s, before the parliamentary annex was built in 1983, it was not uncommon for five to six backbenchers to be sharing a single office.

The Assembly meets usually about fifty to sixty days a year, and as little as thirty in election years. Until 1970 all questions in question time had to be on notice and given to the speaker before the start of the day's proceedings. Questions without notice were permitted for the first time under sessional orders in 1970 and in 1983, more routinely, under standing orders. All speakers of the Assembly have been partisan appointments elected by majority vote in the party room of the governing party or coalition, and many have seen their role as one of assisting to expedite the government's business. Several speakers, however, have made genuine attempts to be independent and impartial in the position.

The role played by the governor as formal head of state has occasionally been politically significant. The Colonial Office attempted to use Governor Sir Matthew Nathan (1920–25) to curb the radicalism of the Theodore Labor government in the early 1920s over such measures as the plan to abolish the Legislative Council, to force retire judges at the age of seventy and to borrow funds from America. While Nathan was opposed to many of Theodore's policies and tactics, he was unsuccessful in dissuading the premier from implementing them. He declined, however, to politicize the office of governor by campaigning against them in public.

In 1987 the governor, Sir Walter Campbell, refrained for intervening in a political crisis over the leadership of the National Party. Campbell was asked by the premier, Sir Joh Bjelke-Petersen, to dismiss his entire ministry as part of a scheme by the premier to reduce the influence of dissidents within his party. Campbell refused and sought a written assurance from the new National Party leader, Mike Ahern, that he had sufficient numbers in the Assembly to govern. Campbell's actions in the crisis were subsequently endorsed by both sides of politics. In a similarly contentious matter involving a ministry, Governor Peter Arnison elected not to intervene in August 1997 after a vote of no confidence was passed by the Assembly in the performance of the Attorney-General Denver Beanland. Arnison apparently accepted Premier Rob Borbidge's contention that, while the parliament had confidence in his government, he was responsible, as premier, for selecting the ministry. It does not appear that the governor decided to take any further advice on the matter, even though a constitutional change in 1977 extended the powers of the governor so as to make the office not 'subject to any direction by any person whatsoever nor be limited as to his sources of advice'. The constitutional amendment also included a provision allowing a governor to dismiss a government 'if he shall see sufficient cause', and one effecting a double entrenchment of governor's office. The latter provision was introduced after the dismissal of Gough Whitlam by Sir John Kerr to allay Bjelke-Petersen's fears that the office of governor could be abolished (see Hughes 1980).

Despite the institutional weaknesses, Queensland has had few major debates about the effectiveness or robustness of its political institutions. A major exception was the Fitzgerald Inquiry into police corruption (Queensland Commission of Inquiry 1989) which, in turn, prompted the setting up of a wide-ranging commission of inquiry (Coaldrake 1989; Hede et al. 1992; Lloyd 1989; Prasser et al. 1990). The Queensland Electoral and Administrative Review Commission (EARC) was designed to recommend changes to the operation of government including procedures to ensure parliamentary accountability and effective public scrutiny of the executive. The commission produced a series of reports and recommendations which have made significant contributions to the analysis of ways to ensure accountability in parliamentary government and which resulted in a major review of political, electoral and administrative institutions. The result was the reform of the electoral system and the passage of laws removing restriction on public assembly, setting up a freedom of information regime, creating anti-discrimination procedures, and providing for public disclosure of donations to parties.

The public service was also reformed along managerial lines, but there did not appear to be any lessening of its politicization at higher levels. This longstanding criticism of the public service persisted in spite of changes prompted by the Fitzgerald Inquiry. The longer term effects of the review of the structures of government are hard to gauge. Existing institutions were largely taken for granted with no suggestions for substantial reform of the office of governor, the organization of Legislative Assembly, the number of members of parliament, parliamentary terms, the role of ministers, or the place of political parties. The question of the reintroduction of an upper house was excluded from EARC's deliberations. A slightly augmented system of parliamentary committees was eventually adopted in 1995 following an extensive report into the effectiveness of parliamentary scrutiny. In 1991 the Goss Labor government put a referendum to the people seeking four-year terms for the Legislative Assembly. Although the premier was enthusiastic for this change, his party appeared less so and the National Party campaigned against the proposal claiming that it would support four-year terms only if three-year minimum terms were included. The Liberals nominally supported the move but did not campaign on the issue and some party members advocated a 'no' vote. With the main parties divided, or at best lukewarm, on the proposal, the referendum failed to pass.

Political parties

The Australian Labor Party

Although Queensland is able to boast the first Labor government in the world – a seven-member minority ministry surviving for just seven days in 1899 led by Anderson Dawson – its creation was the result of a gubernatorial tactic to force the fractious conservatives to form a ministry. After 1899 Labor won the support of the largely working class Catholic community that comprised around one-quarter of the state's population. But Labor remained out of office until 1915 although some Labor members joined ministerialist governments between 1903 and 1911. Labor's support hovered around 35 per cent of the first preference vote from 1893 until 1912 when it increased to 46 per cent and then to 52 per cent at the following election in 1915. From 1915 with only three exceptions, Labor's vote remained close to 50 per cent until the internal divisions leading to the Labor split of 1957, and reached over 53 per cent on three occasions: 1918, 1935 and 1953. The party's main support came from regional Queensland. With the development of the railways, rural areas, mining centres and country towns formed the backbone of the ALP and remained so until Labor began to make inroads into suburban Brisbane after the party gained government in 1989 (see figure 4.1).

With such high levels of support for much of the period, Labor was able to build itself into a hegemonic party for the period from 1915

Figure 4.1 Queensland Legislative Assembly, general elections
1893–2001: vote share of ALP, Liberal and National parties (and their
precursors), and minor parties (% of first preference vote)

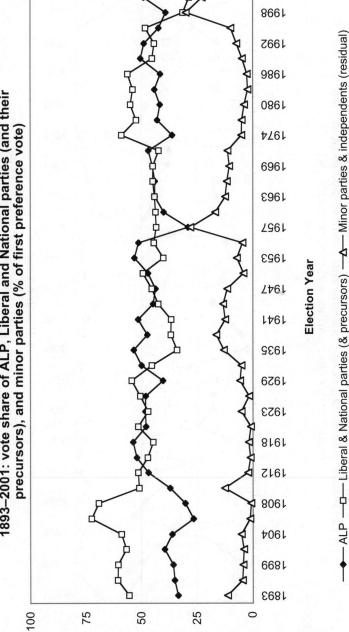

Election Year

ALP ——□—— Liberal & National parties (& precursors) ——△—— Minor parties & independents (residual)

Source: calculated from the Australian Government and Politics Project database, University of Western Australia.

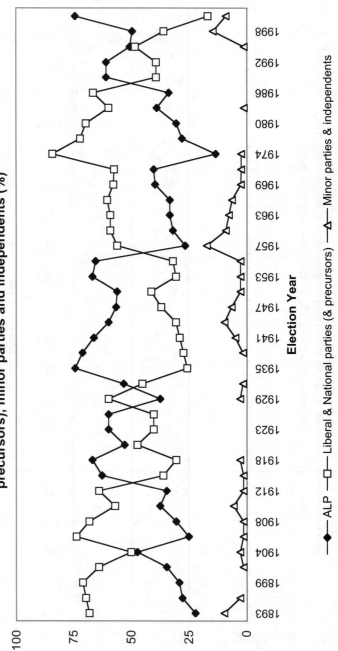

Figure 4.2 Queensland Legislative Assembly, general elections 1893–2001: seat share of ALP, Liberal and National parties (and their precursors), minor parties and independents (%)

Source: calculated from the Australian Government and Politics Project database, University of Western Australia.

until 1957. Its success was not simply an artifice of its electoral appeal and its skilful campaigning, but relied on a powerful organizational machine. Labor's extra-parliamentary organization was dominated by labour unions, especially the Australian Workers Union (AWU), with strong regional networks. Once in power, Labor cemented its position by the strategic use of state resources to deliver electoral support. A favoured strategy was to undertake public works in marginal electoral districts shortly before an election and, using a combination of closed shop unionism and the one-month residency provisions of the Electoral Act, register the day labourers in the electoral district to tip the balance in favour of the Labor candidate.

Both the parliamentary Labor Party and the organizational wing became increasingly bureaucratized and more conservative as Labor continued in office. When Labor lost office in 1957 after winning over 53 per cent of the vote at the 1956 election, it was not because of a sudden swing towards the conservative Liberal and Country parties. Labor lost office because it split into two warring factions as a delayed reaction to the divisions which had split the Labor Party elsewhere in Australia during 1954 and 1955 (see Murray 1972). Premier Gair and many members of his parliament party were expelled from the party by the State Executive and ran at the ensuing election under the label of Queensland Labor. This party managed to win 23 per cent of the vote in comparison with just under 30 per cent gained by the Labor Party. The division of the Labor vote under a first-past-the-post electoral system ensured the defeat of Labor and the consequent victory of the anti-Labor parties (note Jackman 1992). The divisions in the Labor Party lasted long enough for the anti-Labor parties to become entrenched until their defeat in 1989.

Out of office, the Labor Party became increasingly factionalized and internecine conflicts kept the party in opposition (Fitzgerald and Thornton 1989). Labor's revival was not accomplished until it underwent a renewal in the 1980s under the influence of reform-minded members of the party including future premiers Peter Beattie and Wayne Swan. By this stage, Labor had become a party influenced by middle-class professionals whose main message was the need for greater accountability, civil rights legislation and modernization in many areas of state policy including education and health.

The Liberal and National parties

In contrast to the Labor Party, parties that became the Liberal and National parties were slower to organize and establish the attributes of modern mass parties. And, unlike other states, it has been rural-based parties which have been the major parliamentary rivals to the Labor Party. Although a variety of rural and urban interests were represented in colonial parliaments, and a Country and Progressive National Party formed government for one term in 1929 (under Arthur Moore), the conservative side of politics remained divided and weak until the collapse of the Labor Party in 1957. Various rural and farmer groups ran candidates under different banners until a separate Country Party was formed in 1936. While it attracted around 20 per cent of the vote at every election from 1938 to 1974, malapportionment and the divisions in the non-Labor vote ensured that the Country Party consistently won the largest number of seats in parliament after the Labor Party. It renamed itself the National Party in 1974, became a highly professionalized organization and, during the 1980s, aimed to broaden its electoral base by seeking support among conservative groups in urban Queensland.

The forerunners to the present Liberal Party went through various transformations. A Liberal Party first contested a state election under this name in 1915. But the party was a loose association of like-minded candidates and the upheavals of war and depression were matched by a variety of political associations and party labels under which candidates contested state elections. These included the Nationalist Party, the United Party and an association with anti-Labor rural interests between 1928 and 1935 as the Country and Progressive National Party. This variety of party labels for urban conservative candidates at state elections was less apparent at federal elections in the state where candidates used the names of national party groupings – the Nationalists until 1929, and the United Australia Party until its dissolution in the 1940s. After the divisions of the 1940s, the present Queensland Liberal Party was set up in 1949 to select candidates for both state and federal elections.

The collapse of the Liberal Party and its predecessors has been associated with defining moments in Queensland's political history. The party dissolved between 1926 and 1935 and, while a rural and urban conservative coalition formed government between 1929 and 1932 as the Country and Progressive National Party, this lasted only a single term. The Liberals were unable to build on their popular support in the 1940s as the Queensland People's Party and were confined to the south-eastern corner of the state. This allowed Labor to govern during the 1940s despite only once managing to gain a majority of the vote. After 1983, support for the Liberals collapsed when their coalition with the National Party broke down. The party held only six seats after the 1983 election having lost two of their number who defected to the National Party government. By the 2001 state election, the Liberals

Figure 4.3 Queensland Legislative Assembly, general elections 1893–2001: vote share of Liberal Party (and precursors), National (Country) Party, minor parties (% of first preference vote)

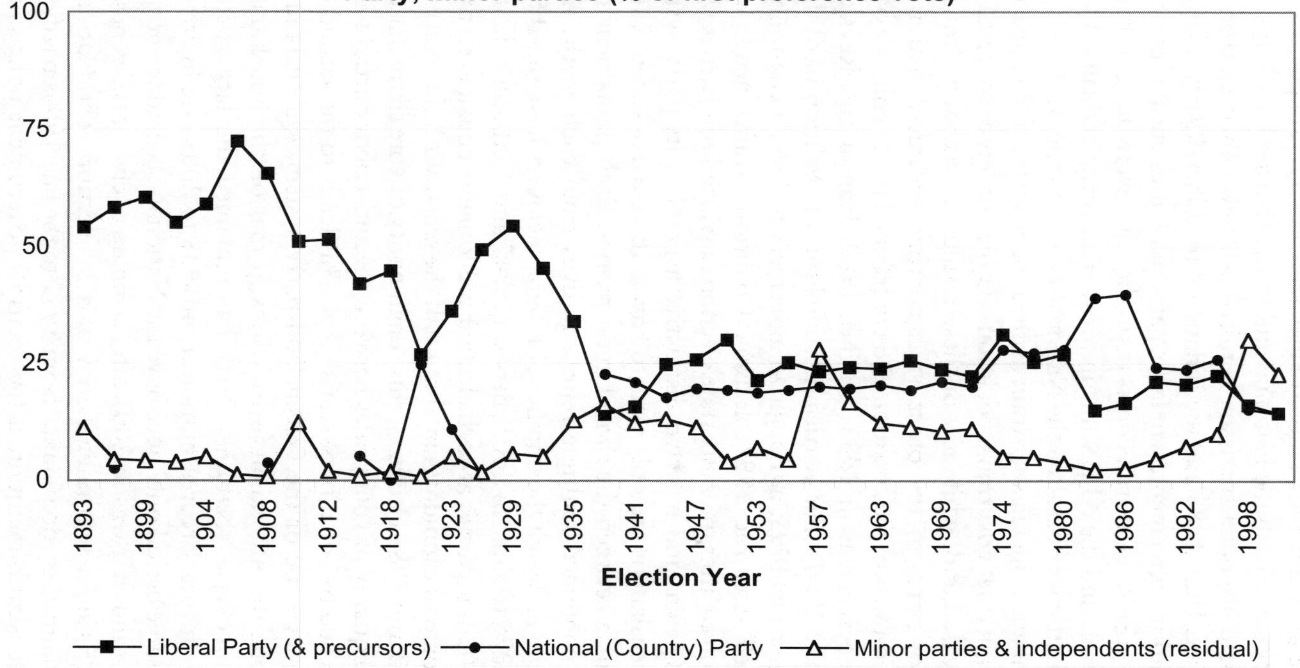

Source: calculated from the Australian Government and Politics Project database, University of Western Australia.

gained only 14 per cent of the vote and held only three seats, two of these by slender margins.

Electoral support for the Liberals has been largely restricted to Brisbane while the National Party has drawn its support from the rest of the state. Both the National and Liberal parties have refused to amalgamate although the issue is raised whenever their electoral fortunes decline. Until 1983 and the collapse of the Liberal Party–National Party coalition agreement, separate party identities meant that, with few exceptions, electoral contests in the city were fought between the Liberals and the ALP, while in provincial towns and rural Queensland, the battle was between the National Party and the ALP. This agreement came under increasing strain as the Liberals tried to enhance their position in the governing coalition. Three-cornered contests gradually increased and, while few of these resulted in a change from one anti-Labor party to the other, such contests became a major source of tension within the coalition and contributed to the collapse of the coalition agreement in 1983 (Hughes 1980; Hamill and Reynolds 1983; Arklay 2000). The parties remained out of coalition until their return to office in 1995, although an agreement to form a coalition had been signed after the 1992 election. Coalition arrangements were again dissolved after the 2001 state election in which both parties fared badly.

Queensland has two distinctive aspects of its party system. First, Queensland is the only state to have a three-party system with a rough balance between the three largest parties. Each parliament since 1938 has contained multiple representatives from each of the main three parties although the number of Liberal members has ranged from thirty in 1974 to three in 2001. Between 1947 and 1980 the vote for the two anti-Labor parties at each election was roughly equal, even though they each stood candidates in about half the seats. With the exception of the 1983 and 1986 elections, this rough parity of vote share has continued.

Equality of vote shares between the anti-Labor parties has not been matched by equality of seat shares. This leads to the second distinctive characteristic of the Queensland party system. Queensland is unique among the Australian jurisdictions in that on the non-Labor side the country-based National Party has remained the largest in terms of parliamentary representation from 1938 to 2001 (see figure 4.2). Over the same period only once have the Nationals secured fewer than twelve seats and that was in 2001 after winning twelve at the general election but losing a seat immediately at a by-election. The National Party's parliamentary dominance from 1957 to the late 1980s pacified regional Queensland, maintained the focus of government policy on regional development and low taxes, and kept the Liberals as the junior member

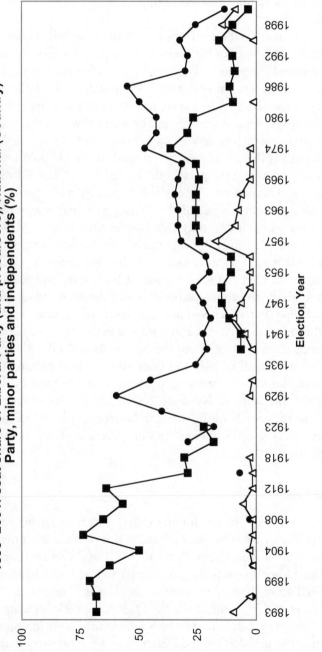

Figure 4.4 Queensland Legislative Assembly, general elections
1893–2001: seat share of Liberal Party (and precursors), National (Country)
Party, minor parties and independents (%)

—■— Liberal Party (& precursors)   —●— National (Country) Party   —△— Minor parties & independents

Source: calculated from the Australian Government and Politics Project database, University of Western Australia.

of the coalition government. But the long stint in government meant that the leadership of the National Party became increasingly attuned to commercial and industrial interests in Brisbane, making the party vulnerable to local mavericks claiming to better represent local and regional interests.

As a result of rural dissatisfaction with the established conservative parties, Pauline Hanson's One Nation Party posed a serious challenge to the traditional three-party system in 1997. One Nation won 23 per cent of the first preference vote at the 1998 state general election and elected eleven members to the Legislative Assembly. The party's policies were a mixture of rural populism and hostility towards the policies of the major parties which were seen as causing hardship and dislocation to 'ordinary Australians'. The party did not fare well in parliament; the One Nation parliamentary party split in 1999 with half forming the City–Country Alliance of Queensland (CCAQ) and the remainder sitting as independents. None of the CCAQ members was returned at the 2001 state election and only two former One Nation MLAs were re-elected as independents. But three new One Nation candidates were elected in 2001 with a statewide share of the vote above 8 per cent.

The principal effect of One Nation at both state and federal elections was to divide the conservative vote and threaten the support base of the National Party. This made the issue of trading preferences between the anti-Labor parties a major issue in the 1998 and 2001 state election campaigns. In 1998 both the Nationals and Liberals agreed to put One Nation ahead of Labor in their allocation of preferences, and most local National Party branches did so in 2001, but not the Liberals (Wanna 2001; Bennett and Newman 2001). The turmoil created by the insurgence of the One Nation Party can be seen as part of a continuing realignment among anti-Labor parties in Queensland, a process which is far from over.

Minor parties

The major source of change for the party system in recent years has been the decline in voter support for the major parties. With the exception of the split in the Labor Party in 1957 and the creation of the Queensland Labor Party (QLP), minor parties and independents had rarely gained more than 10 per cent of the vote in Queensland. For the state elections of 1957 and 1960, the QLP gained 23 per cent and 12 per cent of the vote, but ceased to be a significant player in Queensland politics after the mid-1960s. Independent and minor party candidates had a hard time competing in a vigorous three-party system and did not thrive in the cut and thrust of Queensland state politics. In federal elections for the Senate, however, the successor to the QLP, the Democratic Labor Party, was successful in getting a senator elected at Senate elections in Queensland from 1964 to 1970.

In recent years, however, the Australian Democrats and Greens have made some inroads into Queensland politics, particularly in federal elections. While the Democrats found it difficult to reach 2 per cent of the vote at state elections, the party has elected a senator at every Senate election since 1980 with a statewide vote of between 7 and 13 per cent. The Greens have been more successful at state level but only crossed the 2 per cent threshold for the statewide vote in 1995. In the more competitive electoral pattern of the 1990s and with voter volatility increasing, support for the major parties declined. In 1989 the three main parties received 95 per cent of the vote. By 1992 the figure dropped slightly to 93 per cent, and 90 per cent in 1995. The major drop occurred in 1998 when their combined vote equalled just 71 per cent, recovering slightly in the 2001 election to 77 per cent. While some of the vote went to independents (2 per cent in 1998 and 8 per cent in 2001) most was gained by anti-establishment parties critical of the major party consensus on policy issues such as economic deregulation and the privatization of government services. Pauline Hanson's One Nation Party captured almost 23 per cent in 1998 and again 11.08 per cent in 2001, despite not standing a full complement of candidates. The turbulence in anti-Labor politics in Queensland and the volatility of the electorate will continue to provide an opportunity for the success of minor party and independent candidates.

The electoral system

Elections for the Queensland Legislative Assembly from 1860 until 1912 adopted electoral districts which returned between one and three members but, since 1912, only single-member electoral districts have been used. Enrolment and voting were voluntary and a first-past-the-post (FPTP) voting system was used until 1892. From that date, an optional preferential system of contingent voting (a version of the alternative vote) was used until the 1941 election. This optional preferential system had been introduced in 1892 by a conservative government anxious to prevent the emerging Labor Party from winning seats at the expense of a divided opposition.

Once the Labor Party had emerged as the largest party, it found no reason to change an electoral system that had enabled it to gain and hold power almost continuously from 1915. But the decline in the

Labor vote in the mid-1940s prompted a return to FPTP voting. This was adopted to exploit Labor's position as the largest party in a system with a divided opposition. After the Labor split and the election of a Country Party–Liberal Party coalition government, a preferential system was again adopted for the 1962 state election – this time, a full preferential voting system with the compulsory ranking of preferences for all candidates on the ballot paper. Preferential voting was maintained throughout the coalition's long tenure in office, but following a major review of the state's electoral system by the Electoral and Administrative Review Commission in 1990, all three parliamentary parties accepted a return to an optional preferential system for the 1992 and subsequent state elections.

With the exception of the changes initiated in 1991, previous changes in voting methods can be seen to have been driven by partisan advantage. However, an equally important device for securing partisan gain was the use of electoral weighting to create malapportionment through a system of electoral zones created in 1949 and retained, in

Table 4.1 Queensland Legislative Assembly: voting systems used and governments formed after elections, 1893–2001

Year of first and last election in period	Number of elections in period	Voting System	Governments formed after elections	
			ALP	Non-ALP
1893–1941	19	Contingent voting (a version of the alternative vote with optional preferential voting), two member districts until 1912, single member districts thereafter	9	10
1944–1960	7	First past the post (plurality) voting in single member districts	5	2
1963–1989	10	Preferential voting (the alternative vote) with compulsory expression of preferences in single member districts	1	9
1992–2001	4	Preferential voting (the alternative vote) with optional expression of preferences in single member districts	3	1

various forms, until 1991. Zonal weighting was introduced, together with FPTP voting, by Labor after it had seen its primary vote fall to below 45 per cent at the 1944 and 1947 state elections. The effect of the malapportionment was to favour Labor support in provincial towns, mining areas and other centres of strong ALP support.

The zonal system was retained by the coalition after it won government in 1957 but the system was modified in 1958, 1971 and 1985 to benefit National Party voters. While the zonal system gave a bonus in representation to the anti-Labor parties, and particularly the National Party, it is difficult to conclude that it had the effect of keeping the ALP out of government. As figure 4.1 shows, the combined vote for the non-Labor parties exceeded Labor in most elections from 1957 to 1986. Only in 1972 did Labor significantly beat the coalition in terms of voter support. Mackerras (1990) has argued that the under-representation of the ALP in Queensland during the period was more a result of the single-member electoral districts coupled with preferential voting rather than the effect of malapportionment and zonal weighting. However, his analysis may not sufficiently acknowledge the effects of the zonal system. Hughes (1980, 100) has calculated that the coalition had a two-party advantage over Labor created by the zones of between 1.2 and 9.7 per cent in the elections between 1960 and 1977.

Although the ALP was highly critical of the zonal system after the party had lost office, its attack was blunted because it had originally introduced the measure and Labor had rarely managed to outpoll the combined conservatives. The winner from the system during the 1960s through to the 1980s was the National Party. From the formation of the coalition government after the 1957 election, the Liberals outpolled the National Party (then Country Party) in seven consecutive elections from 1957 until 1974, yet the Liberals remained the junior partner in terms of seats and their place in the coalition government.

Overall, the principal effects of partisan electoral manipulations were threefold. First, the method of counting votes and zonal malapportionment resulted in the familiar effect of enhancing the seat share of the largest party or coalition. Secondly, on the conservative side of politics, the effect of the zonal system from 1957 to 1989 was to over-represent the National Party, allowing it to become the senior partner in their governing coalition with the Liberals, even though the National Party vote was less than the Liberals until 1977. Thirdly, the ALP in opposition was systematically under-represented in the Assembly over ten consecutive elections from 1960 to 1986. An extreme example of this under-representation occurred in 1974 when the ALP polled 36 per cent of the vote but received only 13 per cent of the seats.

A significant change occurred to the electoral system in 1991 as a result of the Fitzgerald Inquiry and the review undertaken by EARC. Before the EARC review in 1990, electoral laws had been a major political issue but, after a thorough investigation and with considerable public input, there was bipartisan support for EARC's recommendations. Single-member electoral districts were retained with equal numbers of electors per seat except for five large territorial seats in the far west and north of the state. The return to an optional preferential system, recommended by EARC, did not stop a concerted campaign by all parties to convince voters at the 1992, 1995 and 1998 elections to continue to give a full allocation of preferences. At the 2001 state election, however, Labor's Premier Beattie urged voters to 'just vote 1' giving a vote to the party of choice but then exhausting their ballot by not allocating preferences to any other candidate. This tactic against a divided opposition helped to increase Labor's representation (49 per cent of the vote giving 74 per cent of the seats in the Assembly) but had the effect of changing the electoral system once again to a hybrid FPTP system, and making the electoral system a political issue.

Patterns of office-holding

More than any other Australian jurisdiction, incumbency in Queensland is characterized by majoritarianism and a 'winner takes all' philosophy. From 1915 to 1996 Queensland had two long periods of office-holding by the same party or coalition; Labor from 1915 until 1957 (with a short break from 1929–32), and a National Party–Liberal Party coalition from 1957 to 1983, continued by the National Party alone until 1989. From 1915 to 2001 there were only six changes of government involving different parties in office, and only eight from 1910 to 2001. The average number of victories per government was seven, while the predominant party continued in office for an average of just over twelve years. Since 1915 only two governments have lost office after a single term, the Moore Country and Progressive National Party government from 1929 to 1932, and the Borbidge National Party–Liberal Party coalition government from 1996 to 1998. Queensland holds the record for the longest run of majority election victories by an anti-Labor coalition in an Australian state (eleven) and also has the second longest run of nine consecutive victories by Labor.

This pattern of dominant partisan majorities has meant that Queensland has had only a small number of minority governments that have held office for about 5 per cent of the period from 1910 to 2000. Although minority governments have not been a prominent feature, there have been some important periods of minority or coalition minority government. One of these occurred in 1983 when the coalition agreement between the National Party and Liberal Party collapsed and the Bjelke-Petersen government decided to continue in minority until the election. Bjelke-Petersen survived for sixty-four days with a minority government and avoided testing parliamentary confidence in his regime by not allowing parliament to meet.

Two other minority governments in the mid-1990s managed to govern with the confidence of the Assembly. The Borbidge–Sheldon National Party–Liberal Party coalition formed a minority government with forty-four seats in the 89-seat Assembly in February 1996 and managed to remain in office until defeated at the general election in June 1998. This was followed by a Labor minority government led by Beattie whose party had won forty-four seats at the 1998 election – with just 39 per cent of the primary vote – and managed to form a government with the support of an independent. Labor remained as a minority government for over five months until it gained a majority by winning a by-election in Mulgrave caused by the resignation of a One Nation member. Other cases of a government lacking majority parliamentary support include the period during which intra-party factionalism had reduced the Gair Labor ministry to a minority government for five months from April to August 1957 when defeat of the budget on the floor of parliament led to a general election. The possibility of minority or coalition government was avoided by Premier Bjelke-Petersen whose National Party government won only forty-one seats in the 82-seat Assembly in 1983 but managed to persuade two Liberals to defect from their party and join the National Party government as ministers.

Coalition government had not been common in the state until 1957. Thereafter coalition government became the norm, continuing for nine consecutive terms until 1983 when single-party majority governments prevailed until 1996, before a further minority coalition government was formed for the period 1996–98. All these coalition ministries were anti-Labor and led by the National Party and its predecessor, the Country Party.[2] Coalition ministries usually consisted of an odd number of ministers with the majority from the National Party and the party with the most seats in parliament. Portfolios were allocated by the premier to suit the political interests of the National Party with this party controlling the departments responsible for public works, transport and industry. The Liberals were usually allocated the positions of treasurer and attorney-general, and the portfolios of health, and industrial relations. As junior partners in the coalition, the Liberals were assigned

Table 4.2 Queensland government: Patterns of office-holding, 1893–2001

Period	Pattern of Government	Predominant party or parties in government	Comment
1893–1915	Periods in office of short duration with frequent coalition governments	Ministerialists (groups of members of parliament who supported a government but were not bound by tight party discipline: they were linked to other members by their support for a particular premier or government)	Governments often relied on ALP support; 5 coalition ministries included former Labor members; there was one minority ALP government in 1899; the period ended with the election of the first majority ALP government in 1915
1915–57	Periods in office of long duration and single party hegemony	Australian Labor Party	Only one break in ALP monopoly of government, the 1929–32 Country and Progressive National Party government during the Depression; the period ended with the 1957 split in the ALP
1957–89	Periods in office of long duration, coalition government predominating	National (Country) Party and Liberal Party	The National (Country) Party dominated the coalition; the last two terms of office were National Party governments, 1983–89; the period ended with the collapse of National Party support
1989–2001	Periods in office of moderate duration	Australian Labor Party	Fairer electoral system; more electoral volatility; two successive minority governments (one a non-Labor coalition); the emergence of Pauline Hanson's One Nation Party and the growing importance of minor parties

'bad news' portfolios and were used as convenient scapegoats by the Nationals for policy failures.

During the twentieth century, four principal patterns of office holding can be identified. Throughout the years of hegemonic government from 1915 to 1989, there was a tradition of long-serving premiers who would depart at a time of their own choosing. The premiership was not usually determined by election outcomes but was passed to the next in line by vote of the parliamentary party. Only four premiers lost office at a general election between 1915 and 1989 – McCormack (1929), Moore (1932), Gair (1957) and Cooper (1989) – although Borbidge (1998) can be added since 1989. After 1911 no premier was ever returned to office after a defeat.

The predominance of stable and well-disciplined partisan majorities supporting the government in a unicameral parliament has meant that few governments have ever been brought down by defeat on the floor of parliament. Motions of no confidence have rarely been put and the Gair Labor government was the only one to be brought down by defeat on a matter of confidence, in the case of Gair, the defeat of his budget in 1957. Hughes (1980) reports that only three, or possibly four, no confidence motions were moved in a twenty-year period from 1957 to 1977. After a change in the leadership of the National Party in 1989, a successful confidence motion was moved by the new Premier Cooper in 1989 to forestall an opposition plan to move a no confidence motion. On losing his parliamentary majority as the result of a by-election in 1996, Premier Goss resigned before a want of confidence motion could be moved in parliament, and the incoming premier, Premier Borbidge, moved a motion of confidence in his government as soon as parliament met.

In terms of the structure of ministries, the number of portfolios in Queensland has generally been smaller than in other states, and has increased less dramatically. Queensland had just eleven ministers and eighteen portfolios until 1957. The existence of coalition government after 1957 corresponded with an increase in the number of portfolios but the number of ministers remained at eleven. The first substantial increase in the number of portfolios occurred in 1968 followed by a larger increase in 1983. The period in which the National Party governed alone (1983–89) and for the duration of the Borbidge government (1996–98) corresponded with the largest number of portfolios (forty-seven) but this figure remained well below that of other states over the same period. As a low-tax state, Queensland premiers appeared to believe that more portfolios would add to the expense of government without improving decision-making. There was a reluctance to use the

creation of portfolios as a way of dealing with new policy areas, preferring to accommodate new issues within existing departmental structures.
In recent decades partisan factors have influenced the number of ministers and portfolios, with Labor generally preferring a smaller and more
integrated array of ministerial portfolios than the conservatives. Labor,
however, has not had to balance the demands of rival parties within a
coalition in the design of its administrative structure.

The categorization of portfolio responsibilities reveals that
Queensland governments have tended to focus on physical infrastructure and resource portfolios (regional development, agriculture, energy,
industry, and land) but have neglected social portfolios (health and
welfare) in comparison with other states (Moon and Sayers 1999).
Between 1890 and 2000 Queensland governments had established the
same number of portfolios in the physical infrastructure and resource
areas as the average of the states combined for each decile but was well
below the average number of portfolios in the social activity area for
most periods.

This is consistent with the policy of Queensland governments of all
political persuasions to have been concerned to protect the interests of
farming and rural communities. By the 1970s Queensland had the
largest number of statutory marketing authorities to protect producers
at the expense of consumers. Many crops remain regulated and enjoy
various forms of state assistance. By contrast, Queensland governments
have been less interested in spending resources on education, and the
plight of indigenous peoples was not given a high priority until the
granting of limited land rights in 1993. Funding for the arts and culture
was very limited until the 1980s as was spending on the environment.
There remain many areas in which Queensland has the lowest per
capita expenditure of any state.

Public policy trajectories

Contests over broad government policy have not been the most important determinant of political fortunes in Queensland. Elections have
usually been about matching the competing parties' promises rather
than policy differences. Patronage and the distribution of government
largess have been important in securing political advantage, with
departmental staff being used to make the most effective use of these
resources.

In terms of policy making, ministers have frequently seen their role
as that of making a series of largely unrelated decisions about
competing interests. Administrative policy has often been made on the

run without much thought about coherence or consistency. By the 1960s, however, some policy debates occurred in such sensitive areas as industrial relations. As a consequence of increasing public protest and the emergence of a new social consciousness in the 1970s and 1980s, the merits of unrestrained development and the exploitation of the environment came under question. This change in public opinion was exploited by the Labor Party and contributed to its success in the 1990s. The party's stress on technocratic competence in dealing with new and existing issues also led to a much greater emphasis being placed on policy coordination.

Consistent with the style of politics in the state, the personality of the premier often had a major influence on policy choices. The Labor Party's Forgan Smith in the 1930s and the National Party's Bjelke-Petersen in the 1970s championed developmentalism. Labor premiers Hanlon and Gair were influential in creating an extensive system of public health care, a policy which was continued by subsequent conservative premiers. Socially conservative premiers such as Nicklin and Bjelke-Petersen opposed the introduction of gambling and longer hotel trading hours. Paradoxically, their refusal to permit reform of gaming and sex laws was found by the Fitzgerald Commission to have contributed to the growth of illegal sex and gambling industries and associated police corruption, which were major factors in the demise of the National Party government.

Labor Premier Goss was more active than his predecessors in pushing the state government to become active in national policy debates (Stevens and Wanna 1993) but, after an initial rush of legislation dealing with a host of reform issues in the state, his government lost the initiative in its second term. The return of a National Party–Liberal Party coalition government in 1996 under Premier Borbidge was associated with an attempt to stress the business virtues of prompt delivery of services and timeliness in decision-making. There was also a reaction to the system of policy coordination dominated by the premier's department which had characterized the Goss government.

When Labor returned to government in 1998 under Premier Beattie its policy agenda was as much concerned with methods as goals, stressing consultation with relevant interests before government decisions were made. Beattie's priorities for government have focused on job creation, 'smart state' initiatives for industrial development, community law and order issues, environmental concerns and regional development. This list of issues dealing with matters of immediate sensitivity to the electorate is in the tradition of most Queensland premiers over the past eighty years.

Transport policy has been one of the thornier post-war issues for government, and its treatment indicates the competing demands characterizing Queensland politics. The state had long neglected expenditure on roads but established an extensive system of state railways as an agency for state development. This did not always suit farmers, many of whom preferred to send their produce by road. In response, government restrictions on road transport were used in an attempt to force rail usage, and a deliberate system of cross-subsidization from the profitable mining railways was used to reduce the price of other freight. Pressures for change forced a modification of this policy by the 1960s but this led to a heavy demand for road funding, much of it met by transfers from the federal government. But the rail system remained and by the early 1990s was a major drain on state resources. As the railways were a significant source of local employment in rural areas, the political cost of closing local lines was high. Governments might have wished to preserve public sector employment but had to accommodate a farming sector intent on using private transport, and an increasing demand for major arterial highways in the heavily populated south-east corner of the state.

Apart from a preoccupation with development, the other characteristic which has been associated with Queensland government has been social conservatism and the use of state authority to regulate behaviour to prohibit various practices thought undesirable. Censorship laws have been stricter than those of most states. In the 1970s and 1980s, cabinets attempted to preclude schools from raising issues relating to human relationships and to insist that creationism was taught in science classes. A police special branch was used on various occasions in the 1960s and 1970s to spy on political opponents and others who chose to protest over government actions. The Bjelke-Petersen government banned street marches and public assembly without a police permit. These impositions have been relaxed by subsequent governments but not entirely removed, public demonstrations still requiring a police permit.

After thirty-two years out of government, the newly installed Goss Labor government declared the need to catch up in a range of policy areas, including civil rights, education and health, the environment, public housing, road funding, prisons, justice, the reform of public trading enterprises, and administrative law. The new era of government activism commenced and the state budget doubled in a decade. The growth of state spending increased under Borbidge and has continued to grow under Beattie, although the rate of growth in public expenditure has tapered off. In policy terms, the Queensland state government remains activist and interventionist and, unlike some other states, has been opposed to privatization and contracting out in areas where governments have been the traditional service provider.

There remains a series of policy dilemmas for Queensland governments: how to retain a relatively low tax regime in the face of national taxation schemes and mounting pressures to increase services; how to reconcile the interests of the congested urban south-eastern corner of the state with the demands of the vast hinterland; how to provide infrastructure and skills to enable the state to prosper while committed to private sector initiatives in development; how to improve the living standards for indigenous peoples while balancing the demands of other underprivileged groups; and how to care for the environment while promoting sustainable development. These policy dilemmas are becoming more acute and now have to be faced in the context of a declining electoral consensus, many disaffected voters and a general suspicion of government. While the characteristic of Queensland politics for most of the twentieth century was stability and predictability, this appears much less likely for the twenty-first century.

Chapter

5

South Australia

Andrew Parkin

South Australia enters the twenty-first century with uncertainty. Its government and political leadership shares with counterparts in every state the challenge of coping with the economic and social insecurity associated with globalization, competition and social change. But South Australia – with neither the population nor the natural resource base upon which other mainland states can draw – feels itself particularly vulnerable.

The affliction is compounded by being a little unfamiliar. While South Australian political developments have never had a dominating influence on national affairs,[1] there have nonetheless been important periods when the state has generated ideas and inspiration disproportionate to its relative size.

Its colonial beginnings in 1836 deliberately eschewed the penal model that provided the foundational administrative and economic structures elsewhere in Australia. Promoting Benthamite liberal ideas, religious freedom and widespread land ownership, the founders attempted to implement a novel plan for the construction of a free settler society. When self-government was bestowed in 1856, it was under constitutional arrangements claimed to be 'the most democratic in the British Empire' (Howell 1986, 157). The colony became something of a democratizing pioneer, pushing ahead with the expansion of the franchise, and some of its policy innovations, like the 'Torrens title' system for land registration and conveyancing invented in 1858, were exported elsewhere.[2] South Australian political leaders were arguably crucial contributors to the federation movement in the 1890s (Bannon

1994; Howell 1996). From the 1920s South Australian arguments were important in establishing a redistributive fiscal mechanism (not incidentally, to the state's advantage) within the increasingly Commonwealth-dominated system of public finance. From the late 1930s successive government-led strategies paved the way to an economic and social transformation that inspired interest and emulation around Australia. First, under Premier Playford in the 1940s and 1950s, the economic base was reshaped from agricultural to urban manufacturing. Later, during the 1970s under Premier Dunstan, South Australia was where policy modernization and professionalization in the human services and cultural management – in fields such as education, welfare services, the arts, community health, urban and environmental planning, multiculturalism, Aboriginal affairs and women's affairs – were first promoted and implemented.

By the 1990s the structural economic changes that have disadvantaged manufacturing industry in general, disadvantaged South Australia in particular. Whereas the state's population growth had once been well above the national average (such as during the 1950s), it is now consistently losing its population share. And its reputation for policy flair – for being able to conjure, through governmental initiative and political will, sufficient innovation and momentum to overcome relative resource and locational disadvantage – has suffered from a severe loss of internal confidence caused by the State Bank collapse of the early 1990s. South Australia in the first decades of the new century faces the possibility of coming to resemble what it had been in the first decades of the twentieth: a mendicant state within a federation whose main centres of prosperity and initiative lie elsewhere.

This chapter traces the governmental and political trajectory which has carried South Australia to this point. It traces how the interaction of policy innovation and conservatism has shaped the state's history. It concludes with some speculation about the prospects for restoring policy confidence and economic security.

Context

A state is a geographically-defined political entity. The character of its geographical base – climate, agricultural potential, water supply, mineral resources, location in relation to international and interstate trading routes, and so on – serves as a consistent constraint on political development, predisposing the influence of some forces rather than others.

South Australia's current territorial limits have been in place since

1911. The initial western colonial boundary, set in the British parliament's *Colonization Act* of 1834 at longitude 132°E, was extended westward to the current 129°E in 1861. Today's northern border at 26°S is identical to that established in 1834, but in the meantime what is now the Northern Territory was added in 1863 and traded away to the Commonwealth in 1911. Even the eastern boundary, apparently static at 141°E since the initial 1834 cartographic determination, has a story. The High Court ruled in 1911 that a surveying error which erroneously gave a strip of South Australian territory to Victoria should remain uncorrected, thus legitimizing the strange kink in the state border as it crosses the River Murray from New South Wales to Victoria (Selway 1997, 19).[3]

Climatological factors have had important political consequences. Agricultural settlement has essentially been limited by climate and water supply to the southern one-third of the state below 'Goyder's Line'. That the capital city is not too distant from most of the best agricultural land has helped Adelaide to dominate in population terms and has deterred the development of any other sizeable urban centres. By the late nineteenth century, South Australia's population was already metropolitan-centric. Members of the state's ruling elite until well into the second half of the twentieth century were typically wealthy rural land-holders who maintained close residential and commercial links with Adelaide but who fought hard and successfully to ensure that Adelaide's population dominance was not reflected in political representation. The absence of much development in the northern outback expanses, apart from a few mining localities and pastoral leases, made it easier in the 1960s and 1980s for pioneering land rights legislation to pass effective control over to Indigenous communities. The mining towns have also made a political impact: for decades, they provided the Labor Party with their primary non-metropolitan parliamentary representation; the brown coal deposits at Leigh Creek underpinned much of the Playford industrialization strategy; Labor Party ructions over uranium mining at Roxby Downs contributed to Dunstan's sudden resignation from the premiership in 1979.

Commentaries on South Australian political history used to remark on the significance of its relatively low proportion of citizens of Irish Catholic descent and the relatively high proportion of non-conformist Protestants, especially Methodists (Reid, Blair and Sainsbury 1960, 340; Jaensch 1977, 7–8). Religion scarcely rates a mention in discussions of today's political affiliations, a mark of the secular character of modern public life and the virtual disappearance of the sectarianism that once affected some aspects of Australian politics. But census figures from 1901 revealed that 14 per cent of South Australians at that time professed Catholic affiliation, significantly below the national figure of 22 per cent, and there was a similar under-representation of Anglicans (29 per cent compared with a national figure of 40 per cent). Conversely, 24 per cent of South Australians at that time identified themselves as Methodists, almost double the national proportion of 13 per cent (CBCS 1908).

The low Catholic proportion may help to account for the weak impact in South Australia of the mid-1950s split that badly afflicted the Labor Party elsewhere. And perhaps – though this can only be speculation – the early prominence of Methodism helps to explain something about the intermixture of conservatism and social reformism to which this chapter draws attention.[4] While it now seems to matter little, South Australia's distinctive religious profile has survived a century of social change, including a significant post-war influx of immigrants from Catholic but non-Irish sources like Italy. The 1996 census found that 21 per cent of South Australians professed Catholicism (compared with a national figure of 27 per cent), 16 per cent Anglicanism (compared with 22 per cent) and 13 per cent an identification with the Uniting Church into which Methodism had been absorbed (compared with less than 8 per cent nationally) (ABS 1999a; ABS 1999b).

An important contextual factor has been South Australia's location – geographically and strategically – within the federal system. The state is close enough to the major population centres in Sydney and Melbourne to be able to supply some agricultural and manufactured goods to those markets but also to be vulnerable to interstate competition. The state's economic profile places it somewhere between the more advanced secondary and tertiary industrial profiles of New South Wales and Victoria, on the one hand, and the resource-centric economies of Queensland and Western Australia on the other. This may help to explain why South Australia has often seemed to be in a pivotal position in intergovernmental negotiations, and why South Australian governments have typically placed a high priority on extracting the maximum advantages to the state through those negotiations and via the system of federal grants (Parkin 1996a).

Traditions and interpretations

Whether or not there are sufficient interstate differences to support claims of a distinctive 'political culture' in South Australia (or any other state) has been a matter investigated and disputed by scholars for some time (for example, Holmes and Sharman 1977; Denemark and Sharman 1994). But it is sufficient to say that each state features a governmental, political and policy system largely independent of the other states, and is thus capable of generating its own distinctive political history and momentum. This political self-sufficiency is what permits historians and analysts to portray what is distinctive about the South Australian experience. Various interpretations, with some threads of consistency, emerge.

The dominant perspective has been labelled by Holton (1986) as 'the Whig theory of South Australian history'. Richards (1986) describes it as 'a recurrent theme, a tenuous continuity, from the colonial origins set in the laissez faire milieu of the mid-nineteenth century, to the incipient Keynesian policies of the late 1930s and the growing role of the state thereafter'. This interpretation portrays a South Australian political culture developing from a 'paradise of dissent' created by the founders of 1836 within which, in contrast to 'other parts of Australia [which] may muddle through in the best British tradition; South Australians attach themselves to some conscious theoretical purpose' (Pike 1967, v).[5] This Whiggish orientation, so the story goes, led to the innovations in electoral reform and women's suffrage later in the century, underpinned the Playfordian urban-industrial transformation of the mid-twentieth century and reached its pinnacle with the 'Dunstan decade' of the 1970s. It helps to explain the finding by Nelson (1985), having reviewed policy innovation in all of the Australian states over an eighty-year period, that South Australia, notwithstanding its relatively small population, stood with New South Wales and Victoria as the 'innovators', ahead of the other three 'rearguard' states.

This interpretation does not provide much explanation for less memorable stretches of political history, such as the first third of the twentieth century when South Australia remained economically retarded and became dependent on support from the new Commonwealth government. It seems at odds with awkward facts like the early recognition of women's suffrage not preventing a relatively belated experience of actually electing women to parliament (Bacchi 1986, 403), and full adult suffrage not being achieved for the Legislative Council or local government until well into the 1970s. The most useful interpretative framework is one that posits two intertwining traditions: a tradition of government-centric policy innovation intertwined with a conservative counter-tradition, each of the two elements having a distinctively South Australian flavour.

System of government

These two elements – policy innovation and conservatism – were visible from the very beginning, manifest in the basic institutional arrangements established soon after colonization and continuing with little change for nearly a century and a half. After settlement in 1836, a twenty-year period followed in which observers in the late 1950s (Reid, Blair and Sainsbury 1960, 335) could still claim that 'the character of South Australian politics was established, and its social and historical traditions formed'.

The initial 1836 arrangements were unconventional. They were laid down in the *South Australia Act* of 1834, marking South Australia as 'the only British colony whose foundation rested upon a parliamentary statute' (Main 1986, 1). Authority was divided between the governor, responsible for general government, and Colonization Commissioners, responsible for land distribution, town planning and the immigration of healthy young settlers in accordance with the Wakefield Scheme for planned development of the colony. Within two years, the tension between the two sources of authority had to be resolved by appointing the governor as the Resident Commissioner. In 1842, the office of the commissioners was abolished and a small appointed legislative council created, the enabling Act of the British parliament providing for an elected parliamentary lower house though this was not implemented.

Self-government was achieved in 1856 with a bicameral legislature that has persisted ever since, making laws for 'peace, welfare and good government' of the state (Selway 1997, 6, 63–74). Its constitution consists of what Selway (1997, iii) describes as 'various statutes, instruments, rules and conventions', all of them in principle alterable by the parliament itself.[6] Many of the relevant provisions are consolidated in the South Australian *Constitution Act*.

Members of the Legislative Council were, from the beginning, elected on the basis of a property franchise and lengthy terms of office, initially twelve years on a staggered four-year basis. The property franchise lasted, with some changes, until 1975, and the staggered terms of councillors still remain in effect. The term for today's 22-member Legislative Council term is specified as a minimum of six years, but with half retiring at every House of Assembly election – now up to four years apart – the typical term is closer to eight years. By contrast, the House of Assembly was created in 1856 on the radical democratic basis of universal male suffrage (expanded to universal adult suffrage in 1895) and featured maximum three-year terms. Today's House of Assembly has forty-seven members, and since 1985 the maximum term of office has been four years from the first meeting of the house after an election.

From the beginning, the popularly-elected House of Assembly – the house in which the government is determined – became the institutional basis for the innovative element within South Australian political life, while the Legislative Council institutionalized the conservative element.

The awkward relationship between the two houses was revealed early. The Council claimed and exercised equal status on legislative matters with the Assembly, except that, under 'Compact of 1857', formalized in 1934 into the current *Constitution Act*, the Council agreed not to amend – though it could still reject – financial legislation. Even on financial legislation it retained the capacity to recommend amendments to the Assembly 'except that portion as provides for the ordinary annual expenses of Government' (Selway 1997, 7). A deadlock procedure was formalized in 1881 but was so convoluted that it was never invoked. The procedure allowed for a double dissolution or for the election of extra councillors after two rejections by the Council of legislation passed by the Assembly, but the restrictive franchise governing Council elections made it very likely that all that would follow from this would be a third rejection from which there could be no further step (Jaensch 1986, 366–72).

The electoral system underpinning the Legislative Council – not just the property franchise but also the malapportionment which meant that rural and urban conservative voters were disproportionately well represented – reinforced its role as a sedate, almost semi-aristocratic, house of review. Its membership until well into the 1960s continued to include descendants of the nineteenth-century landed gentry. A majority was consistently drawn from the major right-of-centre political party (known as the Liberal and Country League or LCL from 1932 to 1975). As late as 1965, when the Labor Party at last won a majority in the House of Assembly election after thirty-two years in opposition, winning more than 54 per cent of the statewide two-party-preferred vote, the Council remained composed of sixteen LCL members against four for Labor.

The Council majority was not averse to keeping even governments of its own party in check if they came too close to trammelling on the rights of property-owners. In dramatic circumstances (Muirden 1978), it came very close to defeating the defining legislative achievement of the Playford LCL government: the state takeover of the Adelaide Electric Supply Company in 1946 to form the publicly-owned Electricity Trust. A majority of councillors consistently regarded many Labor initiatives, whether in the form of early-century pioneering efforts to build the skeletal structure of welfare and industrial relations systems or in the form of the Dunstanite radicalism of the mid-1960s and 1970s, with deep suspicion. The language in the Legislative Council that greeted the advent of the Walsh Labor government in 1965 – vows to defend 'the permanent will of the people' against this mere temporarily popular upstart and to disallow 'class legislation' (Parkin 1981, 3) – would have not sounded out of place in the same chamber a hundred years earlier.

But it was the encounter with Dunstan-led Labor reformism, and an urbane sense of modernization that accompanied it, which led in 1974 finally to the demise of the Legislative Council model of 1856 and to the shaping of today's chamber. A deep schism within the LCL saw dissenting urban-based 'progressives' trying to wrest control from their 'conservative' party colleagues entrenched in the Legislative Council. After the 1973 state election that had seen LCL 'progressives' elected to the Council, full adult suffrage and a statewide proportional representation electoral system were introduced, taking effect in a staggered fashion from the election of July 1975. Today's Legislative Council had been created with the balance of power being held by minor-party and independent members. It retains the same power of effective legislative veto, and the only deadlock provision after an Assembly bill has twice been defeated remains the possibility for a double dissolution followed by a third attempt.

While the legislature's historical odyssey has some distinctively South Australian quirks, the executive branch features familiar parliamentary institutions that are typical of an Australian state government. The cabinet, led by the premier, is drawn from the ranks of parliamentary members of the governing party. While the cabinet itself remains in constitutional terms 'a body without legal form or recognition' (Selway 1997, 77), the appointment of ministers is governed by the *Constitution Act* which limits their number. The maximum permissible number was last increased, from thirteen to fifteen, in December 1997.

The position of premier has been especially significant. The style and attributes of the political leader seemed to have a direct influence on the image and performance of that leader's government. Doubtless such an impact is helped by the relatively small scale of South Australian government compared with (say) the national level or the major eastern states, and probably also by the longstanding administrative dominance of Adelaide over the entire state.

The advent of Premier Thomas Playford (who held the highest office from 1938 to 1965) broke the mould not just in terms of longevity in office but also personal dominance. All the studies and reminiscences about Playford remark on how this 'benevolent despot'

(Cockburn 1991) towered over his colleagues and dominated the government. While Frank Walsh's brief stint as premier (1965–67) was hardly in the same league, his Labor successor Don Dunstan (in office from 1967–68, and 1970–79) projected a flamboyant, activist, reformist image and quickly stamped his authority on the government.

Each of Dunstan's successors also lent their personal style to their governments, the longest serving being John Bannon (1982–92) who offered a restrained managerial approach with a touch of social and cultural flair that was brought to a sudden end by the State Bank collapse.

Electoral system

The electoral system has often been central in shaping South Australian politics. Malapportionment leading to a significant under-representation of metropolitan Adelaide in both houses of parliament played a major role in determining electoral outcomes until well into the 1970s.

Until the 1930s multiple-member electorates moderated the partisan impact of this malapportionment in the House of Assembly. After 1915, for example, Assembly elections were based on eight three-member and eleven two-member electorates, and this seemed to allow enough representation from minority parties to moderate the effect of rural over-representation allowing the Labor Party, for example, to return some non-metropolitan members. In 1932, however, a new system based on thirty-nine single-member electorates was instituted, with a guarantee that country seats would outnumber city seats on a two-to-one ratio. This system strongly favoured the Liberal and Country League and needs to be taken into account when assessing the longevity of the Playford LCL government. There is a scholarly dispute over how Playford's party would have fared under a balanced electoral system (DeGaris 1976; Jaensch 1971; Playford 1982; Stock 1991) but there seems little doubt that Playford won at least some of his nine successive election victories with less than majority support among South Australians.

The effects of malapportionment became exacerbated as the relative population share of Adelaide grew steadily. By 1968 the ratio of country to metropolitan seats had increased to about three-to-one, and one metropolitan electorate had more enrolled voters than the seven smallest country electorates combined. That was the year in which a Labor government, having been elected in 1965, notwithstanding the electoral bias after being out of office for thirty-two years, lost office despite winning 52 per cent of the first preference vote.

The same internal LCL tension between urban-progressive and rural-conservative wings that led to the later restructuring of the Legislative Council contributed to the demise of electoral malapportionment in the House of Assembly. The incoming LCL government of 1968, led by Premier Steele Hall, legislated to increase the numbers in the house to forty-seven while reducing, though not eliminating, the malapportionment favouring rural areas. The bill, virtually guaranteeing that the Hall government would lose office at the next election, passed the House of Assembly with unanimous support and with sufficient momentum for the unreformed Legislative Council, though disturbed by its erosion of rural interests, to allow it to be enacted. The Labor government duly elected in 1970 under the new arrangements kept up the pressure to eliminate malapportionment. This was finally achieved with the support of the urban moderates among the Liberals. A deeply-entrenched principle of representation for well over a century had been overturned (Jaensch, 1981).

This was not the end of the controversy about the House of Assembly electoral system. The notion of electoral fairness had become elevated by decades of debate into a fundamental criterion for governmental legitimacy. But single-member electoral systems, however well apportioned, are not designed to produce a close match between a party's share of votes and share of seats. In the 1989 election the Bannon Labor government was returned to office despite winning just 40 per cent of the statewide first preference vote. While the Labor leadership explained in Playfordian-sounding tones that their 1989 election strategy had naturally been built around winning a majority of seats rather than a majority of votes, it sounded hollow in the context of Labor's own previous moral fervour on the issue of fairness. The outcome was a government-sponsored amendment to the *Electoral Act*, ratified by a popular referendum, henceforth requiring the independent Electoral Commission to draw electoral boundaries in such a way to ensure 'as far as practicable' that the party winning a majority of the two-party-preferred vote won a majority of seats.

This provision required the commission to make predictions about voting behaviour within specific localities. In practice, the commission seems to have concluded that they are best able to meet the requirement by creating more marginal seats, thus enhancing the effect of any electoral swing in support from one major party to the other. An unintended consequence is that the turnover rate is increasing for members of the House of Assembly. The February 2002 election produced another failure to achieve electoral fairness in the sense envisaged. The Liberal Party won 50.9 per cent of the two-party-preferred vote (40.4

per cent of the first preference vote), but it lost office after post-election negotiations between Labor (with 35.2 per cent of the first preference vote) and two independent Liberals whose votes were allocated by the state electoral office to the Liberal two-party-preferred tally.

The introduction of proportional representation for the election of members of the Legislative Council has meant, as in the Australian Senate, that there is a strong likelihood of minor parties and independents holding the balance of power. The February 2002 election for half of the Council, for example, returned five Liberal, four Labor, one Democrat and one Family First Party members. This created an overall Council with nine Liberals, seven Labor, three Democrats, one Independent No Pokies, one Family First and one SA First member, the last named having been elected on the Labor ticket in 1997 but defected later.

Government legislation has to be negotiated with other parties in the Legislative Council in order to secure passage. The Olsen government's (ultimately successful) attempts over 1998 and 1999 to privatize the Electricity Trust provide an example of both the difficulty of passing controversial legislation through the Council and the determination of a government to secure its chosen policy.

Parties and the party system

The modern party system took some time to develop in South Australia and dates, in its current form, from the 1930s. The colonial parliament had featured an unsteady assortment of independents and proto-parties whose solid names, like Conservatives and Liberals, belied their embryonic form. The fluidity of factional groupings in the state parliament produced rapid turnovers of government: between 1856 and 1893 there were no fewer than forty-seven ministries (Howell 1986, 110).

As elsewhere, it was the formation of the Labor Party which produced a consolidation of the party system, but in South Australia this took time. A Labor League had formed in 1882 and managed to get ten members elected to the House of Assembly in 1893 but, by 1902, its numbers had dwindled to five. After the 1905 election, a surge in support led to the first Labor premier, Tom Price, taking office at the head of a Labor Party–Liberal Party coalition government which lasted until 1909. Labor gained office with majorities in the House of Assembly under premiers Verran (1910–12) and Vaughan (1915–17). Interspersed were a number of Liberal governments, with Liberal leader Archibald Henry Peake enjoying a number of separate stints in the premier's office (1909–10, 1912–15, 1917–20).

The 1921 election was notable for the participation of the Farmers and Settlers Party, thereafter called the Country Party, but it was, along with the Liberal League, one of several contending anti-Labor groupings better described as 'more in the nature of coalitions for electoral purposes' than as modern parties (Reid, Blair and Sainsbury 1960, 338). There was a consolidation of several anti-Labor groupings in 1923 into a Liberal Federation. Three-way contests between the Labor, Liberal and Country party groupings then continued, with Labor and Liberal alternations in office, until the amalgamation of the two non-Labor entities to form the Liberal and Country League (LCL) in 1932. One of the conditions of the amalgamation was the guarantee of at least a two-to-one ratio of country to city seats in the House of Assembly.

The LCL proved to be a stable and spectacularly successful anti-Labor force. Richard Butler, who had been premier of a Liberal Party–Country Party coalition government from 1927 to 1930, headed an LCL government that lasted from April 1933 until November 1938. His successor as LCL leader, Thomas Playford, then remained as premier until March 1965. The LCL developed a large membership based both in rural areas and in the eastern and southern suburbs of Adelaide, with an unusually high proportion of women members. By the 1960s the LCL appeared to be entrenched in government.

The Labor Party, meanwhile, seemed correspondingly entrenched in opposition. Much of its energy was taken up by internal party contests over the preselection of candidates and the selection of party officers, both of which were under the control of a union-controlled party machine led by Federal members of parliament Jim Toohey and Clyde Cameron (Stokes and Cox 1981; Stokes 1983). This machine-dominated consensus induced Premier Frank Walsh to make way in 1967 for his somewhat unconventional successor, Don Dunstan, after Walsh had led Labor to an election victory in 1965.

The end of the long period of LCL rule in 1965, followed by a similar period of Labor dominance for most of the next quarter-century (Labor was in office for twenty-two of the twenty-seven years from 1965 until late 1992), had significant consequences for both major parties. On the Liberal side, the schism between the urban progressives and the rural conservatives reached its deepest point in the early 1970s. Steele Hall resigned as parliamentary leader in March 1972, describing his party as 'deeply cleft by the pervasive influence of a number of its members in the Legislative Council' (Parkin 1981, 9). During the 1973 election a group of LCL members, including Hall, rebadged themselves as the Liberal Movement (LM) – a strange 'party within the party' –

and contested the election against other LCL members. The LM was proscribed for LCL members after the election and most LM affiliates returned to the fold. The LCL then proceeded to rename itself as the Liberal Party of Australia (SA Division) but the divisions of the 1970s period took decades to heal.

On the Labor side, consistent electoral success in the 1970s and 1980s apeared to lead to a disintegration of the internal consensus model that had served the party so well in its long years in opposition (Marshall 1992; Summers and Parkin 2000). By the end of the 1970s, overt factionalism, somewhat replicating the Left–Centre–Right structure also emerging in the party in other states and at the national level but with peculiar local idiosyncrasies, had taken the place of the Toohey–Cameron machine. For much of the 1980s the dominance of the moderate Centre Left faction (for which South Australia was the prime national base within the party) provided some stability, though proportional representation rules ensured that the Left and the Right groupings remained visible. During the 1990s the Centre Left evaporated as a major force, seemingly one of the casualties of the electoral devastation caused by the State Bank collapse under the Bannon Labor government. The Left split into two separate warring factions and a new machine – based on an odd alliance between a resurgent Right and one of the Left groupings – had risen to internal party dominance by the late 1990s.

Figure 5.1 charts the long-run patterns of major party support in South Australia over more than a century, from the election of 1893 to the election of 2002. It sketches the trajectory of first preference vote shares in House of Assembly elections since 1893 for the Labor Party and for the major anti-Labor party. What is most evident in figure 5.1 is Labor's long mid-century pattern of predominance in voting support. Tellingly, the Playford era of LCL dominance in office (1938–65) does not register in terms of vote share. While this result was underpinned by electoral malapportionment, the chart ignores the large number of uncontested seats during this period, and the support for the typically Right-of-Centre independent candidates which usually fed into support for the Playford regime. On the other hand, figure 5.1 reveals a trend from 1989 away from Labor and towards the Liberal Party, and twice in this period (in 1989 and 2002) Labor has won governmental office with a minority of the two-party preferred vote.

Minor party and independent members of parliament have been important players periodically in South Australian history. Their occasional prominence before the consolidation of the bipolar party system in 1932 has already been noted, but the pinnacle of support for

Figure 5.1 South Australian House of Assembly, general elections 1893–2002: vote share of ALP, Liberal Party (and precursors), and all other parties* (% of first preference vote)

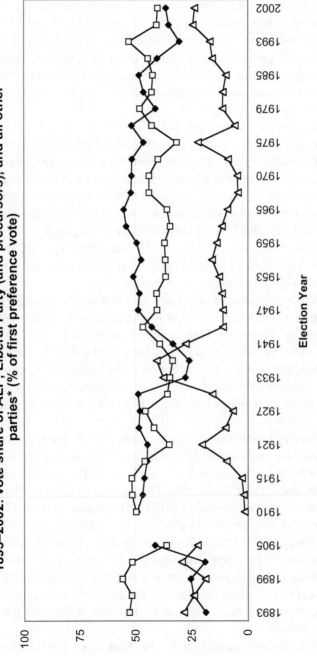

Election Year

◆ ALP   □ Liberal Party (& precursors)   △ Minor parties & independents (residual)

Note: 'other parties' includes the National Party and its predecessors (see text for details); there is no entry for the 1906 election because the Labor Party and the Liberal Democratic Union formed an alliance and ran a joint slate of candidates.

*

Source: calculated from the Australian Government and Politics Project database, University of Western Australia.

independents coincided with the beginnings of Playford's long premiership in 1938. The 1938 election returned fifteen rural-based independents (most of them LCL-supporting) in a House of Assembly of thirty-nine. Their numbers gradually diminished election by election down to just two independents in 1962 and one in 1965 and 1968, but these small numbers became crucial. The two independents enabled a minority Playford government to survive from 1962 to 1965, while the one remaining gave the Hall government its parliamentary majority from 1968 until his support was withdrawn, precipitating an early election, in 1970.

Both major parties have recently suffered from the actions of disaffected members of their parliamentary parties who have either run successfully as independent candidates or resigned from the party while in parliament to sit on the cross-benches. On the Liberal side, the complex Liberal Movement story of the 1970s represents an instance of this, and the October 1997 election saw two formerly safe Liberal rural seats fall to independent Liberal candidates on whose support the Olsen government then became dependent.[7] After the February 2002 election, two former Liberal MHAs who had been elected as independents decided to support a minority Labor government.

Labor has had similar experiences. In 1975 an independent Labor candidate won a safe Labor seat and had to be quickly welcomed back into the party to support the Dunstan government. Another safe Labor seat fell to an independent Labor candidate in the defeat of 1979 and then, in 1989, the Bannon Labor government limped back into office needing the support of two independent Labor members who were later joined on the cross-benches by a third following a party preselection dispute.

When the Australian Democrats formed in 1977, the residue of the Liberal Movement gave the party 'a ready-made constituency in South Australia' which has remained at the core of the party's national strength ever since (Stock 1992, 59). The remaining Liberal Movement member in the House of Assembly (Robin Millhouse) relabelled himself a Democrat and was re-elected twice in that capacity (in 1977 and 1979). The party retained Millhouse's seat in a by-election in May 1982 after Millhouse had been appointed by the Tonkin Liberal government to the Supreme Court in what seemed like a fairly blatant attempt to restore his seat to its former safe Liberal status. Only at the general election six months later was a Democrat presence eliminated from the House of Assembly.

In the Legislative Council, as in the Australian Senate, the post-1975 system of proportional representation has been more favourable

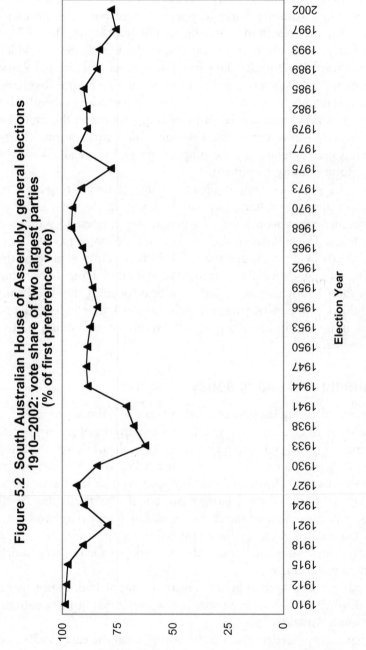

Figure 5.2 South Australian House of Assembly, general elections 1910–2002: vote share of two largest parties (% of first preference vote)

Election Year

Vote share of two largest parties

Source: calculated from the Australian Government and Politics Project database, University of Western Australia.

to the election of Democrat candidates. Since 1979 the Democrats have been able to win one of the eleven seats in each half-election, and gained two seats at the 1997 election.

The embryonic Country Party had been absorbed into the LCL in 1932, but a new Country Party reappeared in response to the LCL's refocusing on metropolitan Adelaide in the late 1960s. In 1973 a Country Party candidate won a rural seat in the Eyre Peninsula which he retained until 1989 under the party's new name of National Party. The National Party was successful in 1997 in winning a rural Riverland seat, and this member, together with the two independent Liberals also elected at that time, was crucial in providing support to the minority Olsen Liberal government. After February 2002 the National Party member has been sidelined by the support of two independents for the minority Rann Labor government.

Figure 5.2 provides some indication of the changing trajectory of independent and minor party support by charting the total share of first-preference votes won jointly by candidates endorsed by the two largest parties. The significant shift away from the major parties in the 1930s is clearly evident, though the 1933 shift, largely explained by the splintering of the Labor Party into official Labor, Lang Labor and Premiers Plan Labor camps, differs significantly from the 1938 shift which follows it and which went largely to non-Labor independents. Also evident is what has been a post-1980 trend towards minor parties and independents.

Government and public policy

The patterns of voting support charted in figure 5.2 above provide little guidance – due to electoral-system effects – to patterns of governmental incumbency. Figure 5.3 provides a better indication of changing patterns of governmental office over the 1893 to 2001 period by charting the share of House of Assembly seats won by the Labor Party, by the Liberal and National parties combined (the particular labels changing over the course of the century), and by minor party and inde-pendent candidates. Getting above the 50 per cent mark – that is, a majority on the floor of the House of Assembly – is the key to winning or retaining government.

The pattern dsiplayed in figure 5.3 can be mapped fairly directly on to four distinct periods of governmental policy making in twentieth-century South Australia.

During the post-federation period lasting until the early 1930s, no clear pattern of party dominance emerges, reflecting a state whose

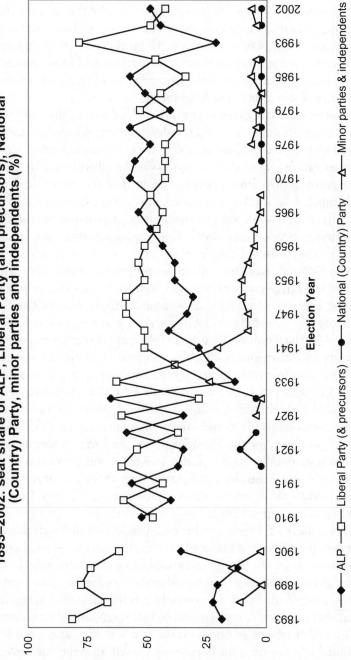

Figure 5.3 South Australian House of Assembly, general elections 1893–2002: seat share of ALP, Liberal Party (and precursors), National (Country) Party, minor parties and independents (%)

□ ALP   □ Liberal Party (& precursors)   ◆ National (Country) Party   △ Minor parties & independents

Election Year

Source: calculated from the Australian Government and Politics Project database, University of Western Australia.

social, economic and political profile was uncertain. At this stage, South Australia struggled within the new federal system. Its agricultural profile was increasingly out of kilter with emerging industrial forces elsewhere. But successive governments, normally through the initiative of Labor administrations and the acquiescence of their successors, put in place the local manifestations of the utilitarian style of Australian government; wage arbitration, the State Bank and other public enterprises, rural railways, urban tramways and arterial roads, plus Australia's first planned 'garden suburb'.

South Australian governments also helped to establish an important institution within the Australian federal system which has, ever since, worked to the state's advantage, or rather, as South Australians would prefer to express it, worked to redress its disadvantages. By the 1920s South Australian premiers were arguing that federation had unfairly disadvantaged South Australia since, along with Western Australia and Tasmania, its economy was based mainly on export-oriented agricultural and mining production, with little manufacturing industry. South Australia thus suffered disproportionately from the costs imposed by uniform Commonwealth-level tariffs on imported machinery and other material used in primary production, and from the extra shipping costs resulting from the effective exclusion under Commonwealth policies of cheaper foreign shipping. In 1929 a special grant was initiated to South Australia by the Commonwealth, and the state thereafter joined Western Australia and Tasmania as a regular recipient of special assistance. From 1933 this was institutionalized by the creation of the Commonwealth Grants Commission, under which South Australia became recognized as a claimant state requiring additional Commonwealth transfers. South Australia was to retain its special claimant status until 1959 and it was renewed, in effect, for the 1970–75 period. In 1982 a more comprehensive and systematic process of horizontal fiscal equalization was applied, again to South Australia's net advantage, through formulas recommended and calculated by the Commonwealth Grants Commission (Parkin and Summers 1996).

From the mid-1930s to the mid-1960s, South Australia entered what is best termed 'the Playford period', though this span also takes in the last years of the Butler premiership of 1933–38 which saw the beginings of what was to become identified as the Playford strategy. As already described, Playford, extending Butler initiatives, instituted a strong and purposeful government-led strategy for industrialization. A small number of key public servants and a public sector ethos which combined innovation with parsimony played an important role in this strategy.[8]

The elements of the strategy included the provision of various inducements to attract business investment to the state, with notable successes including the establishment of the Whyalla steelmaking and shipbuilding industries, new weapons research and manufacturing plants in Adelaide's northern suburbs, the opening up of the Cooper Basin gasfields and new Adelaide-based factories occupied by various multinational corporations including British Tube Mills, Philips Industries and, most significantly of all, the motor vehicle manufacturers General Motors and Chrysler. Some of the inducements came in the form of publicly funded infrastructure – water pipelines, electricity grids, rail extensions and arterial roads – which served to make South Australia a more industrialized and urbanized community.

Perhaps most novel of all, a government housing agency – the Housing Trust – played a major role in developing new housing estates in concert with the industrialization strategy. The provision of low cost housing to the industrial workforce, it was argued, could permit lower nominal wage levels in South Australia and hence produce lower business costs, a major inducement for investment. In the process, the SA Housing Trust came to play a role in the state's housing industry which exceeded by far that played, in relative terms, by a housing authority in any other state. It became something of an international model for an economically strategic, non-welfarist, non-stigmatized form of non-market housing provision (Stretton 1975; Badcock 1989).

Playford's indifference to social and cultural services in a state which, through his own policies, was becoming increasingly dominated by metropolitan Adelaide and its growing middle classes was eventually to contribute to his undoing. The Playford period gave way to a period of Labor dominance with the advent of the Labor governments of the 1970s and 1980s, electorally underpinned by the support of an urban middle class which, in other states, was more likely to support the Liberal Party. The first half of this period was dominated by the policies and personality of Don Dunstan, initially (1965–67) as a minister in the Walsh government when 'it was not uncommon to hear the Walsh Cabinet referred to as the Dunstan Ministry' (Blewett and Jaensch 1971, 36), and later (1967–68, 1970–79) as premier. Much has been written about the 'Dunstan decade' stressing that it was, above all else, a period of policy innovation and modernization (Parkin and Patience 1981).

Many of the policy reforms of the Dunstan decade generated controversy, even cultural shock. In Aboriginal affairs, as Summers (1981, 127) has argued, Dunstan's legislative initiatives in the 1965–67 period as a minister in the Walsh Labor government were 'far ahead of anything else in Australia at the time'. These were policies which turned away from the paternalism of the old order and which promoted the idea of indigenous Australians as equal citizens under the law. The *Aboriginal Lands Trust Act* of 1966 recognized land rights a quarter of a century before the Mabo and Wik High Court decisions. South Australia has been spared most of the division and bitterness of the national land rights debate of the 1990s in large measure because of the Dunstan reforms of the 1960s.

The same innovation characterized Dunstan's social welfare reforms. In 1965 Dunstan inherited the Children's Welfare and Public Relief Board, the nomenclature epitomizing its tradition of charity and paternalism and its staff largely untrained in the emerging profession of social work. Dunstan's *Social Welfare Act* of 1965, along with analogous legislation on such matters as juvenile courts and adoptions, restructured the bureaucratic and ideological meaning of welfare, and professionalized its delivery.

Reformist urban policy in Australia probably reached its apogee under the national Whitlam Labor government of 1972–75. While Whitlam articulated the vision, it was Dunstan and his government which had already taken the initiative. There was flair in what was achieved. Micro-level projects like Rundle Street's pedestrian mall redefined urban spaces. Grander projects like the West Lakes development put public–private partnerships to work. The Land Commission, created to combat land speculation at a time of urban growth, embodied a genuinely radical claim about the role of the public sector. There was also flair in what was consciously not pursued, such as the abandonment of the freeway plans, and even in what was envisaged but not achieved by the legion of architects and planners educating themselves in the design of the phantom city of Monarto (Parkin and Pugh 1981). The same urbane vision inspired other social reforms. Gambling shifted from sinfulness to government sponsorship. Pubs were not only allowed to stay open after 6 o'clock but a new al fresco conception of city spaces and sidewalks encouraged the consumption of good food and fine wine in cosmopolitan public places. If South Australia had been shaped by Methodist sobriety, Dunstanism swept most of that legacy away.

New conceptualizations of the way in which political interests could be envisaged – notions like ethnic affairs and women's policy – took institutional form. By simply defining a sphere of consumer affairs, Dunstan and his governments presided over a minor ideological revolution. Protections like product labelling, warranty provisions, consumer credit regulation, licensing of dealers, proscription of misleading advertising, cooling-off periods and so on were implemented in the face of contest and controversy. Much the same philosophy inspired the State Government Insurance Commission (SGIC). Under Dunstan, arts policy became established as part of the normal repertoire of contemporary Australian government. The Dunstan regime provided the institutions – the Festival Centre Trust, the Film Corporation, the Craft Authority, and others – and, to an important extent, Dunstan himself contributed to the image which propelled Adelaide to national prominence as the place to be in the arts scene.

Government schools have long been a significant expense for state governments, but a self-conscious notion of education policy – of schooling as a purposive activity with social, cultural and economic consequences about which there could be political arguments and strategic choices – came into focus in the Dunstan period. The Karmel Report submitted to the Dunstan government in February 1971 anticipated by several years the Karmel Report to the national Whitlam government, with the same new emphasis on equality of opportunity, curriculum innovation, community education, greater professionalism and less bureaucracy.[9]

This is a remarkable policy record even though economic policy does not figure prominently. It is not that the Dunstan years were characterized by an economic policy vacuum; rather, it is simply that the approach of Dunstan governments in the economic area was conventional rather than unconventional. Like the governments which preceded and followed him, Dunstan's administration advocated tariff protection for local industries and offered a portfolio of incentives to attract private investment. Dunstan's one genuinely radical idea in the economic sphere – industrial democracy – got nowhere.

After the Tonkin interregnum of 1979–82, the Bannon Labor governments maintained much of the momentum well into the 1980s, without Dunstan's flair but also largely without its controversy. The Bannon legacy is now so deeply associated with Bannon's traumatic last years in office – devastated in morale and purpose by the revelation in February 1991 of the disastrous State Bank losses – that it is usually forgotten how benign most of his period in office had been, how there had been a genuine attempt to lead a renewal of Australian federalism through a better Commonwealth–state partnership (Parkin and Marshall 1992; Parkin 1996b) and how Bannon had acquired the slightly unfashionable image of being a careful, moderate manager of the state's affairs, proud of his steady retirement of state debt (Parkin 1992; but note Patience 1992; Kenny 1993).

The gradual deterioration of the South Australian economy coming to the fore in the Bannon years with the recessions of the early 1980s

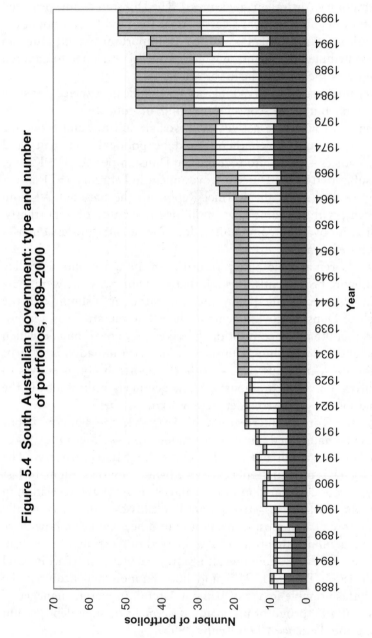

Figure 5.4 South Australian government: type and number of portfolios, 1889–2000

■ Defining Activities ☐ Physical Resources ☐ Social Activities

Source: calculated from the Australian Government and Politics Project database, University of Western Australia.

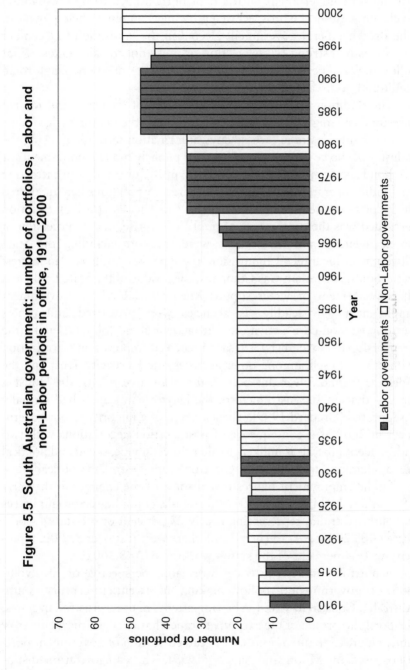

Figure 5.5 South Australian government: number of portfolios, Labor and non-Labor periods in office, 1910–2000

■ Labor governments □ Non-Labor governments

Source: calculated from the Australian Government and Politics Project database, University of Western Australia.

and early 1990s led to the end of the period of Labor dominance. What has replaced it is a period of uncertainty. The collapse of the State Bank left the state government with a debt burden back to its pre-Bannon levels but without the prospect of a growing economy to help pay it off. The Brown Liberal government elected in the landslide of December 1993 was hamstrung by its election promise not to raise taxes. What followed was a period when the government continued one Playfordian tradition but discarded another.

The tradition maintained was the wooing of interstate and foreign investors who might be interested in establishing their cutting-edge industries in South Australia – these days, information technology being the industry of choice – especially after a few publicly funded inducements or tax holidays. Some successes, especially in the novel idea of attracting back-office operations to Adelaide for large corporations headquartered in Sydney or Melbourne, were achieved. The Playfordian tradition discarded was the central role of public enterprise, and a succession of public agencies and investments were sold off including the State Government Insurance Commission, the Pipelines Authority, an interest in the South Australian Gas Company, the residue of the State Bank, and the management of water supply. Meanwhile, levels of government employment fell steadily, as agencies were privatized and others outsourced non-core activities. The accession of John Olsen to the premiership in November 1996 saw a renewed emphasis on privatization with moves to sell, among other agencies, the Electricity Trust and the Adelaide Casino. Over this period, the distinctive role of the Housing Trust – that unique instrument of the Playfordian state – had virtually disappeared (Orchard 1999). The accession of a minority Labor government in 2002 as a consequence of post-election negotiations with two independent Liberals is unlikely to alter the economic, social and political trends characterizing this latest phase of South Australian political life.

Public employment figures reveal some of the change. In the early 1980s there had been over 101 000 state-level public-sector employees in South Australia, representing nearly 23 per cent of the state's workforce (ABS 2001c). As of early 2000, there were just over 87 000, representing 16.4 per cent of the state's workforce (ABS 2001b).

A portfolio analysis provides a revealing perspective on the evolution of governmental policy making in twentieth-century South Australia. Consistent with the broad patterns in other Australian states, the portfolio profile of the executive branch has changed markedly over time. Figures 5.4 and 5.5 utilize the categorization of government portfolios used by Moon and Sayers (1999). The categorization distinguishes between portfolios according to whether they are 'defining' (that is, the core activites of government administration), 'physical' (activities relating to economic activity and physical infrastructure) or 'social' (the provision of social benefits and services).

Figure 5.4 reveals how the nineteenth-century colonial pattern of government devoted essentially to defining and physical activities continued with little change until the 1930s. Even then, the accretion of social activities was modest until the end of the Playford era in 1965, leaving the state in the mid-1960s with a relatively undeveloped social services sector. This accurately portrays government in South Australia as focused on the physical and economic infrastructure of the state, initially through agriculture and mining, joined later by industrial development. Stretton (1975, 143) nicely summarizes the austere and economically focused Playfordian priorities: 'What had been advanced institutions in [Playford's] grandfather's day continued to look good to him ... Central economic planning ran half a century ahead of a central lack of compassion – saving on that was where the winning margins of investment in cheap land, water, power and housing came from.'

Figures 5.4 and 5.5 confirm that it has been the advent of Labor governments – especially the initial impacts of the Walsh government in 1965, the Dunstan government in 1970 and the Bannon government in 1982 – which have both increased the scope of state government port-folio activity in general and added a significant component of social activities in particular. It remains to be seen whether future Labor governments will be consistent with this pattern.

The future

There are three scenarios which might describe where South Australia is heading during the first decade or two of the twenty-first century. Scenario 1 envisages continuing decline and marginalization; South Australia slowly becomes more peripheral to the national and international economy, there is a steady net population loss and the state has a decreasing role in shaping national affairs.

Under Scenario 2, the deepest wishes of South Australian political leaders in both major parties are fulfilled; national and international investors at last realise that Adelaide is the ideal location for large and sustained private capital investment. The state maintains a stable and skilled workforce, good higher education institutions, a high standard of general education and social services, inexpensive housing, fine wines and a generally healthy lifestyle. As a consequence, the state become Australia's high-tech, high-status and high-income equivalent of southern California.

Scenario 3 combines the more plausible elements of the first two into a more modest package. It is the Edinburgh or Minnesota option, with the residents of the state accepting that South Australia is a relatively minor player in national affairs and that some of its best and brightest sons and daughters will leave to work elsewhere. But the state remains devoted to promoting a sense of artistic and cultural excellence, enhancing Adelaide as a city of learning and South Australia as a distinctive place to live in and to visit, creating interesting and challenging jobs for its citizens, and restoring the state's reputation for good government. It would be fascinating to be able to read the year 2101 bicentenary of federation's inevitable revisiting of the history of Australian political life to see which of these scenarios, if any, comes closest to reality.

Chapter

6

Tasmania

Aynsley Kellow

Tasmania's founding as a convict settlement in 1803 continues to shape the state's politics. Its convict origins gave rise to both a prominent role to the state which continues into the twenty-first century and, at the same time, a class divide and a determination on the part of the landed gentry to protect their interests. This latter feature was responsible for a constitutional design which stressed the importance of a property-based upper house of parliament as a conservative brake on government. The role of this chamber, the Legislative Council, although changed from its composition in 1856, has been to resist constitutional and democratic reform to itself, while permitting major changes to the lower house, the House of Assembly.

As a consequence, Tasmania has a distinctive set of legislative institutions in comparison with the other Australian states; a House of Assembly, since the 1998 election, of twenty-five members elected by a system of proportional representation by the single transferable vote from five multimember electoral districts, and a Legislative Council whose fifteen members are chosen by a preferential voting system from single-member electoral districts for six-year terms on a rotating cycle of elections at which two or three councillors are elected each year. The staggered elections in the Council are intended to protect the electorate from any popular 'enthusiasms' which might sweep governments based on transitory majorities in the lower house.

Tasmania has a more decentralized population than the other states and it is much more socially homogenous. The state has seen little recent immigration, interstate or international, with almost 90 per cent of its population being Tasmanian-born. Most of its immigrants are Anglo-Celtic, and its indigenous population, though resurgent, was thought as recently as the 1960s to have been driven to extinction. Tasmania has been affected to only a limited extent by the multiculturalism which is a feature of the current politics of other states. The state's population has been so stable that it has great value as a location for genetic research. There have, as a result, been few divisions to cross-cut, and thus diminish, the class divide, save for strong regional attachments. These parochial concerns stem from the dispersal of the population across the state and a fierce rivalry between regions. The north and north-west regions consider themselves to have claims to be equal, if not superior, to the capital, Hobart, in social status and sporting prowess. The lack of large-scale immigration could be said to have contributed to a conservative and parochial political culture.

But while its population reflects its insular geography, its economy is more open than most states. It relies heavily on exports, principally of primary production including timber, wool, and vegetables of all kinds from the fertile north coast of the state. Its manufacturing base in areas such as textiles has proven to be uncompetitive and its recent economic successes have been in primary products – cheese, salmon and opium poppies – and tourism rather than manufactures. There have been some successes, such as a builder of high speed ferries, but they have not been sufficient to do more than hold a rather precarious status quo. And the policy followed by successive Labor governments from the 1930s to the 1970s of hydro-industrialization based on cheap electricity has created few of the promised benefits and many costs in both financial and environmental terms. The long-term result has been that one of the state's longest-running exports has been its people, especially its young people, who are forced to seek employment on the Australian mainland or beyond.

This has been the 'Tasmanian problem' for successive governments since the 1850s marked the end of transportation, the establishment of self-government, and the discovery of gold in Victoria. The lack of opportunity persists (Felmingham 1993; Rothwell 1997). The Australian Bureau of Statistics made a projection in 2000 which saw the population of the state dropping to half its current size over the next half-century. This, of course, was a projection based on current activity, and did not take account of any success that either local business action or government policy might have in arresting the slide.

It could be that the legacy of Tasmania's colonial past as a penal settlement has led to an expectation that the state rather than private entrepreneurs will look after economic problems, coupled with a conservative tradition and a set of political institutions which make it less likely that any government will be capable of meeting expectations (Davis 1986). Where Tasmania's predicament would suggest the need for a government with a bold, programmatic vision for reform, its political system is characterized by an altogether different style, described by Chapman et al. (1986, 117) as 'the politics of personality, development, opportunism and brokerage'. These are characteristics commonly found in economic backwaters. It would be an oversimplification to suggest that these are features which cause Tasmania's predicament since other geographic, economic and political factors provide more powerful explanations, but they surely do not make it any easier to develop remedies.

A long period of Labor rule, for example, might have been expected to have yielded impressive social democratic reforms, but these are largely lacking in spite of the Labor Party's hold on government from 1934 to 1982 with only one three-year break. The explanation for this lies in the kind of ALP regime Tasmania produced. The regimes of Ogilvie, Cosgrove and Reece ran uninterrupted from 1934 until 1969 precisely because they were not doctrinaire socialist regimes; they were distributive, rather than redistributive in flavour, what Lowi (1964) calls patronage politics. They were focused more on development than dogma. Like many settler societies, Tasmania has become habituated to look to government to distribute the natural resources of the state, once the indigenous inhabitants had been dispossessed of them.

The initial wealth was land, but Tasmania's mineral wealth and forests were also important. It was the formula of harnessing the considerable hydro-electric power potential to the processing of these mineral and forest resources, particularly by using the state's entitlements to capital under the federal government sponsored Loans Council arrangements – the development strategy which became known as hydro-industrialization – which helped to underpin the continuing electoral success of the ALP.

Tasmania's geographical position means that it was never going to be able to position itself as a centre of trade like Hong Kong or Singapore. It was never likely, in the words of P. J. O'Rourke (1998) to 'make everything when you have nothing'. Its endowment of natural resources, like most settler societies, was always going to be the basis of its economy. Like all colonial economies, capital formation was the problem, and the Loans Council ensured Tasmania would have its share of public capital with which to develop its resource endowment. Its problem has been that this reliance on state-sponsored developmentalism has resonated with political factors to militate against consideration of the kinds of programmatic reform which might have produced a more dynamic economy. It is not that Tasmania is a case, to continue O'Rourke's line, that has 'made nothing from everything', but it has made less than it might have out of what it has.[1]

We can explore this theme by considering the development of the Tasmanian political system in the nineteenth century when its basic features were determined, and then move on to explore the way Tasmanian politics has panned out in the century after federation. This exploration is necessarily selective, but a theme which recurs throughout the century since federation is Tasmania's need for economic development in the face of limits put on policies to encourage economic growth by the state's political system. The governmental process has resisted reforms which might have reduced the parochialism and patronage that have limited economic growth. We need to look in turn at the colonial origins of Tasmanian politics, the basic constitutional features of the state, its idiosyncratic electoral system, the patterns of representation and party success, and the broad trajectory of policy and government activity.

The colonial origins of Tasmanian politics

While the first European settlement of Tasmania occurred in 1803, the colony of Van Diemen's Land, as the colony was called until self-government in 1856, was not established as a separate political entity from the colony of New South Wales until 1825 (Robson 1983). The initial constitutional arrangements were for a lieutenant-governor and an executive council, consisting of the chief justice (until 1835), the senior officer of her majesty's forces, the lord bishop (once the diocesan see was established), the colonial secretary, the colonial treasurer and the chief police magistrate (Townsley 1991, 37–41): a list befitting a penal colony. Almost immediately, in 1828, a Legislative Council was established with the lieutenant-governor presiding over six officials and eight nominated non-officials, 'fairly selected from the more intelligent, wealthy and respectable members of the commercial, agricultural and professional bodies of the colony' (Townsley 1991, 42).

The Legislative Council could be controlled by the non-officials, and it exhibited quite some independence from the executive, with a group of non-official members who became known as the 'Patriotic Six' resigning in 1846 as a way of forcing democratic reform. There were further demands for elected rather than appointed representatives, and provision for elections was made in 1851, but on a decidedly undemocratic basis; '[Governor] Denison, always fearing the radical and unruly elements that congregated in towns, gave Hobart two seats and Launceston one out of sixteen to be elected, even though the two towns had 40 per cent of the total population' (Townsley 1991, 46). It is important to note in this regard that Tasmania's convict population had included quite a number transported for espousing radical political causes.

At the time of self-government, therefore, the Legislative Council enjoyed a reputation for keeping the executive accountable, while being established on an electoral franchise which gave weight to regional interests at the expense of equality of representation. When the House of Assembly was established in 1856 it became the lower house of a parliament whose upper house, the Legislative Council, had almost equal powers and had been designed to be insulated from the popular will. While the franchise for the Assembly was extended at the time of federation to adult males and, soon after, to women, a property franchise for the Council persisted into the 1960s. The Council was a chamber which claimed to embody the principle of keeping the executive accountable while resisting democratic accountability itself. The chamber proved to be remarkably resistant to changes in its composition but permitted all manner of experimentation with the electoral system for the Assembly.

In most other respects, the features of parliamentary government we know today were developed before federation, although this did not happen immediately upon the establishment of self-government. For example, the convention that the premier should always sit in the Assembly took time to evolve, and several premiers in the 1860s and 1870s sat in the upper house (Townsley 1991, 114), a practice familiar in Britain at the time but much less so in the Australian colonies. By 1900 the familiar set of parliamentary relationships between the executive and the legislature were well established, but the system of representation in the Assembly was to undergo substantial change. The alterations to the electoral system in the early years of the twentieth century and the emergence of the modern party system were to have important consequences for the style of parliamentary government.

The structure of government

The Tasmanian constitutional arrangements are similar in their institutional form to the other Australian states (Townsley 1976). There are constitutional documents establishing a bicameral legislature and giving formal executive power to the governor acting in the name of the monarch. There is very little constitutional specification of the role of the premier and ministers and no indication of the nature of their responsibilities to parliament. By long established practice, governments are formed in the House of Assembly and the governor acts on the advice of the premier and ministers, only rarely playing an independent role in the formation and operation of government.

The Legislative Council maintains its power to block all legislation including money bills but it has not used the threat of blocking supply since 1948 (Bennett 1986; Townsley 1956). It contributed, however, to a parliamentary deadlock in 1981 over the highly divisive issue of damming wilderness rivers in the south-west of the state which ultimately resulted in the prorogation of parliament and the subsequent electoral defeat of the government. The Council continues to play a significant role as a house of review, frequently forcing governments to accept amendments to their legislation. In spite of an electoral system in the Assembly which (as we shall see) would appear to favour the representation of minor parties, governments have usually been able to secure working majorities and it has been the upper house where governments have had to seek compromises. The power of the Council has been maintained in large part because the voters have consistently refused to elect many members of parties to the upper house, often preferring to choose independents whose standing in local communities and freedom from partisan influence has removed any guarantee that governments can be sure of gaining support for their legislation.

This longstanding parliamentary tension between a government with a working majority in the Assembly has been upset in recent years. The minority Labor government led by Premier Field from 1989 to 1992 was forced to rely on an Accord with five Green independent members of the Assembly (Haward and Larmour 1993; Haward and Smith 1990). A similar dependence on the Greens faced the minority Rundle Liberal government in 1996 to 1998. Both these minority governments were defeated at elections prompted by the collapse of the coalition agreement and the withdrawal of parliamentary support by the minor party.

The formation of these minority governments required independent action by the governor. Until 1989 the functions of the governor in Tasmania had been predominantly ceremonial and uncontroversial since a crisis over the voting of supply in 1924–26, barring some mild controversy over statements of a 'political nature' made by Sir Stanley Burbury during the 1970s (Chapman et al. 1986, 121). This was to change dramatically in 1989 with the election of a parliament where no party commanded a majority (Killey 1991). The previous Liberal Party government under Premier Gray had won only seventeen seats in an Assembly of thirty-five members – one short of a majority – the ALP thirteen, and five Green independents. The Liberal Party was unable to secure the support of any of the Green independents and, in spite of being offered alternative advice, the governor waited until parliament met and invited ALP leader Michael Field to form a minority ALP government once he was satisfied that Field had the support of the Green independents on the floor of the Assembly.

The governor was again required to exercise his powers after the 1996 election which returned sixteen Liberal members of the Assembly, fourteen ALP members, four Greens and one independent. This time the Greens declined to support the ALP but, once the Greens had indicated they would not vote against supply for the new government, the governor invited the Liberals to form a minority government under Premier Rundle.

The governor is granted wide executive powers under the state's constitutional documents, including the possibility of intervening in deadlocks between the House of Assembly and the Legislative Council over the passage of legislation (Lumb 1977). Despite persistent disagreements between the two chambers in 1877, 1899–1904, 1924–26, 1948 and 1980–81, no governor has exercised these powers, leaving the disputes between the houses to be resolved through the political process (Townsley 1956). In these disagreements, the Council is in a strong bargaining position with the government of the day because the Council as a whole can never be dissolved to face the electorate; it is locked into an electoral cycle by which a few of its members are elected each year for six-year terms. The result is that the Council can force an election on the House of Assembly without having to face the electorate itself, although such action without broadly based public support would almost certainly result in constitutional change and the limitation of the Council's powers. But the refusal of the Council to agree with government proposals for the Franklin dam was an important factor in the unseating of Premier Lowe in 1981and the eventual defeat of the ALP government led by Premier Holgate at the 1982 election.

The Legislative Council can be seen as one of the few formal checks on the executive under a constitutional system none of whose key provisions are entrenched by referendum. The existence of an upper house with a system of representation from which party politics has been largely absent has made it difficult for a government to manipulate constitutional rules for its own advantage. The other side of the coin is that Council has used its power to resist changes to its own constitution; changes such as the introduction of compulsory voting for Council elections, not adopted until 1938 (1931 for the Assembly), universal franchise, not adopted until 1968 (1903 for the Assembly) and the removal of substantial malapportionment between Council electoral districts, not adopted until 1995.

The Council has been seen as a bastion of conservatism and there have been campaigns to abolish it, the latest being in 1997 and 1998. But it has managed to retain both its considerable powers and public support by remaking itself from time to time in response to changing public moods. The Council's committee system has recently been playing an increasingly important role in scrutinizing the executive (note Scott and Young 1994). The very small size of the Assembly, reduced from thirty-five to twenty-five in 1998, weakens the ability of the non-governing parties to provide effective opposition and means that, on the government side, the ministry dominates the back-bench. Given these factors, the checks exercised by a powerful and independent Legislative Council on the executive are all the more important.

The electoral and party systems

While the Legislative Council has used single-member districts and majoritarian electoral systems since self-government in 1856, the lower house, the House of Assembly, has adopted the Hare–Clark variant of proportional representation using a single transferable vote system since 1909, after some brief earlier trials (Homeshaw 2001; Newman 1992). This has resulted in a situation which is the inverse of the current pattern in the Commonwealth parliament and the parliaments of New South Wales, South Australia and Western Australia. The Tasmanian upper house uses preferential voting in single-member districts which might be expected to work in favour of the representation of large parties and produce stable partisan majorities, while the lower house uses proportional representation which reduces the threshold for the representation of minor parties and often provides the potential for such parties holding the balance of power.

In the event, neither of these predispositions has been fulfilled. In particular, the sequence of annual rotating elections for members to the Legislative Council, its institutional history and the effects of community politics have prevented the logic of single-member electoral districts and a majoritarian electoral system from working in favour of the representation of parties. The Council continues to be dominated by independent members in spite of the efforts of the major political parties.

The story for the House of Assembly is more complicated. The Assembly used one- and two-member electoral districts with first-past-the-post voting for most areas until 1909. Andrew Inglis Clark, attorney-general in the Braddon government (1894–99), introduced, for the electoral districts of Hobart and Launceston, a variation on the system of the proportional voting system advocated in England by Thomas Hare. The reform was not extended to country districts and was repealed in 1901, but was reintroduced for the 1909 election (Townsley 1991, 144) as an unsuccessful means of blunting the emergence of the Labor Party, which had increased its representation from three to eight seats in the Assembly at the 1906 election. The Liberal Democrats and Conservatives applied the Hare–Clark system to the whole state creating five multimember electoral districts with six members to create an Assembly of thirty members, five fewer than the previous Assembly (Townsley 1991, 233). The move failed, and at the 1909 election the Labor Party won twelve seats and John Earle was invited to form the first Labor administration, a minority government which lasted a week before being defeated in a vote of the Assembly.

There were numerous attempts to fine-tune the system to overcome some of its problems, such as the tendency for a small Assembly with an even number of members and proportional representation to produce hung parliaments. There were concerns as early as 1913 about the failure of the Hare–Clark system to return majority governments (Townsley 1991, 260). Those concerns have persisted in spite of various alterations to aspects of the electoral system, but both governments and the public appear to be committed to the retention of proportional representation.

The ALP proved to be remarkably successful in Tasmania and, as in other states, has usually been the party with the largest vote share since 1912. Its emergence resulted in the realignment of anti-Labor groups as a single party (Davis 1981; McRae 1956) and the establishment of the current party system (Weller 1977). A Liberal Party ran for the Assembly in the 1912 election and regrouped as the Nationalist Party for the 1919 election. Since the formation of the modern Liberal Party, the Country Party (later National Party) has played almost no role in Tasmania; the dispersed pattern of settlement and the strength of community politics has diminished the significance of a simple rural–urban divide.

Throughout the century, the task of finding the desirable mix between the Hare–Clark electoral system and size of the House of Assembly proved to be a continuing one. From 1901 until the 1959 election the House of Assembly had thirty members, but this produced a tendency for tied outcomes, with several post-war ALP governments depending on support from independents or minor parties. The size of the house was increased to thirty-five at the 1959 election, with the

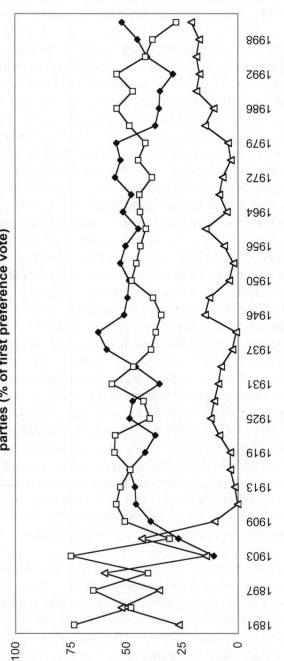

Figure 6.1 Tasmanian House of Assembly, general elections 1891–2002: vote share of ALP, Liberal Party (and precursors), and all other parties (% of first preference vote)

Election Year

ALP ——— Liberal Party (& precursors) ——△—— Minor parties & independents (residual)

Source: calculated from the Australian Government and Politics Project database, University of Western Australia.

number of members representing each of the five multimember electoral districts rising from six to seven. While this had the desired effect of precluding tied votes in the Assembly, it reduced the size of the quota required to gain election, and facilitated the rise of independents. As the Tasmanian developmentalist consensus broke down, first over the Franklin dam issue and then over the Wesley Vale pulp mill proposal, five Green independents were elected to the Assembly at the 1989 election. This led to a minority ALP government under Premier Field whose existence depended on an accord with the Greens.

Sharman remarked in 1997 that Tasmania was witnessing a sea change in its politics, after the Labor–Green Accord of 1989 and the minority Liberal government of 1996: 'Tasmania alone of all the states has clear evidence of a major change to its party system and the dynamics of parliamentary politics in its lower house' (Sharman 1997, 61). The major parties moved to blunt these dynamics in Tasmania shortly after Sharman wrote this but subsequent elections elsewhere, especially in Queensland, Victoria and South Australia, have elevated the importance of independents and minor parties.

By 1998 both major parties had recent experience of minority government dependent on Green support and supported moves to reduce the size of the house to twenty-five (Tasmania 1994), an issue which had been canvassed over a decade before (Tasmania 1984). The adoption of this proposal raised the bar for the representation of the Greens and only one Green member was returned in the Green heartland of Denison at the 1998 election. This reduction in the membership of the Assembly was done, at least nominally, in the name of reducing the size of government, and the size of the Legislative Council was also reduced from nineteen to fifteen (note M. Stokes 1996). This has produced a bonus for the ALP by exaggerating the percentage of seats produced by its share of votes at the 1998 election (from 45 per cent of the vote to 56 per cent of the seats), and simultaneously under-representing the Greens and independents (11 per cent of the vote but only 4 per cent of the seats). This effect is more like the result of a first-past-the-post system rather than one of proportional representation.

While five-member electoral districts minimize the chance of a hung parliament and raise the threshold for minor parties to gain representation, these reforms have also exacerbated existing problems for future governments and oppositions alike by substantially reducing the pool of talent from which cabinets and shadow cabinets can be drawn. It is now possible to form a government with just thirteen members;[2] cabinets typically have eight members, and the government must also provide a speaker and a whip. Apart from the small pool of members, there is a

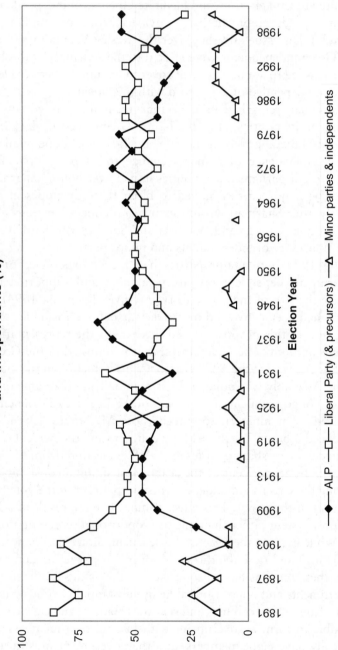

Figure 6.2 Tasmanian House of Assembly, general elections 1891–2002: seat share of ALP, Liberal Party (and precursors), and minor parties and independents (%)

— ALP — Liberal Party (& precursors) — Minor parties & independents

Election Year

Source: calculated from the Australian Government and Politics Project database, University of Western Australia.

diminished fear of demotion to the back-benches, and no chance at all of the executive being checked by back-bench members. The problems for an opposition of twelve or less are even more acute and leaders find it difficult to impose discipline or extract good performance.

While the reduction in the size of parliament was widely regarded by the Greens as a plot against them, it should be noted that the difficulties of both the ALP and the Liberals with minority governments did not begin with the Green electoral success in 1989. The history of the house since the introduction of Hare–Clark has been one of adjusting its size to try to get the formula correct. The size of the house has varied from twenty-five to thirty-five, with other changes to the size of the legislature considered but rejected (Newman 1985).

Problems with the formation of governments have been common. As Sharman et al. (1991, 420) noted, on only five of the ten times the ALP formed government between 1945 and 1990 did it win a majority of seats. The Liberals were in the same position with the Bethune government from 1969 to 1972, having to rely on the Centre Party's Kevin Lyons to form a government. While the main parties were undoubtedly manipulating the electoral rules to their common advantage in putting in place the 1998 changes, they were doing so against a long history of problems with forming governments.

Since 1910 – in other words, since the rise of the modern party system – Tasmania has seen minority government for 38 per cent of the time, with the figure slightly higher post-1945, and coalition government for almost 5 per cent of the time (note Sharman 1990). Much of the long period of ALP dominance, in fact, was a period of minority government, with more than a third of ALP tenure of office from 1945 being in minority government. When compared with the other states, coalition government in Tasmania has been rare, with the mean share of coalition government in other states for the century being five times higher. On the other hand, minority government in Tasmania has been twice as common as the mean in the other states, and ALP governments have been in a minority situation four times as often as their counterparts in other states. This, together with the need to accommodate views of the Legislative Council, has made life difficult for programmatic parties such as the ALP, and favoured brokerage politics.

While the reforms of 1998 certainly weakened the value of the Green vote, it is important to note that its size had been declining since the high point of 1989. From 17 per cent of the vote in 1989, the Greens attracted only 13 per cent in 1992, 11 per cent in 1996, and only 10 per cent in 1998 – only twice the vote of right-populist Tasmania First. And while the reduction in the size of the house certainly diminished the representation of the Green vote, the previous arrangements had actually inflated Green representation in 1992 and, very slightly, in 1996. A more interesting question is why an electoral system so favourable to minor parties saw, throughout most of the century, such a large proportion of the vote going to major parties.

Proportional representation rests on the assumption that accuracy in replicating the pattern of voting support in the community is to be preferred to an electoral system which produces inflated support for governing parties. The 1998 changes reflected a desire to enhance the likelihood of a workable government being formed by a party commanding the largest number of seats. It was anti-Green only inasmuch as the Greens could not command anywhere near enough support to be such a party, and it diminished the influence of all minorities at the expense of the majority.

Other aspects of the Tasmanian electoral system for the Assembly weaken the power of parties and thus weaken party government as a system of government relying on disciplined majorities (note for example, G. Smith 1982; G. Smith et al. 1980). These features also strengthen the representation of diverse interests. First, candidates for election are encouraged to build a personal vote because voters can choose their preferred candidates within a party group. Even if a party's share of the vote is unchanged, the popularity of individual candidates can vary considerably. Individual candidates cannot rely upon a party campaign or party popularity alone to guarantee their election. Parties may group candidates on the ballot paper but cannot rank them in any preferred order. As a result, there are no safe seats and sitting members are defeated at an exceptionally high rate in Tasmanian elections – more than twice the rate in Western Australia, for example (Sharman et al. 1991, 420–1). Party control is also weakened, because candidates cannot be rewarded or punished by placement on a party ticket.

There have been other moves to limit party influence in Tasmania, especially by limiting further the effectiveness of the system parties usually used to direct preferences on the how-to-vote card. First, the so-called Robson rotation has been adopted. This is designed to overcome the effects of the 'donkey vote' – electors voting down the ballot paper favouring candidates because of their position on the ballot. Robson rotation requires the random rotation of names on the ballot, so that there is no single ballot paper format which parties can use on their how-to-vote cards to encourage voters to follow the party-preferred order of candidates. There is also no provision for party ticket voting, as in Senate elections since 1984, where a voter can mark a single party box which indicates that the voter wishes to follow the party-preferred ranking of candidates. While the Robson rotation of candidates creates difficulties for party control of the distribution of preferences, the *Electoral Act* compounds the problem for parties by requiring the permission of each candidate before a how-to-vote card can be distributed and the distribution of such cards is prohibited on election day. As a consequence, candidates campaign on an individual basis, and the influence of parties is diminished.

The competition between candidates on the same party list is also enhanced by the fact that the method for filling vacancies in the Assembly between elections is not to hold a by-election but to recount the votes cast at the previous election, redistributing the preferences of the departed candidate and electing the next preferred candidate. This requires each party to have a pool of candidates from which a replacement can be chosen in the event of a vacancy occurring. As a result, parties usually stand a list of five candidates for each electoral district even though only two or three are likely to be elected from each party, the remaining candidates forming the pool from which occasional vacancies can be filled. This spreads the party vote across all candidates on the party list and further enhances competition between individual candidates.

To attract voters to the party list, parties select candidates who can bring with them a personal following, resulting in the election of many candidates who have a high local profile because of their sporting achievements or commercial visibility. These celebrities owe their election less to the party than to their fame as notables, and bring with them views which do not necessarily reflect the majority views of their party. For other candidates, nomination by a party is a necessary condition for gaining office, though by no means a sufficient condition. Candidates must gain and cultivate a substantial personal following if they are to win and retain office, and the parties are correspondingly weakened in their ability to impose collective views on members. Sharman et al. (1991, 424) suggested that this results in many characteristics of the party and electoral system in Tasmania which lean towards consensus rather than majoritarian democracy, and that 'candidates of the major parties in Tasmania should be seen as teams of independents who happen to run on a party ticket'. Successful members work hard to retain their personal support base and some find unusual ways of doing this – popular legend has it that one would doorknock extensively, repairing sewing machines as he went.

This factor enhances the tendency towards brokerage politics in Tasmania (Herr and Hemmings 1975; Sharman 1977a). The voter has a choice between parties and, within the party list, he or she can select candidates who will support the issues of particular importance to the individual elector. Support can be expressed or withheld on the basis of regional issues and loyalties, reinforcing a longstanding attachment to locality and parochial issues in the state, particularly in the rivalry between Launceston and Hobart. This helps to resolve the paradox of high levels of support for major parties despite the existence of an electoral system which would appear to be favourable to the representation of minor parties and independents (Sharman et al. 1991, 424). If voters can choose candidates representing a diversity of ideals, interests and geographical factors from within a major party list, and add to those from the list of the other main party, there will be little demand for the increased choice that minor party and independent candidates usually bring.

Once elected, members of the Assembly are divided in their loyalties between party and the interests which have elected them. The need to negotiate compromises within the major parties is compounded by minority governments, and the requirement for legislation to secure the consent of the Legislative Council encourages a pattern of brokerage politics and compromise rather than a tradition of programmatic politics.

Parochialism and an economic vulnerability that favours developmentalism are mutually reinforcing. This exacts a price from Tasmania which could benefit from a programmatic approach to policy development. Instead, its political system is sensitive to factors which work to prevent such an approach. This includes, at the start of the twenty-first century, the power of a small but influential Green lobby which has argued against government plans for economic development without providing alternatives which are attractive to investors or the majority of the electorate (Barnett 1999).

Patterns of government and public policy

Until the early 1980s Tasmania had seen a long period of single party dominance, whereas states such as Western Australia had been marked by alternation of regimes (Sharman et al. 1991, 412). During much of the twentieth century the ALP dominated government in Tasmania. It built this dominance on the foundation of developmental politics and successful use of government patronage to maintain its style of brokerage politics. Successive governments from Cosgrove (1948–58) onwards dealt with the perennial problem of economic decline and net migration losses by employing the formula of using access to Loans Council funds and other transfers from the Commonwealth to develop

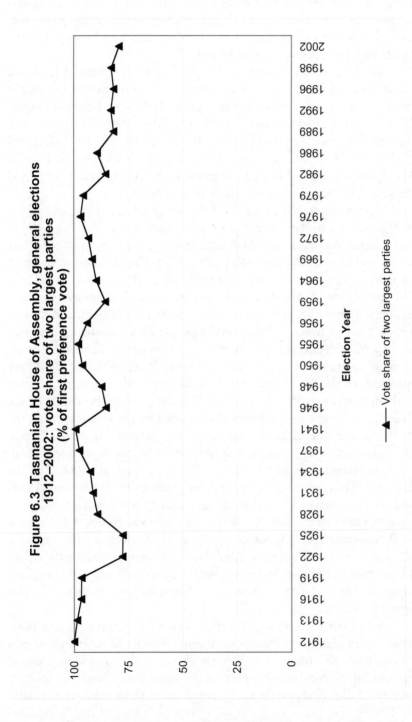

Figure 6.3 Tasmanian House of Assembly, general elections 1912–2002: vote share of two largest parties (% of first preference vote)

Election Year

◄— Vote share of two largest parties

Source: calculated from the Australian Government and Politics Project database, University of Western Australia.

the state's natural resources (Commonwealth Grants Commission 1995), most obviously hydro-electricity, but also forests and mineral resources. The breakdown of the consensus upon which this policy was based led to the end of the era of ALP dominance and ushered in the return of a Liberal government in 1982.

The ALP excelled in managing the political environment of Tasmania for almost fifty years, holding government for forty-five of forty-eight years under nine premiers: Albert Ogilvie (1934–39), Edmund Dwyer-Gray (1939), Robert Cosgrove (1939–47), Edward Brooker (1947–48), Robert Cosgrove (1948–58), Eric Reece (1958–69; 1972–75), Bill Neilson (1975–77), Doug Lowe (1977–81), Harry Holgate (1981–82). The dynastic nature of this period meant that only Ogilvie in 1934 and Reece in 1972 fought elections other than as premier.

Cosgrove managed to ward off the worst effects of the split in the ALP which led to the formation of the Democratic Labor Party (DLP) and a small decline in the ALP vote at state elections during the late 1950s and early 1960s (Townsley 1994, 274). The DLP had more effect on federal politics in the state and managed to elect a senator in 1958. But the shadow of the split and the unwinding of developmentalist politics played their part in bringing this era to an end, beginning in the late 1960s. Premier Reece called upon the people to re-elect his government at the 1969 election and continue 'The golden age of Tasmanian development', while Kevin Lyons of the Centre Party criticized the heavy spending of the Hydro-Electric Commission and its immunity from parliamentary scrutiny (Townsley 1994, 260, 268). The defeat of the Reece government in 1969 was also assisted by the conflict within the ALP over the role of Brian Harradine, an overhang of the DLP split. Harradine was later to run successfully for the Senate as an independent.

A substantial decline in the ALP vote started in 1982 over the Franklin dam controversy (note Commonwealth Parliament 1982) and its vote share declined to 29 per cent in 1992 with substantial inroads made by the Greens. While the slide was reversed so that the ALP rebounded to 45 per cent at the 1998 election, the vote for all minor and independent candidates has held consistently above 15 per cent of the first preference vote for a decade and the vote share of the two largest parties has been declining for over twenty years (see figure 6.3).

This recent pattern would appear to reflect the effect of the post-materialism of green politics; a substantial number of voters, either as a consequence of affluence or lifestyle choice, reject developmentalism because of its continuing threat to the natural environment and the quality of life. It also reflects the concerns of those who feel insecure

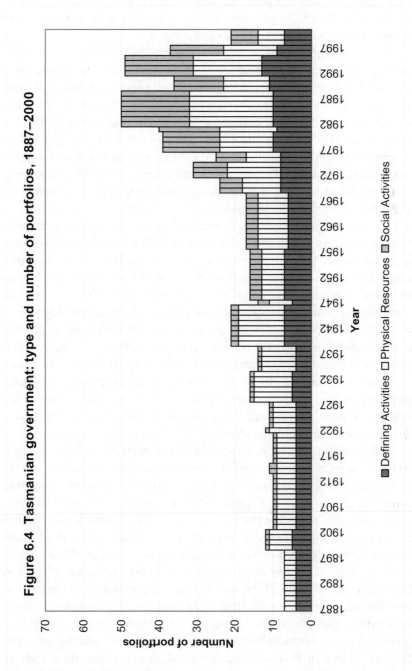

Figure 6.4 Tasmanian government: type and number of portfolios, 1887–2000

■ Defining Activities □ Physical Resources □ Social Activities

Source: calculated from the Australian Government and Politics Project database, University of Western Australia.

because of economic change and who have been alienated by the with-drawal of government services and the changes to the way such services have been provided. These apprehensions made populist answers attractive to about 10 per cent of the electorate who voted for the Tasmania First party at the 1998 state election.

In terms of government activity, Tasmania showed considerable stability for much of the century with fewer than twenty portfolios except for a slight increase during the second world war. Most of these can be classified in Rose's (1976) terms as being engaged in provision of 'defining' and 'physical resources' (see Moon and Sayers 1999), the basic services for the running of government together with portfolios relating to transport, public works, power generation, water supply, agriculture, forestry and industrial development. This reflects the long, stable period of hydro-industrialization and ALP rule, and a stress on economic rather than social issues.

The period since 1969 has been marked by innovation in govern-ment activity, as reflected in the number and type of portfolios (see figure 6.4) with Tasmania appearing to play 'catch-up' with the other states (Chapman 1985). Much of this expansion was in the 'social activities' category seen elsewhere, but there was also an increase in physical resource mobilization activities. There was a bipartisan nature to what can, without exaggeration, be called an explosion in the number of portfolios, with the peak of fifty being reached under the Liberal administration of Robin Gray in the 1980s. Much of the increase during the Gray years came in the physical resource mobilization area, reflecting the reassertion of developmentalism which brought Gray to power, but also a search for solutions to Tasmania's chronic economic problems (Nixon 1997).

This large number of portfolios is all the more remarkable when it is considered that they were filled by members of the parliamentary party commanding a majority in a 35-seat House of Assembly governing a state with a population of around 470 000. Perhaps surprisingly, the period of the Labor–Green Accord saw a reduction in the number of portfolios, followed by a resurgence under the Liberal Premier Groom, then a reduction under Rundle and, finally, a sudden return to around twenty under the Bacon ALP government elected in 1998. In Tasmania, the ALP has not been associated with the growth of government, at least as measured by the number of portfolios, and the reduction in the size of the house to twenty-five members made fifty portfolios an unsustainable number for a cabinet usually of eight members. Even in Premier Gray's period in office, during which he enjoyed larger than average majorities in parliament, there were never more than nineteen government members, and eight cabinet ministers had to take an average of a little over six portfolios each.

The dispute over the damming of the Franklin River divided the ALP and left a legacy of hostility between those who favoured traditional Labor policies and the new professional groups who wanted a more open style of government and more environmentally sensitive policies. Premier Gray came to power by exploiting the pains of an ALP trying to find a way of harmonizing the state's reliance upon a developmentalist formula for political success with policies which appealed to its dissidents. While the disarray of the ALP gave the Liberals a majority of first preference votes for the only two occasions since before the second world war, the Liberal government was caught in the same policy dilemma and it adopted a similar developmentalist formula with even less long-term success than the ALP.

The 1980s marked the end of a broad consensus between the major parties about policies for economic growth but, by the late 1990s, a bipartisan commitment to a more restrained developmentalism had emerged. Both major parties championed resource development less stridently than in the past, and with more environmental controls than twenty years before. 'Micro-developmentalism' became the vogue, attempting to build on the production of specialty foods and such high value and exotic agriculture as pyrethroids, essential oils, and alkaloids for morphine. There has been considerable interest in encouraging the production of wine, in fostering aquaculture, in using the arts as a tourist resource, and in attracting such footloose industries as call centres to take advantage of relatively low real estate costs.

Tasmania has been willing to use the federal system not only to extract transfers from the central government but to pursue policies which have not been shared by other states. This distinctiveness once evident by its resistance to environmental issues has now come full circle; the government has been keen to establish and maintain a 'clean, green' image. This has found unlikely expression in the assertion of state quarantine prerogatives against a World Trade Organization ruling on the importation of Canadian salmon, and in the establishment of a moratorium on field trials of genetically modified crops.

Former agencies associated with exploitative development policies such as the Forestry Commission, now Forestry Tasmania, are expected to operate on a commercial basis with some consideration of the long-term sustainability of tree harvesting. Although 'the Hydro' (the Hydro-Electricity Commission) remains and the Bacon government was elected on a promise not to privatize it, its halcyon days of being a dominant player in the state's public works and industry policy are long passed.

Even the notorious ministerial exemptions are gone; these were used to relieve large companies from having to meet environmental standards in return for investment in industrial development. While searching for economic prosperity, public policy in this area has become more imaginative, responsive and innovative at the beginning of the twenty-first century than it was for most of the twentieth.

Conclusion

Successive Tasmanian governments have tried to adjust the state's institutions and public policies to their circumstances. It is questionable, however, whether the institutions have always permitted an appropriate response to deal with the state's two underlying and related problems, slow economic growth and population decline.

The problems faced by Tasmania in 2001 are much the same as those of a century earlier at the time of federation in 1901. On balance, federation has been good to Tasmania, not only because of financial transfers but also because it has provided a stable economic environment. But the state has paid a high price for its relative lack of growth over the last century; it has failed to create sufficient opportunities to keep the state's population from migrating elsewhere. Successive governments do not seem to have found the answer to speeding up the state's slow rate of growth, and a political system which both engenders and reflects parochialism and patronage has not helped. The state has had long periods of ALP government, but the party could not find a replacement for hydro-industrialization once that policy had failed.

The relative lack of development in Tasmania, combined with its natural beauty and cultural heritage, has proved attractive to those inside and outside the state who have provided a support base for the Greens and other agents of the new politics of post-industrial society. While there are some signs of entrepreneurship in this group, its political influence can be seen more as an impediment than as an agency for economic change. All too often it has become yet another interest to be accommodated in brokerage politics. Those pursuing alternative lifestyles and employed in managerial positions in the public sector might be content with relative economic stagnation in a pleasant environment, but this does little for such groups who are more economically vulnerable.

Whatever might be mapped out as the future destination for Tasmania, it will have to be adopted through the political process. The present system reminds one of the old highlander who, when asked the way to Glasgow, replied 'If I were going to Glasgow I would nay start from here!'. Tasmania might be better served with proportional representation in the Legislative Council and a single-member system of preferential voting for the Assembly. This might create bolder governments based in the Assembly while subjecting them to a partisan accountability that is now blurred by the Hare–Clark system. At the same time, proportional representation in the Council would provide institutional expression for minority opinions in a chamber where such representation would not limit the possibility of programmatic reform.

While Tasmania can choose a destination, it cannot choose its point of departure; the state must work within its present set of institutions. But the consequences of the 1998 changes to the size of parliament and the restructuring of ministerial arrangements have yet to be worked through, and it may be that Tasmania now has a better chance to meet its economic and political aspirations for the next century.

Chapter

7

Victoria

Nicholas Economou, Brian Costar and Paul Strangio

Since the discovery of gold in 1851, Victoria has vied with New South Wales for the position of the most affluent and powerful of the Australian states. For a brief time in the 1880s the population of the Victorian capital, Melbourne, was greater than that of its northern rival, Sydney. This moment of dominance was to be fleeting. For much of Australia's white settler history, from the gold rushes through to the beginning of the twenty-first century, Victoria has been the second state and Melbourne the second city; second, that is, to New South Wales and its capital Sydney in terms of population, economic output, and the intangible notion of power and influence within the Australian federation.

This is not to underestimate the critical importance that Victoria has had on national politics. Victoria played a pivotal role in the moves which led to federation in 1901 and provided many influential delegates to the various constitutional conventions who drafted the Australian federal constitution in the 1890s (de Garis 1974). One of these, Alfred Deakin, played a key role in formulating the Commonwealth Constitution and helped to have it passed by the British parliament. Deakin was to be one of the early Australian prime ministers, and his liberal ideas were to be influential on non-Labor politics (La Nauze 1979). Deakin was one of eleven Victorians who have served as prime minister since federation. Victoria has also provided eleven leaders of the federal opposition.

Because Victoria has been an important state for the manufacturing industry, Melbourne has, until recently, been the preferred home for major businesses. Consequently, when the Australian Council of Trades Union was formed in 1927, its headquarters were located in

Melbourne. Because the new Commonwealth parliament sat in Melbourne from 1901 to 1927, federal administrative agencies were similarly located. It took many years to accomplish the move to Canberra with the Australian Security Intelligence Organisation (ASIO) remaining until 1986, and the Australian Industrial Relations Commission is still based in Melbourne.

Melbourne was the home of protectionism as a way of encouraging industrial growth and defending its manufacturing industry from inter-colonial and, after 1901, international competition. But the change in national economic policy orthodoxy from protectionism to free trade during the 1980s led to significant economic restructuring of the manu-facturing and finance sectors, and may have contributed to the fact that Sydney has been progressively displacing Melbourne as the hub of Australian corporate capitalism. In the 1990s the response of the Victorian Liberal–National coalition government was to shed the state's protectionist past and to adopt wholeheartedly the idea of competition and market solutions in both the private and the public sectors.

The debate over the nature of liberalism is one of the major themes running through the political history of Victoria. From the gold rushes onwards, liberal ideas and 'liberal' politicians have been major players in the development of the state (Serle 1977). The battle between liber-alism and conservatism corresponded with another enduring political theme, the cleavage between rural and urban Victoria. This has had consequences for the formation of governments and the policies they have pursued. The clash between liberal and conservative ideas and the rivalry for political influence between rural and urban interest had the effect of marginalizing the social democratic or democratic socialist alternatives presented by the labour movement and its party, the Australian Labor Party (ALP) (Rawson 1977).

Labor has been spectacularly unsuccessful in Victorian state poli-tics. On the rare occasions where it has gained office, it has faced a powerful parliamentary upper house, the Legislative Council, which the ALP did not control until 2002, save for a three-week period after the 1985 election. Labor politics has not been central to the history of Victoria's political and economic development (note Gollan 1960), although the Victorian branch played a major role in such momentous events in national ALP history as the split in the party in the 1950s. Rather, Victoria has been a liberal state where the main political battle has been between liberals and their conservative opponents, sometimes operating from within the same political party. The evolution of the Australian variant of liberalism owes much to Victorian political history where liberalism has encompassed both social interventionism and the neo-classical version practised by the reformist Liberal-led coalition governments of the 1990s.

Society, politics and government

Immigration and self-government

Victorian politics and society have been shaped by two waves of immigration, the first prompted by gold and the second as a result of post-1945 European migration. The first major gold rush to the state occurred in 1851, the same year that Victoria was established as a separate colony and broke away from New South Wales. The new colony was provided with a constitution by the British parliament under which a governor was to administer the colony in conjunction with an appointed executive and with the advice of a Legislative Council composed of land-owning appointees. The lack of popular representation did not appeal to the settlers on the goldfields, and the diggings were to provide the impetus for the move to a more democratic system of self-government.

The discovery of gold transformed perceptions of Victoria, especially in the minds of intending immigrants, from being a colonial outpost to a land of hope and opportunity. This influx was to be a major challenge for the colonial administration and its new governor, Charles Hotham. With an appointed Council to advise him, the governor sought to provide, amongst other things, orderly regulation of mining activity. This was to become a serious source of complaint with the diggers, who linked grievances about the license system with demands for democratic reform of the system of government.

The most well-known incident of tension between miners and Hotham's government occurred in Ballarat in 1854 when a stockade was constructed near the site of the Eureka hotel to defend miners from police and troopers dispatched to enforce the license regulation. A violent encounter between the miners and the military ensued in December that year that led to casualties on both sides. Serle has pointed out (1977, 183) that the number of miners involved in the uprising was small as a proportion of the total mining population, and that claims that the fields were a hot-bed of radicalism need to be seen in the light of the orderliness of most of the diggings. Yet, it was clear that the influx of miners as free settlers altered the political balance in Victoria.

By 1856 Victoria was to have a bicameral parliament with a lower house, the Legislative Assembly, elected by manhood suffrage using the secret 'Victorian' ballot. The powerful Legislative Council was also made an elected chamber but on a property franchise which favoured large landholders (Holmes 1976, 12–20; Wright 1992, 17). This basic structure has continued to the present with most changes relating to the method of selecting representatives rather than the powers and functions of the legislature and the executive. The Assembly gained universal franchise in 1909 and has been elected from single-member districts since 1904 using preferential voting (the alternative vote), with voters required to rank all candidates (full preferential voting) since 1916.Various changes have been made to the election of members to the Legislative Council and to the extent of malapportionment in the chamber, but its composition and its power to block legislation remain a topic of controversy (Harkness 1999, 68–71).

Post-war change

The end of the second world war provided the next major influx of population. Partly in response to concerns about its small population relative to the region, and partly out of a desire to stimulate economic growth, the post-war federal Labor government commenced a major immigration program. Whereas Australia had had immigration programs before, the post-war version was to be different in that it would accept people from European nations other than Britain.

The flow of migrants to Melbourne in particular was to provide the basis upon which the Victorian capital would be transformed into a multilingual and cosmopolitan city. This change was to result in Melbourne shedding its prior reputation for teetotal, social conservatism which can be seen as a reflection, in large part, of the social and political influence of the Protestant churches. Melbourne had emerged as the home of 'wowserism', a conservative outlook in which the drinking of alcohol was seen as antithetical to the social good (Dunstan 1968). Hotels had to close at six o'clock in the evening, and cafés and restaurants were not allowed to sell wine. Prostitution was criminalized (but flourished anyway) and gambling other than on a race-track was strictly forbidden. Retail shopping on weekends was frowned upon and, in the case of Sunday trading, strictly forbidden. The playing of organized sport on the Sabbath was discouraged until the 1970s.

By the 1980s Victorian society had been transformed by the variety of cultures and ideas to which the state had been exposed in the previous thirty years; censorship of the arts had been liberalized, licensing laws relaxed and then deregulated, retailing hours extended, and gambling laws relaxed (although the proliferation of poker

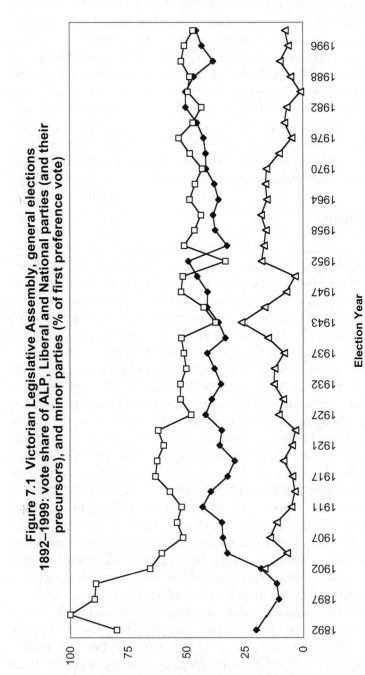

Figure 7.1 Victorian Legislative Assembly, general elections 1892–1999: vote share of ALP, Liberal and National parties (and their precursors), and minor parties (% of first preference vote)

Election Year

ALP ——— Liberal & National parties (& precursors) ——△—— Minor parties & independents (residual)

Source: calculated from the Australian Government and Politics Project database, University of Western Australia.

machines and compulsive gambling was to become the source of controversy). The state aspired to be a leader in the arts, and a massive new cultural complex was constructed on the southern bank of the Yarra. Politicians and planners also began to identify Melbourne's diverse culinary culture as a potential economic asset particularly if linked to tourism, and this led to official recognition of multiculturalism's culinary legacy (Rubenstein 1999, 260). Once lampooned as a dreary and bland place, Melbourne was now projected as an exciting, tolerant, modern and, above all, diverse city.

Despite being so many years apart, both the gold rushes and the post-war migratory wave left similar political legacies, one being the economic, social and political cleavage between rural and metropolitan Victoria. The division between land-owning conservatives and liberal-democratic miners and their urban relatives provided a source of conflict in colonial times which has not disappeared from Victorian politics. For many years, this conflict played itself out in battles over Victoria's electoral system (Holmes 1976, 82–9). It also expressed itself in the emerging party system, particularly in the rivalry that existed between the anti-Labor parties (Costar 1985a, 162; Costar 1999, 88). Throughout the state's political history, the rural–urban tension has been a backdrop to debates about the role and function of the Legislative Council.

The existence of the National Party (formerly the Country Party until a name change in 1975 for the 1976 state election) symbolizes this divide. For much of Victoria's political history, the party has sought to defend an electoral system substantially malapportioned in favour of non-metropolitan voters. The National Party's ability to win representation under Victoria's single-member majoritarian electoral system used for both the Assembly and the Legislative Council has often put it in an influential position. This has been so despite its comparatively small vote share of between 5 and 10 per cent of the Assembly vote since the late 1950s (see figures 7.2, 7.3). The party's ability to hold the balance of power in the Legislative Council from 1955 to 1970 and from 1982 to 1992 allowed it to shape the legislative policies of successive government and, until 1983, to resist electoral reforms aimed at achieving greater voter equality between town and country (Costar and Economou 1992b, 202).

The Liberal Party, as the major anti-Labor party since 1945,[1] has also had its block of rural constituencies, particularly in the western district of the state. This has blunted its enthusiasm for electoral reform; the issue split the Liberal Party in the early 1950s with the expulsion of former Premier Tom Hollway and the formation of the

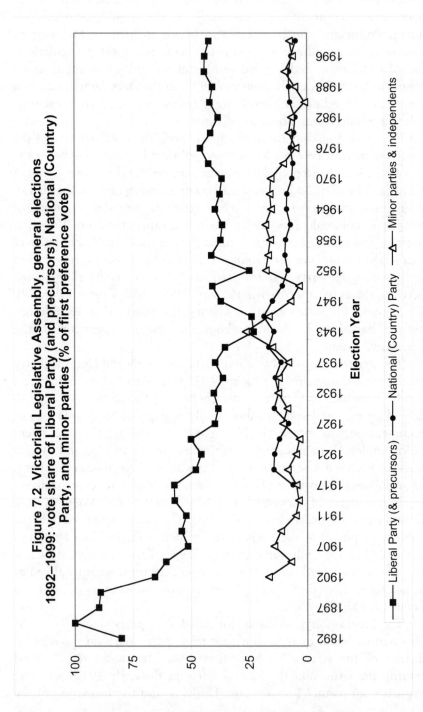

Figure 7.2 Victorian Legislative Assembly, general elections 1892–1999: vote share of Liberal Party (and precursors), National (Country) Party, and minor parties (% of first preference vote)

Source: calculated from the Australian Government and Politics Project database, University of Western Australia.

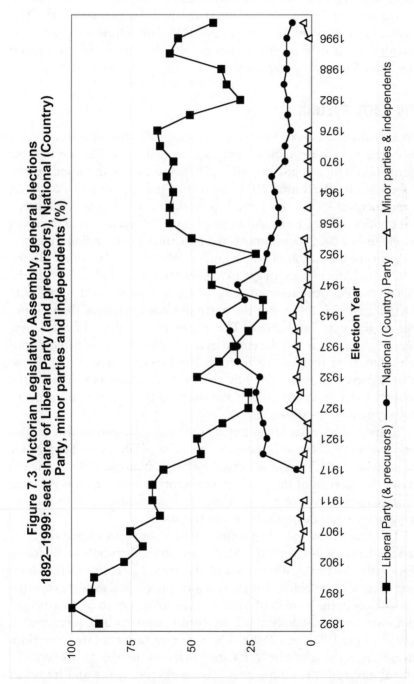

Figure 7.3 Victorian Legislative Assembly, general elections 1892–1999: seat share of Liberal Party (and precursors), National (Country) Party, minor parties and independents (%)

—■— Liberal Party (& precursors)   —●— National (Country) Party   —△— Minor parties & independents

Source: calculated from the Australian Government and Politics Project database, University of Western Australia.

Electoral Reform League (West 1965, 28). But the core of Liberal Party support is to be found in safe electoral districts in the affluent bayside and eastern suburbs of Melbourne, and the party has demonstrated a much greater ability to win marginal suburban electorates than the ALP (Costar and Economou 1992a, 27–31). This electoral geography provides much of the explanation for the dominance of the Liberal Party over Victorian government.

The party system

Three distinctive eras in Victorian politics are discernible during which the state's party system underwent major realignment. The first of these commences with self-government in 1856 and ends with the emergence of the Country Party after 1917 and its first participation in a coalition government in 1923. This period spans the era of pre-party, ministerialist politics dominated by shifting parliamentary coalitions of members loosely linked by a commitment to a particular policy, admiration of a leader or the aspiration of holding office. While candidates were elected to state parliament were to group together to form a Labor Party in the 1890s; the Political Labor Council was not established until 1902 (McQueen 1975, 293); and the party did not gain more than 30 per cent of the vote until 1904. The emergence of the ALP as a new contender for office had the effect, as in all other states, of forcing anti-Labor interests to coalesce to form the Liberal Party. By 1917 the Liberal Party had been joined by the Victorian Farmers Union (as the Country Party was then called), and the principal actors in the modern party system were established.

In spite of its volatility in terms of the succession of ministries, this period was one of consensus on several major policy issues. Support for the protective tariff was seen as vital by both capital and labour alike to ensure the survival of the state's manufacturing sector, as was the need for state intervention to provide the infrastructure necessary to support manufacturing, industrialization and transport.

This was the period when major state corporations such as the State Savings Bank of Victoria, the Melbourne and Metropolitan Board of Works, the Victorian Railways and the State Electricity Commission were created. The belief that these major public bodies were essential participants in the growth of Victoria's economy was to be an article of administrative orthodoxy until the corporatization and privatization policies of the 1980s and 1990s. The Victorian variant of state socialism has not been the result of ALP nationalization but the consequence of Liberal governments taking over private electricity, gas and transport companies to guarantee the service needs of a mixed capitalist economy.

The second phase in Victorian politics stretched from 1924 – the year of no fewer than five separate minority governments, one of them Labor – to 1952 and the election of the first majority government since 1918. During this period majority governments were a rarity, with minority administrations the norm. Coalitions were brief and often turbulent and, in comparison with the politics of other states, there were bizarre alliances between the Labor and Country parties. Changes of government were precipitated by defeat in parliament rather than loss of an election. From 1913 to 1952, only five governments out of a total of thirty-one lost office as a clear consequence of election defeat, the remainder being cut short by parliamentary want of confidence motions, denial of supply, coalition collapses or changes of parliamentary leader.

During this merry-go-round of ministries, party politics displaced personality as the source of volatility and the question of reforming the state's electoral system – or, to be more accurate, resisting the call to reform – emerged as the pivot around which political alliances revolved. In this, the Country Party was a key player even when it split in 1926 and again in 1937 (Costar 1985b, 99). Any proposal to reduce the malapportionment which gave rural voters significantly greater power than metropolitan voters would see the Country Party use its balance of power in the Assembly to bring down a ministry and replace it with another minority or coalition government.

An unlikely island of stability in this sea of volatility was the comparatively longstanding Country Party minority governments headed by Albert Dunstan between 1935 and 1945. These governments were supported first by the ALP and, after 1943, the United Australia Party (UAP) in the Legislative Assembly. Holmes (1976, 8) attributes the longevity of the Dunstan premiership to the Country Party leader's skill in keeping the fragile support for his party intact and his ability to court rural electorates with promises of government programs that would be considered, in today's political parlance, as examples of crass vote-buying. The Dunstan years coincided with continuation of the great depression and the outbreak of the second world war. According to Holmes (1976, 87), the Dunstan approach to administration was one of 'parsimonious neglect' of public services to the point where Victoria began to lag behind other states in the provision of health, welfare and education. This approach was to put great strain on the ALP commitment to support Dunstan and, in 1943, a minority Labor administration headed by John Cain (Sr) was formed. This lasted for four days while the Country Party and the UAP

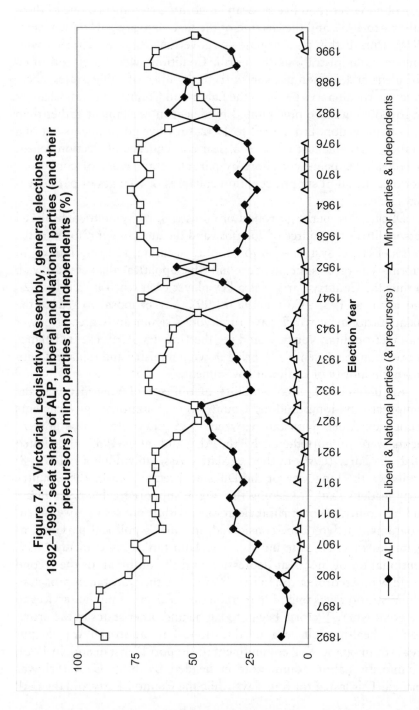

Figure 7.4 Victorian Legislative Assembly, general elections 1892–1999: seat share of ALP, Liberal and National parties (and their precursors), minor parties and independents (%)

ALP ——◆—— Liberal & National parties (& precursors) ——△—— Minor parties & independents

Election Year

Source: calculated from the Australian Government and Politics Project database, University of Western Australia.

negotiated a coalition. Victoria returned to rotating ministries with the issues which had led to the fragmentation of anti-Labor politics, and the seemingly endless controversy over electoral reform, returning to centre stage.

In 1952 a new era began in Victorian politics with the voters electing their first majority government since 1918 (see figure 7.4). Moreover, this first majority government for thirty-four years was a Labor administration led by John Cain (Sr). Cain had already had two terms as premier, the first being his four-day tenure in 1943, and the second a post-war ministry formed with the support of the Country Party that collapsed in 1947 when the Legislative Council denied supply in retaliation for federal Labor government's attempt to nation-alize the private trading banks. The 1952 Labor government came to power partly because of the fragmentation of the non-Labor parties over that perennial problem of electoral reform (White 1982, 148). The Cain government addressed this matter with its 'two-for-one' electoral redistribution which dismantled the malapportionment the Country Party had spent so much time defending. From 1953 to 1965 Victoria's Assembly boundaries were based on those of the Commonwealth with each federal electoral district divided into two equal state electoral districts.

Labor was to be denied any long-term benefits of this victory, as the Cain government was destroyed in 1955 by an internal party schism. This was the product of complex internecine struggles for power between the party's union-based Left and their adversaries, the Industrial Groups. The 'split' was to affect the ALP across Australia, but in Victoria it was particularly divisive and took on a powerful ideo-logical dimension as the Catholic Church became involved (Murray 1972). The Melbourne diocese of the Roman Catholic Church was virulently anti-communist in the wake of the rising tensions of the cold war. The Archbishop of Melbourne, Daniel Mannix, unlike some of his brother bishops in other states, was an ardent supporter of an organiza-tion known as the Catholic Social Studies Movement – the Movement – run by B. A. (Bob) Santamaria which had close but informal links with the right wing of the ALP. Santamaria was a skilful political operative and commanding orator of Italian immigrant background who held syndicalist views as well as being avowedly anti-communist (Murray 1972, 44–65; Santamaria 1997, 65). Against an international back-drop of growing tension between the United States and the communist states, of which the Soviet Union appeared to be leader, allegations made by Santamaria that Labor had been infiltrated by communists were particularly damaging. The Labor split divided parliamentary loyalties, led to the defection of some unions to the newly formed Australian Labor Party (Anti-Communist) later renamed the Democratic Labor Party (DLP), and fragmented a sizeable part of Labor's vote.

This division of the Labor vote was to benefit the Liberal Party as the newly formed DLP issued how-to-vote cards that directed preferences away from the ALP. The effect was to be long-lasting. As figure 7.1 indicates, Labor's primary vote took a long time to recover and the strong flow of DLP preferences to the Liberal Party enabled it to win a series of elections. This led to an era of stable, one-party majority Liberal government from 1955 to 1982 in which there were long-serving ministries and long-serving premiers. Electoral reform continued to be a matter for dispute – vote-weighting was reintroduced in 1965 – but it was no longer the catalyst for political crisis as it had been until 1952.

When the ALP gained office at the 1982 state election, it began a decade of majority rule for the party. Even when the anti-Labor parties won back office in 1992 as a Liberal Party–National Party coalition government, the Liberals had a majority of seats in both the Legislative Assembly and Council. The period from 1952 to 1999 can thus be viewed as a distinct era in Victorian politics during which both the Liberal and Labor parties won clear parliamentary majorities. This came to an end after the 1999 election with the formation of a minority ALP government under Premier Bracks.

The shift from volatility to stability in the period after 1955 altered the nature of the political debate. Whereas electoral reform had been a recurring theme in political debate during the pre-1952 period, public policy issues were the dominant concern after 1952. The Country Party (renamed National Party in 1975), which had played a critical role in government alternation before 1952, diminished in importance. The Liberal Party's dominance of Victorian anti-Labor politics in the 1960s allowed its premier, Henry Bolte, to pursue one of his major political objectives, the marginalization of the Country Party. The Liberal Party claimed rural affairs as one of its policy strengths and flagged this by changing its name to the Liberal and Country Party at state elections from 1950 to 1964 as part of an abortive attempt to eliminate the Country Party (Costar 1985b, 22). While the Country Party's successor, the National Party, continues to play an important role at the margin of the state's parliamentary politics, it must compete for influence with other minor parties and independents who, since the 1990s, have gained a similar share of the vote.

Minor parties

The DLP's dramatic impact upon Victorian politics manifested itself in the internal affairs of the ALP and in the state's voting behaviour and election outcomes. But the impact was limited to the role of spoiler. Notwithstanding its ability to return senators from Victoria, the DLP never won a seat in the Victorian parliament, a consequence of the adoption of the single-member preferential voting system for both the Assembly and the Council. This meant that the DLP's role in state politics could never be more than seeking to exercise indirect influence over election outcomes through attempts to direct the second preference votes of its supporters. But the failure of the party to win parliamentary representation did not dampen the DLP's enthusiasm for participating in electoral contests or prevent it from being an important influence in Victorian electoral politics until the early-1970s.

For other minor parties which have emerged from time to time, the use of single-member districts and preferential voting for both houses of the Victorian parliament have limited their influence. The Australian Democrats are a case in point. The founder of this party and the party's first senator for Victoria, Don Chipp, was formerly a Victorian Liberal MHR for the electorate of Hotham. With each Senate election since 1977 (except 1993), Victoria has returned an Australian Democrat senator, yet the Democrats have been minor players in Victorian politics (Warhurst 1997). The Democrats have not been alone in this. The rise to prominence of Green parties of various shades in the national contest has not been replicated to the same extent in Victoria. Pauline Hanson's One Nation Party was capable of winning votes – and seats – in federal contests and in state elections in New South Wales, Queensland and Western Australia. In Victoria, however, One Nation has been a very weak performer in both federal and state contests. Victoria has not been a happy hunting ground for minor parties.

The Liberal Party and its predecessors

Historically Victoria has been an important state for Australian liberalism. Victorians were able to give practical form to liberal philosophies which espoused the importance of state intervention to provide for equality of opportunity and to encourage the materialistic progress of society. These practical applications of interventionist liberalism took the form of the development of the protective tariff as a means of encouraging the state's manufacturing sector, the institution of an arbitration and conciliation system, the creation of a secular state education system, and in the creation of public corporations to deliver services private investment would not or could not provide.

Parliamentarians who subscribed to liberal beliefs were prominent in Victorian politics from colonial times and Rawson notes (1977, 47) that a 'liberal' party was already present in Victorian politics by 1880. The strongest political challenge to colonial liberalism came not from Labor, but from conservatives and especially those representing rural electorates. Only with the emergence of the Labor Party did liberalism and conservatism find ways of working together to meet the challenges posed by a more disciplined and better organized ALP. This imperative underscored the development of anti-Labor parties, although the tensions between liberal and conservative outlooks, and between rural and urban representation, had a major impact on the form and nature of this emerging party politics.

The fragmentation and internecine division that characterized non-Labor politics extended beyond the rise and fall of the Nationalists from the 1917 to the 1929 state elections, and the UAP from 1932 to 1943. The creation of the Liberal Party following the Albury conference of 1944, at which the remnants of the UAP were refashioned into a new anti-Labor party by former prime minister and UAP leader Robert Menzies, was linked to the establishment of autonomous state divisions (West 1965, 222; Holmes 1976, 101–8; Aimer 1974, 1–20). The Victorian division of the Liberal Party was soon to revisit the internecine tensions that had plagued the UAP. As usual, differences over electoral reform and, by extension, conflict with the Country Party were to play a critical role. These divisions within the newly created Liberal Party contributed to Labor's unprecedented electoral success in 1952.

The Liberal and Country parties' failure in the 1952 election was to be a temporary setback. The fierce divisions within the ALP at the 1955 election resulted in a Liberal and Country Party (Liberal Party) victory which was to be the starting point of a long period of Liberal rule. It was also to be the beginning of an era marked by the personality and approach of the then Liberal and Country leader, Henry Bolte, who was to be premier of Victoria for a record seventeen years and whose party was to hold office continuously from 1955 to 1982, another record period of unbroken rule.

Bolte was the embodiment of the Liberal Party's rural conservatism (Blazey 1990, xvi). He was famous for his espousal of socially conservative views and his intolerance of protesters and street marches. Bolte linked social conservatism with economic pragmatism and state intervention in the economy. This included the provision of subsidized energy and subsidized transport for Victoria's primary producers, and a policy of decentralization with offers of tax concessions to companies which would relocate from Melbourne to regional centres. Once famously declaring that not a drop of water that fell north of the divide would ever find its way to Melbourne, the Bolte government provided farmers with easy access to subsidized water.

The transition in the Liberal leadership from Bolte to Rupert (Dick) Hamer in 1972 represented much more than a simple change of leader. The ascendancy of Hamer heralded a new political style. As Holmes (1976, 194) observed, Hamer had a much more conciliatory and inclusive approach to policy making than the authoritarian Bolte.

Under Hamer the Victorian government became increasingly involved in the planning and coordinating of the state's economy and the provision of social and welfare services. This process was assisted by the election of a federal Labor government headed by Gough Whitlam who sought to increase Canberra's role by making ever-greater Commonwealth financial grants to the states for these policy areas. Notwithstanding the capacity of Whitlam's New Federalism to antagonize the states, the increase in the flow of public funds was welcomed by state governments.

Hamer was removed from the premiership in a party room coup in 1981, the ostensible reason for which was alarm at the slowdown in private sector investment in Victoria. He was replaced by his former education minister, Lindsay Thompson. Hamer's departure heralded the end of the era of Liberal dominance which had been eroded by a series of policy and political problems that arose in the 1980s. In addition to an economic slump, the Liberal government had also been tainted with allegations of impropriety; some Liberal Party members appeared to have made substantial financial gains from the sale of public land in the outer suburbs. This Land Deals affair was to provide the backdrop for the 1982 general election which brought an end to the long years of Liberal government. The party was not to win office for a decade by which time both the political context and the style of leadership had changed markedly.

The Labor challenge

Labor's historical inability to win elections and form governments has been a major feature of Victorian politics. From 1902, the year when the party's organization was finalized, to 1982, Labor had only been in government a total of 102 months. Of these brief periods in office, Labor had formed a majority government only once, the 1952–55 John Cain (Sr) government that was to end in disarray following the 1955 split in the party (Jupp 1983, 78–9). The split and the leakage of support to the DLP was one of the reasons why Labor was confined to the political wilderness during the long years of the Liberal ascendancy. Another was the propensity for the party's organization to be subject to bitter internal divisions. The creation of the DLP resulted in several large unions and influential labour movement officials deserting the ALP. Their departure meant that the party organization became dominated by the industrial Left, making the Victorian ALP one of the more ideological and left-wing of the ALP branches (Jupp 1983, 81).

The split was clearly an important contributing factor to Labor's post-war record of failure and Labor's revival did not occur until after the DLP collapsed in 1975, but it does not account for Labor's historically weak performance before the second world war. Opinion differs as to why Labor had been so weak in a state that has always had a strong manufacturing sector and a highly unionized workforce. Historical overviews stress the consensus that emerged between colonial liberals and organized labour over the need for state intervention generally, and in support of the protective tariff in particular – the so-called 'Lib–Lab Alliance'. Both labour and business could see the need for the tariff as a defender of manufacturing interests and, by extension, the saviour of employment. Victoria's highly decentralized industrial relations system was also prepared to be responsive to labour demands. In the light of this consensus, the need of a Labor Party capable of pursuing worker interests and demands through the policy-making system was diminished (Rawson 1977, 49; McQueen 1975, 299).

Labor's relatively poor performance in Victoria can also be linked to the state's electoral system and geography. Substantial rural and regional malapportionment has been only part of Labor's problem. Of greater significance has been that Labor's core constituency has long been clustered in and around the industrial suburbs of western and northern Melbourne. The concentration of Labor support in confined localities has meant that the party has always won seats with substantial wasted majorities. The more evenly dispersed nature of anti-Labor support has helped the Liberal and National parties to enhance their parliamentary representation relative to the size of their vote. This pattern of voter support is still a feature of Victorian elections.

Internecine division and difficult electoral conditions have contributed to Labor's failure to have a greater impact upon the governing of Victoria. The 1950s looked as though it would be a Labor decade but failed to be so because of the split in the party. The next opportunity for Labor did not arise again until 1982 (note Hay and Warhurst 1979). By this stage, factionalism within the Victorian ALP had been tempered by two factors: intervention by the federal wing of the party in 1971 which sought to constrain the power of the industrial Left, and the emergence of a more formalized factional system in which independents held the balance of power (see Hudson 2000). The Cain (Jr) government came to power because of a major voter swing against the Liberals, particularly in the previously solid Liberal electoral heartland in the eastern and south-eastern suburbs (Costar and Hughes 1983; Economou and Costar 1999, 248; Hay et al. 1985). Apart from the echoes of the Land Deals scandal, there was no single reason why the Liberals lost the 1982 election. The result reflected the electorate's disenchantment with the later years of the Liberal ascendancy and a desire for a fresh approach to running the state. Consequently, Labor was elected not on the basis of any grand design or a manifesto promising anything other than more resources for health, education and public transport. As a result, the style adopted by the Cain ministry soon after its election was one of careful and cautious management of the state's fiscal and policy affairs. It was paradoxical that the Labor experiment would end in 1992 amidst public perceptions of fiscal incompetence and policy inertia on the part of Premier Cain and his eventual successor, Joan Kirner (Cain 1995; Murray and White 1992, 132–6).

Labor's opponents had warned that the parliamentary wing of the ALP was merely a front for one of the more militant wings of any of the ALP's state branches. But some of the first controversies to beset the new Cain government were over industrial relations with public sector unions. A particularly bitter dispute with the Royal Australian Nursing Federation and its secretary, Irene Bolger, led to the closure of state hospitals. The Cain government also zealously pursued the Builders Labourers Federation, having the union deregistered and some of its leaders, including the secretary Norm Gallagher, imprisoned. A bitter demarcation dispute erupted when the Cain government sanctioned the installation of floodlights at the Melbourne Cricket Ground – much to the chagrin of local residents – and then awarded the contract to the Ironworkers Federation, a former DLP-affiliated union. This marked the return in 1984 of four unions that had left the party in 1955 as a result of the split. The Victorian electorate approved of the Labor government being tough with the trade unions, and Cain's approval ratings were measured in some opinion polls to be as high as 74 per cent.

The Cain government also set about instituting reforms to retailing, licensing and gambling and prostitution (Gorjanicyn 1992, 127). Typically, these reforms were preceded by an extensive expert inquiry that would make recommendations to the government. A spate of shootings also put gun control on the agenda, and here the Cain government's bid to toughen gun ownership laws precipitated a series of anti-government rallies from some rural pressure groups. The pursuit of a more extensive national park network also brought mountain cattlemen and timber workers out on to the streets. Farmers, too, protested against aspects of the Cain government's move to deregulate the dairy industry. The rural–urban divide was still palpable in Victorian politics, but, notwithstanding this, the government exuded a quietly capable managerial style, and Labor was re-elected in 1985.

It was the aftermath of the 1987 stockmarket crash along with the decision taken by the federal Labor government to slash Commonwealth transfers to the states that started Labor's decline. As part of its bid to secure conservative middle-class votes in the eastern and south-eastern suburbs of Melbourne, the Cain government had sought to counter the claim that Labor was a high tax government. Consequently, Labor promised to freeze indirect taxes and the price of state sector-provided services such as electricity, water and gas. This 'family basket' pledge was made just at the time when the state's property boom, from which significant land taxes had been earned, came to a halt. The reduction in Commonwealth general purpose grants further reduced the Victorian government's room to manoeuvre and state debt started to rise (Considine and Costar 1992, 5–7).

As part of its attempt to manage Victorian economics and society, the Cain government utilized state agencies to coordinate the transition from an industrial to a post-industrial economy. Part of this process involved the formation of the Victorian Economic Development Corporation (VEDC). The VEDC was supposed to coordinate the raising of venture capital to allow innovative technology-based corporations to begin production in Victoria. Conservative critics of the scheme argued that the Corporation achieved very little and that some venture capital programs were, in fact, corrupt. While a royal commission exonerated the VEDC of any wrongdoing, the public perception that there was something wrong with the VEDC led to the 1989 resignation of deputy premier Robert Fordham.

In 1990 the Australian economy moved into severe recession, and Victoria, with its heavy economic dependence upon the manufacturing sector, was particularly vulnerable. Manufacturing sector unemployment began to rise. Meanwhile the Australian banking sector began to unravel in the wake of the stockmarket collapse, and again Victoria was hard hit. Two institutions figured prominently. One of these was the Pyramid Building Society which had taken advantage of changed federal laws designed to encourage banking sector competition. In late 1990 despite an earlier reassurance by Treasurer Rob Jolly that the Society was financially sound, Pyramid collapsed and closed its doors. The effect on community confidence was immediate and devastating. Angry investors and account holders besieged the government, with some literally camping out in front of John Cain's house in a bid to have the government do something about this crisis. A compensation package involving the application of a petrol levy to bail out Pyramid account holders was eventually agreed to, but this came too late for the government. Cain and Jolly in particular were held personally responsible by many account holders for the building society's failure.

The Pyramid fiasco was just the beginning. It was soon revealed that the government-owned State Savings Bank of Victoria (SBV) – a venerable institution which had been created in the aftermath of the 1890s financial collapse and had grown on the back of its home mortgage business – was on the verge of collapse. The reason for this collapse was that the bank's board had decided to appropriate a former merchant bank, Tricontinental, in order to participate in the large corporate loan program that the private banks had been pursuing during the 1980s (Armstrong 1992, 45). Unbeknown to the SBV board, but apparently common knowledge amongst the financial community, Tricontinental was dangerously exposed to massive corporate debt defaults. Tricontinental's acquisition had thus rendered the SBV insolvent. The state's financial crisis seemed to be getting worse. In the midst of all of this, the tramways union blockaded the central business district for a week, and, in so doing, caused retail business to plummet. It was all too much for Cain, and in 1990 the premier resigned citing lack of loyalty amongst his cabinet colleagues as his reason for leaving politics. Cain was replaced as leader by former education minister Joan Kirner who thus became Victoria's first female premier.

Premier Kirner attempted to deal with the problems created by these economic convulsions. The Pyramid compensation package was enacted. The government began to prepare the state-owned energy sector for privatization. Cuts to government expenditure were instituted in a bid to reduce the ballooning state debt. The SBV, meanwhile, was sold to the Commonwealth Bank. Labor hoped that the high approval rating for Kirner might translate into electoral success, but Labor's days in power were numbered and the Liberal opposition threatened to use its majority in the Legislative Council to block supply and force an early election. In a desperate bid to save itself politically, Labor dispensed with social democratic ideals and embraced neo-classical liberal notions about the need to downsize its administrative structure. There were

other panic responses. Cain had withstood demands for total liberalization of the gambling industry throughout his time as premier. Kirner
announced that Victoria would finally get its own casino, although the
Labor approach preferred a series of small casinos spread across the
state. Gambling taxes were identified as a valuable source of revenue
that could offset the losses sustained from reductions in Commonwealth
transfers. These measures were not enough to save Labor from defeat at
the state 1992 election.

The period of Labor government between 1982 and 1992 was an
unprecedented era in Victoria's political history. Given the paucity of
Labor administrations, this ten-year era represented a willingness by the
Victorian community to explore the opportunities of the social democratic alternative to liberalism and conservatism. For all its associations
with a sharper ideological approach in internal party politics – the
Victorian ALP was, during this period, the strongest state for the party's
Socialist Left faction – the Labor governments of 1982 to 1992 were
moderate and managerial in their approach. In a bid to stave off fiscal
crisis, they even embraced neo-liberal ideas such as corporatization and
privatization of public sector corporations.

Where Labor's legacy was most pronounced was in the role the
Cain and Kirner governments played in hastening the liberalization of
licensing, retailing and gambling laws. While a case might be made that
the Hamer government was beginning to move in this direction before
it was overtaken by the Land Deals scandal, the fact remains that it was
Labor that finally legalized prostitution, liberalized liquor laws, and
opened the way for the establishment of casinos in Victoria. On the
other hand, Labor's attempt to oversee venture capital investment and
its attempt to defend some public sector corporations had resulted in
failure. For all its moderation, Labor was by 1992 viewed as a party
that had been fiscally reckless and beholden to radical elements in the
Trades Hall.

The Cain government also sought to modify the Victorian
Constitution and made changes to the state's electoral system. Cain's
early period as premier was marked by apprehension about the powers
of the Legislative Council and the state governor. Cain was no doubt
influenced in his approach to the Council by the role it had played in
undoing governments headed by his father, and the primary objective
behind his reforms was to address the Council's power to block supply
and force the Assembly to an election (Costar 1992, 204).

The modifications to the Victorian Constitution passed in 1985
were quite extensive. They provided for an extension of the term of the

Assembly from three years to four, and for the Legislative Council from six years to eight. The number of seats in the Assembly was increased from eighty-one to eighty-eight. The old two-zone electoral system was abolished and replaced with a system under which Assembly electoral districts would have a number of voters within a 10 per cent variation of a state-wide quota set by dividing all the voters in the state by the number of electoral districts. This abolished malapportionment in the Assembly for the second time in Victoria's history.

The Legislative Council was to comprise twenty-two provinces made up of four, contiguous Assembly electoral districts. Each of these provinces would have two legislative councillors, one of whom would be elected for a maximum eight-year term at each Assembly. Significantly, the Constitution was amended to provide for election of half of the Council with every Assembly election thereby denying the upper house the power to force elections on the Assembly without having to face the voters itself.

The Cain amendments to the Constitution dealt with two other contentious matters; the power of the upper house to force premature elections on the executive, and the so-called 'reserve powers' of the governor – the power of the governor to use the authority of the office without advice from the premier or ministers. On the question of the tenure of the executive, section 8 of the *Constitutional Act* provides that a government cannot be dismissed by the governor for the first three years of its four-year term unless the government loses the confidence of the lower house, or if a government-designated 'bill of special importance' was rejected, or if supply was denied. Meanwhile, Part IV of the Act dealing with the Executive Council states (section 87E) that the premier is the source of advice to the governor when the governor exercises the authority of the office.

The Labor years produced significant policy change and institutional reform that affected the Constitution, the parliament, the office of the governor, and the electoral system. This had all been done despite the lack of an ALP majority in the upper house. Along the way Labor won two more electoral contests, although 1988 was to be a particularly close result. The onset of financial collapses and the fiscal crisis that confronted the state destroyed Labor's credibility, notwithstanding the high public approval for Joan Kirner. Labor was in serious disarray by the time of the 1992 election, and was subsequently defeated in a landslide that replicated some of Labor's worst electoral performances during the post-split period of the 1950s and 1960s.

Public policy and the Kennett revolution

In 1992 Victoria elected a Liberal Party–National Party coalition government headed by Jeffrey Kennett as premier. In the context of Victoria's political history, the fact that former antagonists such as the Liberal and the National Party could be in coalition was remarkable. Though he was not the author, Kennett abided by the coalition agreement signed between National Party leader Pat MacNamara and then Liberal leader Allan Brown in July 1990. The coalition agreement had been formulated after Labor's very narrow win in the 1988 election as a way of maximizing the anti-Labor vote. By 1992 this imperative had gone, but Kennett and McNamara maintained the agreement nonetheless. Unbeknown to the Nationals, this agreement would tie them to an economic reform program involving the rationalization of government services and the abolition of local government institutions which would alienate sections of the coalition's rural constituency.

The new coalition government under Premier Kennett was to have a dramatic impact on Victorian politics through public policy and changes to public administration rather than through institutional reform (Costar and Economou 1999). Nearly every government activity and state corporation was subject to radical reform. Notions of a career public service were substantially modified (Alford and O'Neill 1994), although this process had commenced under the Cain premiership with the establishment of a Senior Executive Service.

The Kennett government justified these policies by pointing to the need to address Victoria's fiscal crisis and ballooning state debt. The public appeared to approve as Kennett replicated his 1992 landslide in 1996. Both elections gave Kennett's Liberal Party clear majorities in both the Legislative Assembly and the Legislative Council (Economou and Costar 1999, 122). There were few parliamentary or, given the dejected nature of the Labor opposition, political impediments to the Kennett government.

At the time of Kennett's first ministry, all spheres of government in Australia were reviewing the scope and nature of the role of the state in economy and society. The idea of 'economic rationalism' was at its zenith, an approach to state, economy and society based on the advocacy of the minimal state, the privatization of community assets, and the reduction of the tax burden for the productive elements of the economy (Capling et al. 1998, 89–100; Hughes 1998; Pusey 1991). The Kennett government came to office committed to eliminating the state's public debt, to rationalizing public service numbers, to selling off the public sector, and to establishing an environment conducive to business development (note Webber and Crooks 1996). The popular face of this approach lay in the Kennett government's staging of major events such as the Formula One Grand Prix car race – enticed to Victoria from South Australia – and the opening of a large new casino complex at Southbank in Melbourne. In public policy terms the Kennett revolution manifested itself in dramatic reductions in numbers of state-funded teachers, nurses and public servants and the privatization of nearly every form of state government service delivery. Venerable Victorian statutory corporations such as the railways and tramways, the Gas and Fuel Corporation and especially the State Electricity Commission (SECV) were fragmented and sold to private interests, or in some cases, to foreign public corporations.

School properties which had become vacant under the rationalization of state education were demolished and sold for private development. Former state enterprises covering scientific research were also sold to private interests. Gambling industry deregulation led to a substantial proliferation of electronic gaming machines in hotels and clubs across the state. Large numbers of Victorians were spending ever increasing amounts of their income on gaming, thereby assisting in the growth of state revenue. Planning deregulation led to the proliferation of multi-dwelling urban development even in the affluent suburbs of Melbourne. An extensive new freeway system (Citylink) was developed by a private construction consortium in return for a thirty-year monopoly of toll revenue. Local governments were required to disband their workforces, sell off their buildings and equipment and adopt compulsory competitive tendering. This was a form of privatization in which at least 50 per cent of local government functions had to be contracted out to private operators. The Kennett government also suspended local councils and local government elections as a prelude to forcing a rationalization of the number of urban municipalities and rural shires.

Alterations to the form and nature of the Victorian public service were central to public sector reform under the Kennett government (Alford and O'Neill 1994). Rationalization of public service numbers and a crackdown on public service union industrial militancy were only part of the story. Significant changes were also made to the upper echelons of the service. First amongst these was the introduction of short-term contracts with the premier rather than individual ministers for the senior executive service. The contracts included arrangements for performance-based remuneration. Because rationalization was the primary objective in the government's approach to the public sector, senior executive performance bonuses were inevitably tied to the achievement of budget savings. Not only was morale in the lower reaches of the service adversely affected, the requirement for the public service to give frank and fearless advice became less important than the private sector principle of being a team player.

One public sector institution that caused Premier Kennett and his colleagues political problems and proved to be difficult to reform was the office of the state auditor-general. As leader of the opposition, Kennett had used reports from the auditor-general which were critical of the administration of previous Labor government to good political effect. The premier's goodwill towards the office, and to the auditor-general, Ches Baragwarnath, evaporated once the Liberal and National parties were elected to government. The auditor-general put pressure on Kennett's government in a number of ways. He was highly critical of the tendency of the government to blur the distinction between private and public interest, a matter that touched the premier personally when it was revealed that an advertising company owned by his family had won state government contracts. Allegations that Liberal family members and supporters were recipients of government contracts and consultancies were a recurring theme during the Kennett years. So, too, were revelations of inappropriate use of state government-issued credit cards and expense accounts by senior bureaucrats, ministers and even the premier himself.

The auditor-general also made a contribution to the controversy over privatization when a wide-ranging review of the Kennett government's sell-off of public assets found that all but the sale of the old SECV had been at below market value. With the Labor opposition reduced to a parliamentary rump spending most of its time in internal factional battles, the auditor-general and some of the news media, including the Australian Broadcasting Corporation's Melbourne newsroom and the *Age* newspaper, emerged as the most effective critics of the Kennett government's style and approach. The state government responded with an attempt to exert pressure through the boardroom at David Syme and Co., the owners of the *Age*, to staunch what it saw as excessive editorial criticism. It also sought to corporatize the office of the auditor-general. This decision caused discontent within the Liberal party room, and the resignation of one-time leadership aspirant, Roger Pescott MLA, necessitated a 1998 by-election in eastern suburban Mitcham that the Labor Party won with a 16 per cent swing – the first sign of a renewal in Labor's electoral standing since the 1992 and 1996 defeats.

The Kennett revolution can be seen to have been confined to public administration. There was virtually no change to Victoria's constitutional and institutional arrangements save for the changes to the public service. Kennett had, at one point, expressed an interest in doing away with certain types of by-elections but, after an outcry in which the premier was accused of being anti-democratic, this idea was dropped. The premier's jaundiced view of the performance of local government and its representatives did not extend to the state parliament where calls to reform the Legislative Council were steadfastly ignored. The Kennett government appeared to have no interest in, nor time for, institutional reform amidst its extensive changes to the public sector.

But the Kennett government succeeded in turning the state's public finances from being in debt to returning substantial surpluses. It had succeeded in reforming local government where so many before it had failed. It had sold off large parts of the public sector, and it had succeeded in reducing the size of the public service. The Kennett approach was venerated by the business sector, and Kennett was lauded as a dynamic leader who, unlike other politicians – and especially the Liberal prime minister of the time, John Howard – could promise and deliver a pro-business policy agenda. The scope and extent of the application of neo-classical thinking to public policy was dramatic, if not revolutionary, in a state where liberalism, conservatism and social democracy had previously agreed on the desirability of a large, state public sector. The Kennett government stood apart from its predecessors, Liberal or Labor, precisely because of the way it abandoned the commitment to interventionism that had historically underpinned Victorian liberalism. The social liberalism of the previous era, in which the state was expected to buttress a system of private ownership and manufacturing capitalism, had been swept aside by a more market-oriented, small-government ideology.

The Kennett government's undoubted achievements were not made without cost. The government's treatment of the auditor-general alarmed a community that has shown in the past that it takes the issue of administrative propriety very seriously. Meanwhile, the government's approach to health, education and local government damaged some regional and rural communities where there had always been a significant economic dependence on the public sector. At the 1999 state election these regions rebelled, and, contrary to the expectations of political commentators, Kennett and his colleagues were bundled out of office and a minority Labor government put in their place under Premier Bracks (Woodward and Costar 2000, 125–33). In a result that had historical echoes, the Labor ascendancy was achieved with the assistance of three rural independent members of the Legislative Assembly. Without a majority in the lower house, and with the Liberals still holding a majority in the Legislative Council, the ability of the Bracks government to undertake legislative reform was constrained. Once again Victorians had elected a minority government whose hold on executive power depends on the approval of members of the Legislative Assembly representing rural electoral districts. In this sense, Victorian politics had turned full circle.

Victoria and national politics

With the largest number of federal electoral districts after New South Wales, Victoria has always been important to national politics. Victory for one or other of the major political parties in marginal Victoria seats has often provided the basis for success in national elections. Victorians have historically been well represented in federal coalition and Labor ministries.

Rivalry between Melbourne and Sydney has been longstanding in Australian history, but in the post-second world war period Victoria and New South Wales have had occasion to work together, particularly in inter-governmental forums. The key common concern here has been one of fiscal balance since the *Uniform Tax Act* of 1942 and the federal financial relationship that subsequently emerged. Victoria and New South Wales argue that, as the two big states with the largest populations and economies, they have been forced by the Commonwealth to subsidize the public finances of the other states (Considine and Costar 1992, 281–4). Development and growth in Western Australia and Queensland during the 1960s and 1970s has resulted in these states having much stronger economies. This has made their subsidization under current federal–state relations particularly galling to premiers and treasurers from New South Wales and Victoria, and there have often been instances of the two states seeking to exert pressure on this issue (Keating and Wanna 2000). Outnumbered by the less populous states and the Commonwealth, these attempts at forcing a new deal on federal–state relations have had limited success. On the other side of the ledger, Victoria has also been an innovator in exploring ways to reform the federal system to give more coherence to state policy making (Victorian Parliament 1998) but here too change has been hard to accomplish.

Conclusion

From colonial times when its population was swelled by the discovery of alluvial gold, to the rise of cosmopolitanism driven by post-war migration, Victorian politics has been a complex mix of conservatism and liberalism. Victoria had also been a crucible for exploring the idea that the state can intervene in social and economic life to advance social welfare and the development of business.

The evolution of large and powerful statutory authorities delivering education, energy, transport and such agencies as the Melbourne and Metropolitan Board of Works were a characteristic of Victorian politics for most of the twentieth century. These corporations were not developed by Labor in pursuit of democratic socialist ideals but bequeathed by Victoria's liberal and conservative politicians. The status and influence of these agencies was entrenched by the contrast that they provided with the volatility of Victorian parliamentary politics, particularly in the period between the two world wars. They embodied the idea that public sector agencies could provide the planning and direction which was missing from a parliamentary system that was incapable of providing ministries which could be assured of surviving from one election to the next, let alone ensuring the passage of legislation through a bicameral parliament.

The split in the ALP in the 1950s and the formation of the DLP had the effect of ushering in a long period of majority governments under a recently reborn Liberal Party. This enabled the Liberals to preside over the period of post-war growth in Victoria and establish a pattern of one party majority government which lasted for almost fifty years. Over that time, both the major parties had substantial periods in office but used their political resources very differently. The Bolte era of the 1950s and 1960s can be seen as conforming to the normal pattern of state politics with its stress on the provision of services and brokerage politics to balance the never-ending demands of interest groups and constituents against some broader idea of the public interest. Social conservatism and economic constraint were the watchwords rather than ideology or grand plans for social or economic engineering. The Hamer period of office in the 1970s corresponded with a greater sophistication in the administration of government and the burgeoning of social policy and lifestyle concerns.

This style of politics reached its peak with the return of an ALP government under Premier Cain (Jr) in 1982. While it continued and extended the changes to the focus of government introduced by the previous regime, its distinguishing characteristic was its concern with institutional reform. This included not only changes to the state's constitutional, financial, and electoral systems, but attempts by the premier to reform the operation of the federal system and intergovernmental relations. But regimes are often remembered for their failures rather than their successes, and the collapse of the Pyramid Building

Society and the State Saving Bank colours assessments of Labor's decade in office.

The ALP defeat which followed in 1992 ushered in a government with a radical agenda for administrative reform. Just as Victoria could be said to have been a pioneer in developing the delivery of public goods and services through crown corporations and non-ministerial public sector agencies, under the Kennett government it came to epitomize the move to the privatization of the public sector and the use of the market mechanism for the delivery of government services.

This confirms the impression that Victorian government and politics has more often been an outlier than close to the norm of the other Australian states. This has been as true of its experience of volatile party government as it has of the divisions within both Victorian Labor and anti-Labor camps. It is equally true of its experience of the extension of government services and intervention in the economy around the end of the nineteenth century as it has been of the privatization of government services at the end of the twentieth century. With the election of the minority Bracks ALP government in 1999, it is not clear whether the state is on a trajectory towards conformity with mainstream politics or, in line with the experience of much of the previous century, towards a period of innovation and change.

8

Chapter

Western Australia

Jeremy Moon and Campbell Sharman

Western Australia was the last colony to decide to join federation, just as it had been the last to gain self-government. Both of these characteristics can be explained by apprehensions about political representation. Federation in 1901 meant trusting a new and distant national government to safeguard Western Australia's interests in areas of trade and tariffs where the colony was especially vulnerable, and the granting of self-government, some thirty years after the eastern colonies, had been delayed for Western Australia in large part because of the small size of the European population concentrated in the south-west corner of a vast territory.

From its founding, politics in Western Australia has been more strongly shaped by distance and isolation than any other state. This has been as true for politics within the state as it has for relations with the rest of Australia and the wider world. In both political and economic realms, the state has been acutely aware of the costs, and occasional benefits, of separation from the bulk of the nation's population in the south-east of Australia. And within the western third of the continent which comprises Western Australia, more than two-thirds of the state's current population of just under two million lives within a hundred kilometres of Perth. The rest are dispersed in a few moderately sized regional centres and many small farming communities, forestry, mining and fishing enterprises, Aboriginal settlements, and a growing number of communities dependent on tourism. These extend from the cool temperate forests of the south-west, through farming land, scrub and desert to the tropical climates of the north and north-west coast.

Isolation has given West Australians a sense of distinctiveness and awareness of being on the edge of the continent, politically as well as geographically. The two-hour difference in time zones between Perth and Canberra and the commercial centres on the eastern seaboard is a constant reminder that West Australian interests can be easily overlooked. A similar feeling towards the state government is often shared by those who live outside Perth, particularly those in the north of the state for whom the struggle to get fresh vegetables and a daily newspaper is a major logistical exercise.

This has made the issue of representing small communities that occupy a large territory a defining theme in the design and operation of political institutions in the state. While Britain claimed Western Australia in part as a strategic response to French expeditions to the region, it was not enthusiastic about spending money for settlement. The foundation of the Swan River colony in 1829 was as much a commercial undertaking as one driven by government (Statham 1989c). It struggled to survive in the early years and the slow growth of European settlement was the major reason for the delay in achieving self-government, although the colonists had gained a limited form of representative government in 1832 (Black 1991b). At the time when the other Australian colonies were gaining parliamentary government in the mid-1850s, Western Australia had petitioned Britain for convicts to be sent to the colony to speed economic development. The use of convicts continued until the late 1860s when agriculture, forestry, mining and especially wool had become well-established as industries capable of sustaining the colony (Crowley 1960, 32–43).

Even when self-government was finally achieved in 1890, the constraints of a small population concentrated in one region of a large territory were made clear in a number of sections of the West Australian *Constitution Act*. The Act reflected the views of the British Colonial Office that the huge area of the colony meant that it might be divided into several smaller and more manageable territories, an idea which persisted into the 1920s (Ellis 1933, 183–92). While the lower house, the Legislative Assembly, was directly elected, albeit on a restricted property franchise, the Act provided that the direct election of members of the upper house, the Legislative Council, was not to come into effect until the European population reached 60 000.

Unlike other colonies, the significant Aboriginal population in comparison with new settlers was recognized in a provision in the *Constitution Act* (section 70) to ensure that a proportion of government resources was available for Aboriginal welfare. Notwithstanding the good intentions of some in the Colonial Office, local settlers resented this provision and eventually secured its repeal (Johnston 1989). This action was consistent with the neglect and mistreatment of Aboriginal residents of the state for most of the last century (Bolton 1987).

With the discovery of gold in the eastern goldfields, the 1890s became a boom period for the colony, its European population exceeding 60 000 by 1893. At the same time, the growth of population raised issues of representation both within the colony and in relation to the acceptability of federal union. The question of the regional weighting of votes for electing members to both houses of the colonial parliament became a contentious issue and one which continues to be in dispute over a hundred years later. In addition, the rapid increase in the proportion of the colony's population living on the goldfields further complicated the vigorous debate over Western Australia's participation in a federal union of the Australian colonies (de Garis 1999). But by late 1900 a majority of West Australian voters accepted that to be left outside the new federation was riskier than being one of the original states of the Commonwealth in 1901.

System of government

Western Australia entered federation with a set of political institutions which followed the well-established pattern for self-governing British colonies. Legislative power was exercised by a bicameral legislature in concert with a governor appointed by the British crown. Executive power was exercised by the governor who was, on almost all occasions, to act on the advice of a premier and ministers who had the support of a majority of members of the lower house of the legislature, the Legislative Assembly (Boyce 1991). Following the tradition of British parliamentary government, the office of premier, the role of ministers and their relationship with the parliament and the governor were not specified in a constitutional document, a situation which continues today (Galligan 1991; but note WACOG 1996). But, in common with the other Australian colonies, there were significant departures from the British tradition. The setting out of the state's parliamentary structure in a Constitution Act which required special procedures to amend and was open to judicial review made the West Australian Constitution a higher law in a way more familiar to the United States than the British style of constitutionalism (Sharman 1991).

Western Australia continued the pattern of strong bicameralism common to the other Australian colonies and the new Commonwealth government. The Legislative Council had almost equal powers to those of the Assembly and followed the model of South Australia, Victoria and Tasmania in making the Council an elected rather than a nominated house. Its conservatism was ensured by a substantial property qualification for voters and later by malapportionment which had the effect of giving the non-Labor parties control of the chamber until the 1990s. Relations between the Council and the government majority in the lower house could be strained, especially during periods of Labor government when the Council blocked or amended substantial parts of the government's legislative program (Okely 1991; WARCPD 1985). Such situations reinforced the ideological hostility of the Labor Party to the upper house and for many years the party was committed to abolition of the Council. This changed with the electoral reforms negotiated by the Burke Labor government in the mid-1980s which reduced the extremes of malapportionment and introduced proportional representation for elections from 1989. As a consequence, the very substantial powers of the Council, its fixed term of office, the absence of deadlock procedures, and substantial malapportionment remained in 2001 but the Legislative Council's political legitimacy has been greatly enhanced by having the same franchise as the Assembly and by its reflection of the diversity of opinion in the state as a result of proportional representation (Stone 2002).

As a consequence of the controversy over the role of the Senate and the governor-general in the dismissal of the Whitlam government in Canberra in 1975, some members of the state Labor Party argued for a reduction of the powers of the West Australian upper house and the state governor. This prompted the Liberal Party–National Country Party coalition government led by Charles Court to amend the *Constitution Act* in 1978 so that any change to the powers of the governor or any reduction of the powers or alteration of the composition of either house of state parliament would require a constitutional referendum (section 73). This was a radical reversal of the trend to reduce limitations on the government's ability to amend the state's Constitution, and would ensure that, for the first time, any major restructuring of the state's constitutional structure would need broad popular endorsement. Although the 1999 Commonwealth referendum on a republican head of state failed to pass, it raised many questions about the response of state governments and the consequences for state constitutions of moving to a republican executive (WACC 1995, ch.3). For Western Australia, such changes would require a constitutional referendum and, if they occur, will prompt the biggest changes to the state's constitutional arrangements since the granting of self-government in 1890.

Looking at the West Australian governmental system over the

hundred years since federation, and the hundred and eleven years since colonial self-government, the most striking characteristic has been the lack of change. The institutions of government and the administration of justice have proved remarkably resilient in coping with massive changes to the context of government and the expectations of voters. The population of the state is now more than forty times its size in 1890 and yet the number of state parliamentarians has barely doubled (Stone 1998). The office of governor is almost unchanged, and the role of the premier and cabinet is much the same as a century ago. The dynamics of parliamentary politics have changed since 1890 but this is overwhelmingly the result of the rise of political parties rather than any change to parliamentary structures.

Parties and the party system

Political parties play such a central role in our current system of representative democracy that it is hard to think of political activity without them. Yet, for the first two elections under self-government in 1890 and 1894, there were no clear party labels and a party system recognizably similar to the present one did not emerge until 1914 (de Garis 1991). Until then, politics were strongly influenced by local notables, many of whom were returned as members of the Legislative Assembly unopposed. This reflected the dominance of local issues and the small size of the electorate; the average enrolment in 1901 was less than 2000 for each electoral district. For the first decade of self-government John Forrest, the first premier, was the dominant figure in state politics until he moved to the Commonwealth parliament in 1901. Forrest was a Conservative and a Protectionist but such party groupings were loose and changeable associations with little formal organization or electoral significance, their members often bound together only by the need to maintain office in the Legislative Assembly (de Garis 1977, 306–28).

The Australian Labor Party

The engine of change was the Australian Labor Party (ALP). The party began as an association of unions representing, miners, rural workers and urban labour, coupled with a sprinkling of individuals who wanted radical social change. In 1901 there were a number of candidates associated with a nascent Labor Party, and by 1904 the ALP emerged to gain 42 per cent of the vote and form a minority government under Henry Daglish for twelve months from August 1904 (de Garis 1977, 328–41). At the election of 1911 under the leadership of John Scaddan, the ALP won control of government with 53 per cent of the vote, a level of support not exceeded until the 1983 and 1986 election victories of Brian Burke. Although the ALP saw its vote share suffer as a result of the conscription crisis in 1917, it was firmly established as a major party and, for all but a handful of elections since 1914, has won more votes than any other single party (see figure 8.1).

The significance of the rise of the ALP was not just in its electoral success. Its internal structure brought new, and controversial, features to party organization. The idea of a party which had continuing existence between elections and which required candidates standing under its name to pledge to follow party policy, and the decisions of the parliamentary party, were seen by some as an attack on the essence of representative democracy (Bongiorno 2001). In addition, the strong organizational links between the ALP and the trade union movement – a Trades and Labour Council as a coordinating body for trade unions separate from the ALP was not established until 1962 – led to the charge by its opponents that the party was simply the instrument of organized labour and could not govern in the interests of all. But the success of the ALP both in the electorate and in being able to form a disciplined block of votes in the Legislative Assembly had the long-term effect of forcing conservative interests to organize along similar lines.

Although the ALP had been committed to 'state socialism' since 1899 when a resolution to this effect was passed at the first Trades Union and Labour Congress (Pervan and Mitchell 1979, 130), the stance of the party in office was governed more by pragmatism than ideology. This was partly the result of the natural conservatism of the parliamentary party, and partly the result of the influence of moderate unions within the ALP. As heavy state government involvement in many aspects of economic development and the provision of services was taken for granted from early in the state's history, the ALP was, in some senses, the natural party of government until the end of the second world war. It was in power for twenty-four of the thirty-six years between 1911 and 1947.

The organization of the party during these years was decentralized, 'in response ... to the pattern of development in an economy based on agriculture and mining. It was in these industries and accompanying services such as transport that the greatest number of unionists were to be found, scattered in regional centres throughout much of the state' (Mitchell 1983, 165). This dispersed structure and the representation of both local union and local branch members in the same branch organization until 1962 enabled the ALP to articulate the concerns of a wide range of West Australian voters and claim a disproportionate share of

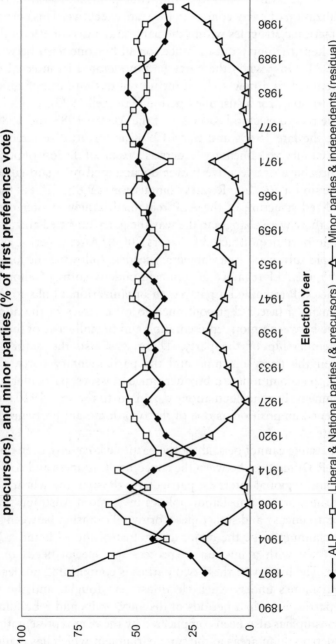

Figure 8.1 West Australian Legislative Assembly, general elections 1890–2001: vote share of ALP, Liberal and National parties (and their precursors), and minor parties (% of first preference vote)

Source: calculated from the Australian Government and Politics Project database, University of Western Australia.

government until the late 1950s. Mitchell (1983) argues persuasively that the large-scale capital investment in the state from the 1960s and the growth of metropolitan Perth led to a change in the balance of power in the ALP organization in favour of urban-based unions and a centralization of party control in the state executive. This corresponded with factional struggles within the party and a loss of electoral support which kept the party out of office for all but one term between 1959 and 1983. Only when the party had moderated its internal divisions and adapted to a new style of media politics and campaigning did it return to office for a sustained period (Mitchell 1983).

The record electoral successes of the ALP in 1983 and 1986 soured during the late 1980s and early 1990s as the ALP suffered from the disgrace of its parliamentary leaders as a result of the loss of public funds and the abuse of executive power documented by a subsequent royal commission (WA Inc Royal Commission 1992). While the highly centralized structure of the ALP remained largely unaltered from the 1980s, there were changes in the way the party operated and an increase in the importance of factions (Sayers 2000). After a period of turmoil and rapid turnover of parliamentary leaders following the loss of office in 1993, the ALP regained government under Geoffrey Gallop in 2001.

The ALP remained a party with organizational links to the union movement, a factor that continued to raise issues of the appropriate balance between union representation and the influence of the rank and file membership of the party. There was also the natural tension between the party machine and the parliamentary party, the latter having to accommodate a broader range of issues, particularly when in government. But the fluctuations in ALP fortunes since 1920 have never threatened its position as one of the two dominant party groupings in the state.

The same cannot be said for the parties which have been opposed to the ALP. Differences between the concerns of business and commerce in Perth and regional interests, particularly those in the wheat belt, have made the story of non-Labor politics in Western Australia since 1914 one of an uneasy and sometimes stormy relationship between a Liberal Party claiming to be the major antagonist of the ALP and a National Party (NP) with a mission to protect the special needs of country people. The history of these two parties is complicated not least by the various names under which elections were fought, and the fact that both parties have had periods of disunity, splits and rebuilding. Their relationship has also been complicated by the over-representation of the non-metropolitan areas in the state parliament which has made the NP a vital component for almost all non-ALP governments.

The Liberal Party

The origins of the Liberal Party were in loose associations of like-minded members of parliament who reflected the commercial and property interests in the community. It also appealed to those who were suspicious of the union influence in the ALP and apprehensive about the political changes advocated by some in the party. The increasing electoral success of the Labor Party in 1904 had led some members of parliament to see themselves as forming a block of 'Liberals' in opposition to the ALP, but the term Liberal Party 'did not come into general use until 1911' (Black 1979, 192). For the next thirty years, the Liberals[1] had some electoral successes but the party had perennial problems with maintaining an effective party machine, with the issue of fund-raising, and with the endorsement of candidates (Black 1979). To add to the party's problems, the emergence of the Country (now National) Party from 1914 meant that the Liberals had to compete with both the ALP and a rival non-Labor party.

Some of these difficulties can be traced to the fact that the Liberals were not comfortable with the idea of a party machine which could instruct the parliamentary party. Overall responsibility for policy rested with the leader and the parliamentary membership of the party which chose the leader. This meant that, while the party needed funds for electioneering and some means of endorsing candidates, both these processes were often heavily influenced by sitting members and small groups of wealthy donors (Black 1979). It was not until the re-creation of the federal Liberal Party under Menzies in 1944 that the party acquired an organization which matched that of the ALP with a large rank and file membership. After a period of organizational transition, Black (1979) argues that the Liberals entered a period of hegemony in 1959 which lasted until 1983. In addition to generally favourable economic conditions, this was aided by an efficient party structure and the ability to expand the Liberal Party's electoral base into areas previously held by the NP. The defeat of the Liberals at the 1983 by a resurgent ALP marked a change in the style of politics (Moon and Fletcher 1988). Only when the ALP was tarnished by scandal and poor management did the Liberals return to power in 1993.

Campaigning for elections is now largely a statewide activity and the Liberal Party has long had a state executive and conference structure providing a large measure of central control. Nonetheless, the Liberals have retained a more decentralized organization than the ALP and, in particular, the selection of candidates is predominantly the choice of members of the local branch. This has proved a source of both strength and weakness. It has provided an opportunity for local members to participate in a critically important party function, but it has been a source of tension within branches throughout the life of the party, sometimes leading to the multiple endorsement of Liberal candidates for the same seat, or unsuccessful candidates running as independents. There have also been occasions when disputes have been brought to the state executive over the recruitment of members to local branches where preselection contests were hotly contested. Overall, however, the Liberals are now entrenched in their position as by far the biggest non-Labor party and the natural home for those on the conservative side of politics.

The National Party and its precursors

The Liberal Party has not always been able to claim this status. Once the Country Party had emerged as an electoral force in 1914, it was unclear for many years as to which of the two non-ALP parties would become dominant. It was only after 1947 that the Liberal Party became the major conservative party in terms of its vote share, and after 1959 in its share of seats in the Legislative Assembly. The Country Party had grown out of the West Australian Farmers Settlers Association (FSA) as part of an Australia-wide radicalization of farming politics closely associated with the growth of wheat farming and agrarian populism (Graham 1966). It was Australia's first country party and set out to ensure that the economic importance of rural production was reflected in government policies which took into account the needs of those living outside Perth (Layman 1979). Rather than remain a lobby group, the FSA set up a political party which borrowed some of the organizational characteristics of the ALP (Graham 1966, 87). The success of the new party was greeted with dismay by the Liberal Party which has been forced, with only one exception in 1996, to rely on the support of the Country Party, and its successor, the National Party[2] to gain a majority of seats in the Legislative Assembly.

Until 1924 the Liberal and Country parties had a similar share of the popular vote but since that date there has been a gradual decline in NP electoral support. The depopulation of agricultural areas and structural change in the West Australian economy provide much of the explanation (Layman 1979, 175–6) but another factor has been consistent pressure from the Liberal Party for it to become the only party on the conservative side of politics. The strategy of the Liberals has included calling itself the Liberal and Country League between the 1950 and 1968 elections and using its position as the stronger partner

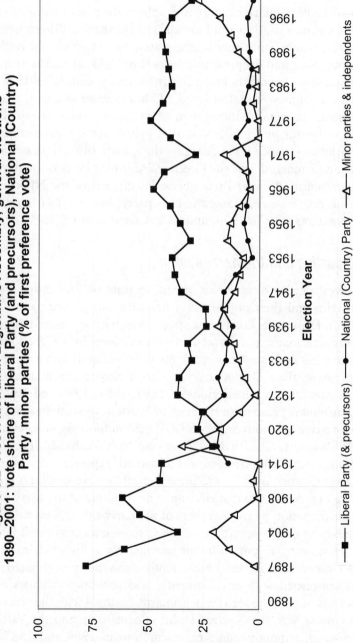

Figure 8.2 West Australian Legislative Assembly, general elections 1890–2001: vote share of Liberal Party (and precursors), National (Country) Party, minor parties (% of first preference vote)

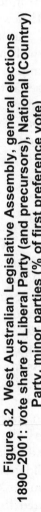

Source: calculated from the Australian Government and Politics Project database, University of Western Australia.

in coalition governments to give preference to Liberal Party policy concerns and take credit for rural policies.

The tensions associated with coalition government have led to divisions in the National Party (NP) over relations with the Liberal Party and caused a particularly acrimonious split in the party from 1978 until the 1986 election (Gallop and Layman 1985). At the 2001 election, the party gained only 3 per cent of the statewide vote and, although the party vote share had dropped to this level in 1953, at that time it held nine seats, seven members being returned unopposed. In 2001 it won five seats, all contested, and it faced a Labor government with a strong commitment to remove the system of malapportionment which has worked in favour of the NP. Now that proportional representation in the Legislative Council is encouraging the growth of such parties as the Australian Democrats and the Greens WA, it may be that the days are passing when the Liberal Party needs the support of the NP in either house of the state parliament. The party lost its last House of Representatives seats in 1974, and its last senator in 1977.

Minor parties and the party system

The newest parties to make an impact in state politics differ in both their origins and their organization from the established parties. The Australian Democrats are a centre party which grew out of dissatisfaction with the major parties at the national level in 1977 (Warhurst 1997) and has preserved a primary focus on national rather than state politics. Australian Democrats have won Senate representation in Western Australia in the elections of 1983, 1987, 1999 and 1998 and gained at least 3 per cent of the vote in Western Australia at House of Representative elections since 1977. Their support at state elections since 1980 has averaged around 2 per cent with no chance of representation until the adoption of proportional representation for the Legislative Council from 1989. Since then, they have won two seats at the 1996 Legislative Council election. The structure of the party allows direct participation by the members of the party through postal ballots on issues of major importance, including the selection of candidates.

A stress on participation by the membership is also a characteristic of the Greens WA. As the name implies, this party originated from groups concerned with environmental and anti-nuclear issues in the early 1980s. Again, the focus was primarily national with the precursors of the Greens WA, the Nuclear Disarmament Party and the Valentine Peace Group, winning Senate representation in 1984 and 1987. The Greens WA won Senate seats in 1990 and 1993 and have won around

5 per cent of the statewide vote at House of Representatives elections. But the Greens have also been strongly focused on state issues and especially on the question of logging in old growth forests in the south-west of the state. The party gained one seat in the Legislative Council at the 1993 election, three seats in 1996 and five at the 2001 election, giving them the balance of power in the chamber. In contrast, the NP retained only one seat.

The most recent contender for votes in West Australian politics has been Pauline Hanson's One Nation Party. The party made a dramatic entry at the 1998 federal election and, although it did not win any seats, it gained over 8 per cent of the West Australian vote for the House of Representatives and 10 per cent for the Senate (Sharman and Miragliotta 2000). A vote share of this size under a preferential voting system made it a threat to the major parties in terms of the flow of preferences. In a similar performance at the 2001 state election, it won almost 10 per cent of the statewide vote and three seats in the Legislative Council, and its vote share of over 9 per cent and the effects of its preferences in Legislative Assembly seats was credited with helping to defeat the Liberal–National Party coalition government of Richard Court.

The importance of these new parties is not only in the indication of changing political values in the electorate. The size of the non-major party vote has reached close to record levels since the emergence of the current party system and raises the question of whether the state's party system is in the process of major change after a long period of relative stability.

If politics is seen as a struggle for office between two large party groupings, with the ALP on one side and a coalition of the Liberal and National parties (L–NP) on the other, the pattern of vote shares of these two groupings is illustrated in figure 8.1. This shows that, after a period of initial turbulence, by 1920 a pattern had been established in which the vote share of both major party groupings had a long-term percentage share of the vote in the mid-40s, with the ALP's share varying between 36 and 53 per cent, and the L–NP between 35 and 55 per cent (see figure 8.1). It should be noted that the pattern of vote share has not always corresponded with the share of seats won or with success in gaining government, as will be examined below. This is partly the result of the vagaries of the electoral system and malapportionment and partly a consequence of the number of uncontested seats which averaged some 20 per cent of the seats in the Legislative Assembly until the 1960s.

There are two factors which need to be kept in mind when examining the apparently orderly pattern of ALP and L–NP struggle for electoral dominance since 1920 in figure 8.1. The first is the category of L–NP itself. Figure 8.2 shows that the non-ALP share of the vote has changed its composition over the years and makes very clear the impact of the NP after 1911 and its steady decline in electoral support after 1943.

The second exception is the importance of votes for 'All minor parties and independents'. This figure has varied from a high of 35 per cent in 1917, to close to zero in the early 1980s and back to over 28 per cent in 2001. This category covers a number of small parties which have gained more than 2 per cent of the first preference vote at general elections and includes independent candidates if their combined vote exceeded 2 per cent. Independents have attracted enough votes to cross this threshold in a majority of general elections, but they have had relatively little importance in the operation of the Legislative Assembly. Their period of greatest success was the period between the 1930s and the 1950s when they gained a significant share of the vote and won at least one and as many as four seats. Independent candidates may become more common if the apparent disillusionment with the major parties continues; independents have gained at least one seat at every general election for the Assembly since 1993 and four were elected at the 2001 state election.

Significant minor parties at Assembly elections since 1917 have included the National Labor Party from 1917 to 1924 and the Democratic Labor Party from 1959 to 1971, both of which had broken away from the ALP: Greypower in 1989, and Pauline Hanson's One Nation Party in 2001. In addition, the Australian Democrats and the Greens WA have become increasingly important at state elections since the 1993 election. They have gained seats in the Legislative Council as did the One Nation Party in 2001 but, excluding the NP and related parties, no minor party has won a seat in the Assembly since 1924.

A final note on the West Australian pattern of partisan competition for votes concerns the combined vote share of the largest two parties, the ALP and the Liberal Party. Their combined vote has moved from 46 per cent of the vote in 1917 to a high of 94 per cent in 1986. Since then there has been a steady decline so that in 2001 the figure was less than 70 per cent, the lowest it had been since 1943. This reflects the growing share of the vote won by minor party and independent candidates. While there is no reason to think that the vote share of the largest two parties must continue to decline, a vote share below 70 per cent begins to produce erratic results in electoral outcomes under a single-member district electoral system. This is because of the effect of a large number of three-cornered contests and the dependence of major party candidates on the flow of preferences for election. This may mean that the neat pattern in figure 8.1 may be less orderly in the future.

Little has been said about the party system for the Legislative Council because, in most respects, the competition for votes was between the same participants as those in the Legislative Assembly until the introduction of proportional representation for the Council from the 1989 election. The distinguishing characteristic of the Council has been in its system of representation and the malapportionment which ensured that the non-metropolitan areas of the state had three-quarters of the seats in the chamber, a figure which has ensured that metropolitan votes have had only a third of the weight of non-metropolitan votes (WACOG 1995).

Federal elections in Western Australia

As a part of a federation, West Australians have also participated in the election of members for the Commonwealth parliament. Elections for the House of Representatives and the Senate have provided additional forums for party competition but, in broad terms, these have had the same contestants and have followed a similar pattern of support as at Assembly elections. This is not to say that there have been no differences in performance; there has been a long-term trend for West Australians to favour the ALP in state elections more than they do for federal elections (Sharman and Sayers 1998). Non-ALP representation in the Senate has been complicated by the question of the Liberal Party and the National Party running joint tickets. Disagreements over the choice of candidates and their position on the ticket led to the discontinuation of joint Senate tickets in Western Australia in the 1950s, an indication of the breakdown of relations between the two parties, and the decline in National Party support.

Having to compete in multiple electoral forums has presented parties with a substantial organizational challenge. The choice of Senate candidates, for example, requires a party to make a statewide choice, whereas the selection of lower houses candidates, both state and federal, can be determined by individual electoral districts. The need to make these different choices has had important effects on the organization of parties, as has the fact that, in order to match state and national parliaments, parties have had to set up national as well as state party machines. Establishing the current system has been a complex process which has taken a long time, and parties in Western Australia have shown a wide range of solutions both between individual parties and within the same party over time. The ALP is a good example of change;

its federal structure has varied from the absence of any organization at all at the national level, to the situation in 2001 which gives the national body the power to intervene in state branches and veto the selection of candidates for federal elections.

Representation

Issues of representation have already been touched on but there are some aspects of the West Australian parliamentary system which deserve special note. In terms of its basic characteristics, the story is a straightforward one. On gaining self-government in 1890 there was a property qualification for electors for the lower house which was not removed until 1907. Votes for women had been secured in 1899 and Western Australia was the first state to have a woman elected to parliament (Edith Cowan in 1921), and the first to have a woman premier (Carmen Lawrence in 1990). Discrimination against Aboriginal voters was not finally removed until 1962. The state was one of the last to adopt compulsory voting for its lower house in 1936 for the 1939 election but had had compulsory enrolment of electors since 1919 (but note Black 1991a, 118). A first-past-the-post (plurality) electoral system with single-member districts was used for the Assembly from 1890 until 1907, when an optional preferential system was adopted. This made the state the first to use preferential voting as a way of encouraging electoral cooperation by anti-Labor candidates in response to the rising ALP vote. The current system of preferential voting with the compulsory expression of preferences was put in place in 1911.

Malapportionment

All Australian states have experienced malapportionment in one or both of their parliamentary chambers since federation, but Western Australia is unusual both in the continuation of systemic and substantial vote-weighting from the beginning of self-government into 2001 and in the effects that malapportionment has had on political competition.

The representation of communities by single-member districts independent of their population often leads to large discrepancies in the number of voters in each electoral district. There is, in other words, a conflict between the principle of equal representation of individuals – the so-called 'one-vote one-value' test – and the principle of community representation. Given that Western Australia has been characterized since white settlement by a concentration of population in Perth and small communities elsewhere in the state, the pressures for community representation have been high (WACOG 1995). This has resulted in malapportionment so that non-metropolitan seats for the Legislative Assembly have usually contained many fewer voters than metropolitan seats. Such a system can become an issue of fierce partisan controversy if one party consistently benefits from this kind of vote-weighting.

This has not been the case in Western Australia for much of the period since 1901 for two reasons. The first is that the over-representation of the farming communities in the wheat belt and the south-west of the state have been matched by over-representation of the goldfields, mining, and Labor-leaning communities elsewhere in the state. Until the 1960s this meant that the ALP was as much a beneficiary of malapportionment as the non-Labor parties (Buxton 1979). The other and related reason for the tolerance of malapportionment has been that, as is shown in figure 8.3, malapportionment has not prevented an alternation of majorities in the Legislative Assembly which has given Western Australia a pattern of more even alternation in office between the ALP and L–NP parties than any other state.

Its almost unbroken experience of opposition from 1959 to 1983 and the urbanization of the ALP since the 1960s has made the party much less tolerant of vote-weighting. Even so, in its electoral reforms of 1987, it accepted a 2:1 population ratio for metropolitan to non-metropolitan seats in the Legislative Assembly, and a 3:1 ratio for the Legislative Council. This accommodation was forced by the need to get a package of legislative reforms through the Council with the support of the NP, and it is likely that vote-weighting will continue to be an issue until it is substantially reduced.

The most consistent beneficiary of vote-weighting has been the NP. A comparison of figure 8.4 with figure 8.2 indicates that the NP's share of seats was usually double its vote share, and until the 1950s sometimes very much higher than this. The picture is complicated for the years up to 1960 by the large proportion of NP seats which were uncontested but the fact remains that the electoral system made the NP a much more potent parliamentary party than its vote share would suggest. A counter intuitive conclusion from this analysis is that the party which has suffered most from malapportionment has been the Liberal Party in being forced to accommodate the NP in coalition when, under an equally apportioned electoral system, NP support may not have been necessary.

Uncontested seats

A distinctive feature of West Australian elections has been the large number of uncontested seats until 1968 (Buxton 1977, 36). An average

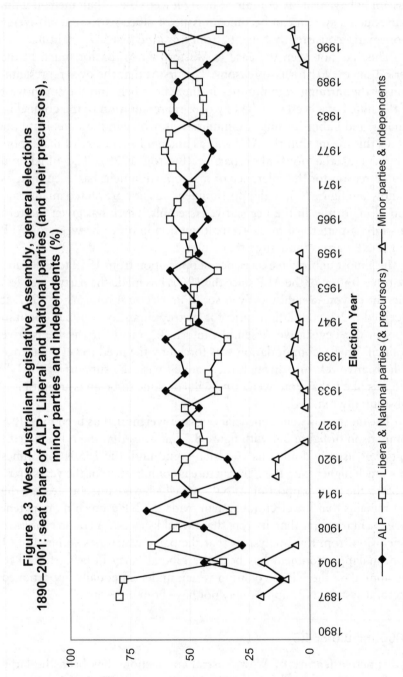

Figure 8.3 West Australian Legislative Assembly, general elections 1890–2001: seat share of ALP, Liberal and National parties (and their precursors), minor parties and independents (%)

Source: calculated from the Australian Government and Politics Project database, University of Western Australia.

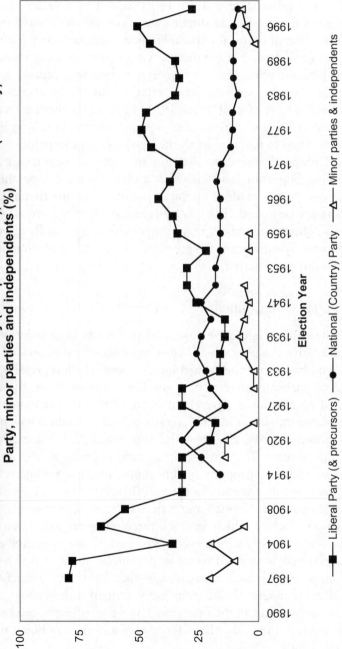

Figure 8.4 West Australian Legislative Assembly, general elections 1890–2001: seat share of Liberal Party (and precursors), National (Country) Party, minor parties and independents (%)

Source: calculated from the Australian Government and Politics Project database, University of Western Australia.

of 20 per cent of seats at all state elections since 1890 have been uncontested, with an average of 27 per cent for elections up to 1968, the last uncontested seat being won in 1983. This was a markedly higher rate than in any other state and can be explained by a variety of factors. Chief among them was the dominance of community politics even after the formation of political parties. Finding candidates and campaigning in small or dispersed communities with a popular local member was often difficult, particularly when parties had few central resources, campaigns were essentially local affairs, and the local member had incentives to be re-elected (Black 1991, 124). At the other extreme, very safe ALP or Liberal seats were seen as not worth contesting by candidates who had to find almost all the resources for campaigning on their own. Only with the centralization of party organizations and the increasing importance of television and statewide campaigning have the biggest parties made it a point of honour to ensure that all electoral districts are contested. The 1971 election marked the arrival of a new style of politics in the state where the politics of a centrally driven partisanship finally submerged the previous decentralized, community-based tradition of party activity.

The Legislative Council

The role of the Legislative Council has already been mentioned as a representative chamber which began as a conservative check on government and has been transformed into a house which represents a wider range of partisan interests than the lower house. From the time the Council became an elective chamber in 1894 until the major reforms which came into effect in 1965, its structure had features which made it both a conservative chamber and one which did not easily fit the demands of party. To its over-representation of non-metropolitan areas could be added its property qualifications, multiple voting, small (and voluntary) enrolment and low turnout (Black 1991a, 131–8). Members of the Legislative Council were elected from multimember districts (provinces) each of which returned three members with fixed six-year terms, one member retiring every two years. These staggered elections with relatively long fixed terms in provinces, some of which covered very large geographical areas, meant that legislative councillors had considerable independence from party control if they could maintain community support in their province. As a consequence, the Legislative Council had some of the characteristics of a non-party house until well into the 1960s.

The Legislative Council was transformed by the changes which were put in place for the 1965 election, which brought its franchise and electoral rules into line with those operating for the Legislative Assembly. But the Council retained fixed six-year terms for its members although they were elected from two- rather than three-member provinces, one member retiring every three years. After 1989 staggered terms were abandoned and the whole membership of the Council was elected by proportional representation from five- and seven-member districts for fixed four-year terms. These alterations were beginning to bring about the changes in the role of the chamber which have become typical of such reformed upper houses using proportional representation – the loss of government control, the balance of power held by minor parties and independents, and an institutional concern with the scrutiny of legislation and committee work (Stone 2002).

Government and public policy

Federation required the transfer of some areas of jurisdiction to the new Commonwealth government, but the bulk of administrative responsibility for delivering the services which affected the daily life of West Australians remained with the state government. This has continued to be true in spite of the growth of the Commonwealth government, its involvement in most areas of public policy since the 1970s and its dominant position in revenue-raising after it acquired a monopoly in raising income tax in 1942. For West Australians as for other Australians, problems with the health system, schools, policing, transport, land use and local government are all matters in which the state, and now territory, governments play by far the dominant role. This reflects the dispersal of Australia's population and the fact that now, as in 1901, the centre of gravity for political activity is based in the states. This has kept the state governments as vital players in the federal system and, as in the case of Western Australia, the principal avenues for articulating the concerns of the political communities which comprise the federation.

All states have had to cope with the demands for social services and the infrastructure for transport and economic development but the latter have been particularly important for a state as large and isolated as Western Australia. For much of the century, communications with the rest of Australia were poor. Until the construction of the transcontinental railway in 1917, all interstate transport was by coastal shipping, as was most communication with the north of the state. The construction of a surveyed road from the eastern goldfields linking Perth to Adelaide was not commenced until 1941 and the last section on the South Australian side of the border was not sealed until 1976. The final section of a sealed road from the north-west of the state to Darwin was completed in 1986, the last component of the national highway around Australia. Air travel is now a vital component for the transport of people and freight within the state and to other parts of Australia but the expense is a constant reminder of the large distances to be covered.

This situation has made the provision of links with outlying communities a major theme in the state's politics often coupled with policies intended to encourage trade, economic development and population growth. John Forrest's government responded to the opportunities and challenges of the gold rush of the 1890s by extensive government spending on railways, port facilities and telegraph links, and by building, dams, reservoirs and the ambitious pipeline to Kalgoorlie in the eastern goldfields.

In the first decade of the twentieth century the emphasis shifted to government support for agriculture. Most significantly, the government played a key role in the opening up of the wheat belt. Farming was supported by the construction and subsidy of railways, the creation of state farms, water searches, advice services, assisted migration and the creation of a state-owned agricultural bank with cheap loans for land improvement projects. In addition, the government lent support to the timber industry in the south west and the pastoral industry in the far north. The initiatives of the early years of the century were extended through such projects as publicly owned abattoirs, saw-mills and hotels, and all manner of agricultural marketing agencies. Moreover, the state was developed through myriad public works and road and bridge building. The mining industries also received substantial government support, including through the School of Mines and state-owned crushing batteries and laboratories. In 1917 a department of industry had been created to encourage the local production of foodstuffs, footwear and clothing. Later it turned to the more ambitious task of exploiting the state's natural resources, through support for fertilizer production and tractor manufacture. At various times the state also owned brick and engineering works.

This style of government-driven development continued through the 1920s, the depression of the 1930s, and the years immediately after the second world war. In addition, power generation, water supply, and rail services for agriculture and industry were often heavily subsidized through the pricing policies of public utilities, and the provision of land at low cost. As a result of these activities, by the mid-1950s the government was 'the largest employer in Western Australia, as well as the greatest landlord and customer' (Crowley 1960, 356).

But the 1950s and 1960s saw changes to the state's development policies as government turned to promoting large-scale extractive and processing industries. There was a switch of emphasis from development through state-owned enterprise, associated with the ALP governments of the early post-war years, to the L–NP coalition's development through joint ventures with private capital. In the words of Minister for Industrial Development and later Premier, Charles Court, it was the responsibility of the state to 'actively go out and seek the assistance of those who had the necessary finance and technical knowledge to develop these resources' (Head 1986b, 177). Charles Court believed that this was particularly true of the remote north of the state which would not be developed by private capital alone. There was also a change in the focus of development politics from supporting infrastructure for domestic agricultural, mineral and industrial activities, towards overseas markets (Head 1986b). If the older style of development was illustrated by the growth of Kwinana industrial complex to the south of Perth and the Ord River Dam scheme in the far north, the new style was shown in policies to encourage iron, alumina and nickel mining projects, and the multi-billion dollar north-west shelf gas project off the Pilbara coast (Harman and Head 1982).

The high point of government-business collaboration occurred under the Burke ALP government from 1983 to 1986 (Gallop 1986) when the commercial activities of this administration led to the label 'WA Inc' being applied to Burke's style of government (Stone 1997). The collapse of many of these commercial schemes lost West Australians hundreds of millions of dollars and the secretive, incompetent and procedurally inappropriate way in which these obligations had been acquired (WA Inc Royal Commission 1992; Stone 1993) led to the disgrace and defeat of the ALP in 1993.

The new government under Richard Court was committed not only to dismantling the discredited institutions of WA Inc, but also to adopting a new style of government. Together with other Australian governments, it adopted policies of corporatizing and privatizing state instrumentalities, and contracting out government services. This 'small government' stance meant a smaller public sector in terms of direct employment but not necessarily in terms of the regulation of social and economic activities or in terms of government outlays. As the century closed, the effect of these policies remained politically contentious and the election of the Gallop ALP government early in 2001 means that they are likely to be reviewed.

In broad terms, however, the continuing themes in West Australian government have been the provision of services to its citizens, reducing the effects of distance and isolation on those who live outside Perth, and the encouragement of economic development for the benefit of Western Australia and the wider Australian community. The rhetoric and mode of achieving these goals may have changed, but the goals persist.

Western Australia and the federation

As well as permitting the state political communities considerable autonomy in the way they govern themselves, one of the advantages of federalism is that it gives political leverage to states which feel they are suffering unduly from policies pursued by the national government. At various occasions over the last century, all states have had periods during which tension with the national government has become a major political issue, but only in Western Australia has the tension reached the stage of a popular vote for secession.

Federation caused considerable dislocation in the pattern of public finance and created a heavy dependence on the new Commonwealth for the transfer of funds. While this remained a source of friction between state and Commonwealth governments, two other issues became highly contentious because of what West Australian governments saw as the discriminatory effects of Commonwealth policies on the state. These were the tariff on manufactured goods which forced West Australians to pay more for their machinery for the benefit of factories in New South Wales and Victoria, and the combination of new industrial relations laws for maritime labour and the limitations on the use of foreign vessels, both of which greatly raised the cost of coastal shipping on which the state was heavily dependent for transport to and from the rest of Australia.

There was a series of inquiries into the special needs of Western Australia and the effect of national policies on the state which, together with similar claims from South Australia and Tasmania, led to the creation of the Commonwealth Grants Commission in 1933 (Reid 1979). This body was more an attempt at a political solution than an economic one, since it decided early in its existence that it would not compensate any state for the costs directly resulting from being part of the federation. Instead, it made grants on notional indicators of special need (Mathews and Jay 1972, 153–6).

The sense of discrimination was enhanced by the effects of the depression and the devastating effects of the fall of international prices for agricultural commodities on which most of Western Australia's wealth then depended. These factors culminated in moves for the state to secede from the Commonwealth and revert to being a self-governing dominion like New Zealand (Western Australia 1934), a movement which eventually persuaded the state government to hold a referendum on secession. When the vote was held, two-thirds of West Australians voted to secede, a message which was compromised by the election of a government which was against secession. Although the secessionist movement was eventually ended by emergence from depression and the unwillingness of the British government to agree to the request for Western Australia to secede (Besant 1990), the factors which had prompted talk of secession have not disappeared. Chief among them is the sense that West Australians are not being listened to in the framing of national policies. From this perspective, talk of secession is less a demand for autonomy than a cry for local concerns to be taken seriously by a distant national government whose concerns are too often focused on issues of importance only to the most populous components of the federation (Hiller 1987; Hiller 1989; Stevenson 1981).

In other respects, Western Australia has had periods of support for strong national government. Its voting record in constitutional referendums until the 1960s shows that it was more in favour of expanding the scope of national jurisdiction than any other state. This paradox might be explained by the heavy dependence of the state on transfers from Canberra and the view of West Australians that a strong central government was one way of checking the dominance of New South Wales and Victoria in the federation (Sharman and Stuart 1981). Since then, the state has been one of the least supportive of attempts by the national government to alter the Constitution, perhaps explained by the state's economic growth and a perception of Canberra as an impediment rather than a facilitator of the state's growth.

Conclusion

The epithet 'Cinderella state' has been applied to Western Australia because of its transition from a community which struggled to survive, to one of the wealthier components of the federation (Crowley 1960, 407). This transformation has been accomplished in large part because of the discovery of natural resources which have been in demand by the rest of the world. Even though most of these projects have been driven by private capital, their success has been dependent on the infrastructure and administrative framework which can only be provided by government. From the first exploitation of gold in the 1890s to the continuing north-west shelf gas project initiated in the 1970s, governments have been both the facilitators and beneficiaries of the economic growth that has followed these developments. Governments may not be as directly involved in building plant and owning infrastructure as they were, but their regulatory role has, if anything, increased. The protection of the environment, the recognition of Aboriginal land rights, and the ever-growing list of health and safety concerns are all matters for which governments have acquired responsibility.

If West Australian governments have been auxiliaries in the process of economic development, they have had a primary role in dealing with the needs and aspirations of its citizens. In a perverse way, the isolation of the state has been of major assistance. It has helped to weld together a disparate and largely immigrant community through a shared sense of distance from the rest of Australia and the danger of neglect of the state's interests by a distant national government. The same factors that have made West Australian sporting teams disproportionately successful have been mobilized by both major political groupings to assert the distinctive needs of the state and the right of the West Australian political community to make rules which suit its priorities. Even after the revelation of major shortcomings in the state government in the 1980s, West Australians still trusted their state government more than the one in Canberra (Denemark and Sharman 1994).

This has not meant that all has been peaceful in politics within the state; the political contest has been vigorous and strongly shaped by rivalries between Labor and non-Labor parties. But the pattern of representation, more by accident than by design, has ensured a rough balance between the two largest party groupings. This and the moderating effect of strong bicameralism coupled with fifty years of economic growth has meant that the political system has not had to cope with highly divisive issues. This may change in response to the problems created by the growth of population, particularly in Perth and the south-west corner of the state, the degradation of soil and water, climate change, and the vagaries of globalization and patterns of national and international trade. But the record to date has been that the West Australian political and institutional system is highly resilient and will deal with new issues as just another variation on the politics of coping with the competing demands of its citizens and the idiosyncrasies of its geography and natural endowments.

Chapter

9

Australian Capital Territory

John Warhurst[1]

The Australian Capital Territory (ACT), with a population of 310 000, is the newest and geographically smallest of the nine self-governing political jurisdictions in Australia. But the government and politics of Canberra as the national capital have already been the subject of considerable analysis (see, in general, Pettit 1998; Halligan and Wettenhall 2000b).

The territory achieved self-government from the Commonwealth of Australia in the *Australian Capital Territory (Self-Government) Act* of 1988, following a lengthy transitional period (Grundy et al. 1996; Juddery 1989). The first ACT government was appointed following the first territory elections in February 1989.

There was considerable opposition to self-government before it was finally achieved (Lindell 1992; Follett 1997). The community feared an increased taxation burden if financial responsibilities were devolved from the Commonwealth government. In 1978 an overwhelming majority (62.7 per cent) in a Commonwealth government-sponsored plebiscite preferred the existing arrangements to either self-government or municipal government.

The ACT has other distinguishing features. It is virtually the city-state of Canberra: the national capital and the seat of national government (Wettenhall 1998a). It contains the national political institutions of Commonwealth parliament, government, public service and High Court. It is still a public service town, despite cuts to public service numbers. But since 1998 the private sector has been larger than the public sector (54 per cent of wage and salary earners in 1999).

Nevertheless, the Commonwealth government is the major employer and Canberra is, as a consequence, a distinctively middle-class residential community. Average weekly earnings are well above the national average. In 2000 they were $808 per week compared to the national average of $734 (ABS 2000a).

It is the only Australian jurisdiction that is completely enclosed within the boundaries of another jurisdiction, the state of New South Wales. Some of its workforce lives in neighbouring New South Wales and as much as 20 per cent of ACT services are utilized by non-residents. In recognition of its place as a regional centre, a larger area with 50 000 people is designated as the Australian Capital Region (Pettit 1998, 25; Birtles 2000).

The legislature is the Legislative Assembly. There is no upper house of parliament. There is also no local government within the ACT with the Legislative Assembly performing both territory and local government functions. The ACT also elects two members of the House of Representatives and two senators to the Commonwealth parliament. As a consequence, a considerably larger than usual representative burden falls on the members of the Assembly. The role of head of state is performed officially by the governor-general, but this occurs only rarely. In practice the chief minister, the territory equivalent of a state premier, is both head of government and head of state. This has led to the suggestion that the ACT, alone among Australian jurisdictions, is already a de facto republic (Lindell 1992; Carnell 1999, 18).

In its short history of self-government, the ACT has achieved some distinction. As one of the two Australian jurisdictions that elects its lower house by proportional representation, it has an unbroken record, after five elections, of minority government. The characteristic style of its government has been described as 'coalition-building, minority government and plural decision-making' (Wettenhall 1998a, 14). It has a reputation for a liberal approach to social issues, such as addictive drug-taking and euthanasia. It has flirted with the idea of introducing citizen-initiated referendums (Williams and Chin 2000, 31–2) and an independent has held a cabinet post. Two of its six chief ministers, Rosemary Follett and Kate Carnell, have been female, their terms in office accounting for the great bulk of the period since 1989.

From creation to self-government

The ACT was created under section 125 of the Commonwealth Constitution which provides for the creation of a seat of government in New South Wales, but at least 100 miles from Sydney (Atkins 1978). In

1911 the new and largely unpopulated territory was transferred to the Commonwealth from NSW jurisdiction. In 1915 Jervis Bay, on the NSW coast, was added to the ACT. In 1927, the Commonwealth parliament moved from Melbourne, where it had been sitting since federation in 1901, to a new parliament house in Canberra.

The administration of the territory was attached to such departments as home affairs, interior or territories and was usually the responsibility of a relatively junior Commonwealth minister. As Canberra grew, the responsibility became more important. After the prime minister, Sir Robert Menzies, decided to give priority to Canberra's development through the transfer of all remaining Commonwealth departments from Melbourne, he created the National Capital Development Commission (NCDC) on 1 March 1958 (Grundy et al. 1996, 2). The NCDC, with responsibility for all aspects of the planning of Canberra's development, became the key agency in matters concerning the ACT. It was perceived by local citizens as 'a major, if not the, principal organ of territorial government' (Grundy et al. 1996, 6). The NCDC controlled planning and land development in a time of rapid population growth resulting from the arrival of public servants in the 1960s and 1970s.

Representation of ACT citizens began controversially with the 1929 election of one person to the three-member Federal Capital Commission. From 1930 until 1970 members were elected to the partly-elected Advisory Council, beginning with three and ending with eight. From 1974 until 1982, all eighteen members were elected to a Legislative Assembly. (The Legislative Assembly became the House of Assembly on 2 June 1979.) The Assembly ceased to exist on 30 June 1986. Notwithstanding their titles, neither had law-making power, and both performed solely advisory roles (Grundy et al. 1996: appendix 2 lists all elected representatives).

After thirty-eight years without representation in the Commonwealth Parliament, representation for the residents of Canberra began at the December 1949 House of Representatives election with a single member, initially with voting rights restricted to territory matters. Jim Fraser (Labor) held this seat from 1951 until his death in 1970. From May 1974 population growth led to two (and briefly three) ACT electorates. Then, from the December 1975 elections, the ACT was awarded two Senate places although with more limited tenure than senators from the states.

The political complexion of the ACT during these years was superficially Labor. Atkins (1978, 12) comments that 'for more than twenty years Canberra was regarded as a Labor Party stronghold'. But, as she suggests, this may have partly been a consequence of opposition to the long period of coalition government at the Commonwealth level from 1949 to 1972. Once Labor won federal office, the position of anti-Labor parties began to improve. At the first election for the Legislative Assembly in September 1974, Labor won only four of the eighteen seats to the Liberals' eleven (together with five independents and two Australia Party members). In addition, Labor lost one of its two House of Representatives seats in the December 1975 anti-government swing that also saw the Liberal senator, John Knight, outpoll his Labor rival (see also Juddery 1983). According to a 1975 study of the ACT electorate as reported by Atkins, 'the ACT had not been a Labor Party stronghold, in fact not a party stronghold at all, but a community with strong potential support for independents' (Greg Snider, quoted in Atkins 1978, 14).

Constitutional features

The ACT's constitutional system is laid out in the *Australian Capital Territory (Self-Government) Act* of 1988, and in subsequent amendments to that Act (for a summary see Pettit 1998, 77–9; also Lindell 1992). This document is an Act of the Commonwealth parliament. It confers on the Legislative Assembly the 'power to make laws for the peace, order and good government of the territory'.

Under the Act, the Assembly has two types of limitations on its power. The first includes limitations shared with the states as the components of a federal system. The second set relates to the absence of constitutional guarantees for the existence of self-government for the territory or for the protection of its government or jurisdiction. Under section 29 of the Act, the Commonwealth parliament may exempt its own members and, more importantly, the parliamentary precincts from enactments of the Assembly. Of greater significance, the Commonwealth parliament may override the ACT Constitution whenever it wishes to do so. It did this in 1997 to preclude a territory from enacting euthanasia legislation. This was the consequence of a strong anti-euthanasia lobby which led to the passage of a private member's bill through the Commonwealth parliament to override the Northern Territory's euthanasia legislation. The Commonwealth intervened again in 2000 to limit territory legislation on leasehold land.

A distinguishing feature of the ACT system of government is the absence of a governor or an administrator as the formal source of executive power within the ACT system of parliamentary self-government. In the absence of such an office, the Assembly, at its first meeting after an election and after having elected its presiding officers, elects a chief minister as head of government. The chief minister, in turn, may appoint up to four other ministers. The chief minister signs all ACT legislation into law (Carnell 1999, 18).

The Assembly sits for a three-year fixed term but the chief minister can be dismissed by a vote of no confidence. In such a circumstance an election must be held within ninety days. The governor-general, acting on the advice of the Commonwealth government, can disallow an Assembly enactment within six months. The governor-general can also, in situations in which the Assembly is not managing its affairs effectively, dissolve the Assembly and appoint a commissioner. But an election must still be held within ninety days.

The Assembly has thus far managed its affairs without the intervention of the governor-general. For instance, it has twice managed changes of government, in December 1989 and June 1991, when chief ministers have lost the confidence of the Assembly. It has also managed to survive a mini constitutional crisis in mid-2000 when the budget was initially rejected because it provided funding for a heroin-injecting room, before the government engineered a compromise with independents (Bennett 2000a; Centenera 2000; Clack 2000; Hull 2000).

Electoral and party systems

The ACT Assembly contains seventeen members. They represent three electorates: Brindabella (five members) in the south; Molonglo (seven) in the centre; and Ginninderra in the north-west of the territory (five). The Assembly sits for a fixed three-year term with elections initially held on the third Saturday in February before being moved to October from 2001 onwards.

The five Legislative Assembly elections have been conducted under proportional representation. Initially, in 1989, a modified D'Hondt method was used but proved to be so cumbersome (it was two months before the result was finalized) that it had to be modified further for the 1992 election at which time the Hare–Clark variant of proportional representation by the single transferable vote was supported by an advisory plebiscite. Since then, Hare–Clark has been the preferred method. In 1995 it was enshrined in the Constitution by referendum.

Proportional representation has weakened the influence of the major parties, Labor and Liberal, and played a part in the representation of minor parties and independents in the Assembly. The highest vote for the two major parties combined has been 73.4 per cent in 2001, after falling to its lowest total of 65.4 per cent in 1998.

The election results are displayed in figure 9.1 (see also Halligan and Wettenhall 2000b, 20). At the first election on 4 March 1989 five parties and groups shared the success. The most distinctive feature was the relatively low vote for the major parties and the strikingly high votes for opponents of self-government and some other groups. The Australian Labor Party received the strongest support but its 22.82 per cent won it only five seats. The Liberal Party's 14.87 per cent won it four seats. The No Self Government Party won three seats (11.47 per cent), the Residents Rally (opposed to certain planning decisions and to a Canberra casino) four seats (9.62 per cent), and the Abolish Self Government Coalition one seat (7.50 per cent). Labor, after considering a coalition, formed a minority government, later losing it after seven months, and later still regaining it.

The second election on 15 February 1992 saw the return of the minority Labor government and some consolidation towards a two-party system. Labor achieved close to a majority government. Its 37.3 per cent share of the vote won it eight of the seventeen seats. The Liberal opposition won six seats (27.2 per cent) and the Michael Moore Independent Group, led by a former member of the Residents Rally, won two seats (5.24 per cent). The Abolish Self Government Coalition won one seat (6.61 per cent), but organized anti-self-government sentiment was fading.

The third election on 18 February 1995 led to a change of government. For the first time the Liberals polled higher than Labor. The Liberals (40.5 per cent) won seven seats to six by Labor (31.6 per cent). The ACT Greens, standing for the first time, won two seats (9.1 per cent). Michael Moore was returned (7.1 per cent for his Independent Group), and he was joined by another independent, Paul Osborne (5.6 per cent).

The Liberals retained their position as the minority government in the fourth election on 21 February 1998 against the odds, given that the Howard Liberal–National Party coalition government was now in office at the federal level (Newman 1998). They maintained seven seats to the Labor Party's six. Both major parties, especially Labor, lost ground to minor parties and independents. The ACT Greens lost one of their seats to a second Osborne Independent, while Moore and Osborne were both returned.

At the most recent election on 20 October 2001, the Labor Party increased its vote share by 14 per cent to win 41.7 per cent of the vote, the highest vote share won by any party since self-government. This gave the party eight seats and the ability to form a minority government supported by the ACT Greens member. This election was also notable for the failure of any independent candidates to gain election.

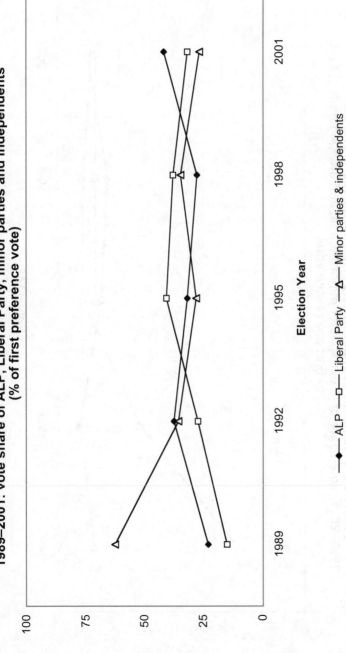

Figure 9.1 Australian Capital Territory Assembly, general elections
1989–2001: vote share of ALP, Liberal Party, minor parties and independents
(% of first preference vote)

Source: calculated from the Australian Government and Politics Project database, University of Western Australia.

Figure 9.2 Australian Capital Territory Assembly, general elections 1989–2001: vote share of Greens, other minor parties, and independents (% of first preference vote)

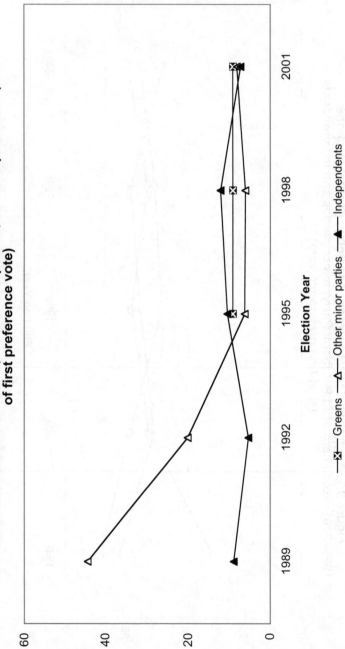

Source: calculated from the Australian Government and Politics Project database, University of Western Australia.

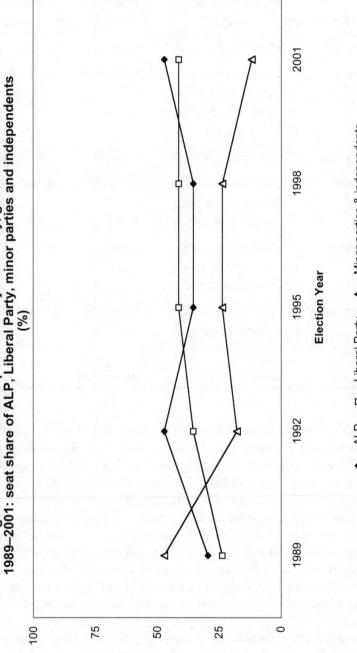

Figure 9.3 Australian Capital Territory Assembly, general elections 1989–2001: seat share of ALP, Liberal Party, minor parties and independents (%)

Source: calculated from the Australian Government and Politics Project database, University of Western Australia.

Table 9.1 Australian Capital Territory: chief ministers, parties in government, parliamentary support for governments and periods in office, 1989–2001

Chief Minister	Party and parliamentary support	Start of period in office	End of period in office
Rosemary Follett	ALP minority government	11 May 1989	5 December 1989
Trevor Kaine	Liberal Party, Residents Rally and No Self-Government Party coalition minority government	5 December 1989	6 June 1991
Rosemary Follett	ALP minority government	6 June 1991	9 March 1995
Kate Carnell	Liberal Party and Moore Independents coalition minority government	9 March 1995	27 April 1998
Kate Carnell	Liberal Party and Moore Independent Group coalition minority government	27 April 1998	18 October 2000
Gary Humphries	Liberal Party and Moore Independents coalition minority government	18 October 2000	12 November 2001
Jon Stanhope	ALP minority government	12 November 2001	

The anti-major party tenor of the electoral system has been assisted by a number of electoral rules, all copied from Tasmania at the time of the 1995 referendum on the electoral system. They include the prohibition on the distribution of how-to-vote cards within 100 metres of a polling booth; the use of Robson rotation to vary the order in which party candidates appear on the ballot paper; and the absence of 'above the line' voting so that voters are required to rank candidates in their own preferred order rather than one predetermined by a party. These provisions have been the subject of controversy and the Pettit Report recommended that how-to-vote cards be available to voters in each polling place, even if they are not allowed to be distributed outside (Pettit 2000, 41).

Until the 2001 election, the Labor Party had not been as successful in the ACT jurisdiction as Federal voting figures would lead one to expect. Labor has continued to dominate Federal House of Representatives representation since self-government in 1989, only suffering a single defeat in the 1995 by-election for the seat of Canberra (Bennett 1997). Yet it has failed to translate this support into a majority in the Assembly (Warhurst 2000). Prior to 1995 it was the dominant party but shared time in office with the Liberal Party. Since 1995 it was in opposition, until it regained office in 2001.

Labor's relatively poor performance has been a consequence both of its own limitations and of its failure to match the personality of Kate Carnell, Liberal chief minister from 1995 to 2000. As measured by her election results, Carnell has been the most popular political figure in the ACT since 1995. Carnell's triumph in personality politics enabled her to develop an image distinct from that of her Federal counterparts whose success in March 1996 threatened her prospects of re-election. Not only did John Howard's government institute cuts to the public service but Howard himself alienated Canberra's citizens by his decision to live in Sydney in preference to the prime minister's official residence in Canberra, The Lodge. Carnell distanced her administration from Howard's by clear policy differences and by running under the name of the Canberra Liberals (Hughes 1998).

ACT Labor achieved separate branch status in 1973 (Juddery 1983, 215). It is the only Australian Labor Party branch in which the Left faction has been clearly dominant. This has given the party an image and a leadership that has seemed, at times, out of character with ACT society (Warhurst 2000). Since the party's 1998 defeat, a transformation has taken place in the party's parliamentary leadership team under a new unaligned leader, Jon Stanhope, who led the party to office in 2001.

Labor's 'old Left' ideological position had weakened its position in relation to both the Liberal Party and minor parties and independents. Two types of minor parties and independents have challenged Labor. The first represent an older Catholic Labor Right. Both prominent independent Paul Osborne and Minister for Urban Services Paul Smyth (MHR for Canberra, 1995–96) come from this tradition. Osborne also benefited from being a former Canberra Raiders rugby league star.

The second represents a post-materialist, white-collar vote that has long polled well in the ACT. Canberra is a natural home for the Greens and the Australian Democrats. While the latter have been poorly organised and unsuccessful in gaining representation until 2001 despite earlier Australia Party/Democrats success prior to self-government, the Greens have been represented in the Assembly since 1995.

Government

ACT government has evolved steadily since 1989 (Follett 1992; Wettenhall 1998a; Wettenhall 1998b). The first Assembly was hindered by disunity and by the inexperience of its members. Only one of its first members had previous legislative experience (Labor's Bill Wood had served in the Queensland Legislative Assembly). They all faced a relatively clean slate as far as machinery of government was concerned.

Slowly the new political institutions took shape. The standard ministry has had four members. The first Labor ministry was led by the chief minister, Rosemary Follett. She was replaced by a loose coalition (known as the Alliance government) between the Liberals, whose leader Trevor Kaine was chief minister, and the Residents' Rally and the No Self Government Party. Follett then returned to office between 1992 and 1995.

Considerable progress in developing ACT government was made over those first six years or so (Halligan and Wettenhall 2000a, 19–23). Several public inquiries accompanied these developments. The creation of a new and separate, independent ACT public service was the largest task. This was effectively formally concluded with the passage of the *Public Sector Management Act* in 1994.

The ACT public service has aimed to be distinctive in its approach to its structures and processes and a leader in public service reform (Halligan 2000). The governments in office since 1995 have organized the public service into six departments, roughly equal to the number of ministers.

Kate Carnell's two terms of office as chief minister gave a high priority to redesigning governance structures and processes. She entered office with a declared preference for breaking down the traditional style of Westminster government in the ACT. From the time of her election as Liberal Party leader in May 1993, she had emphasized community participation and council-style government (Wettenhall 1998a, 12). Since then her preferences and initiatives have created considerable debate about ACT governance. Included among her stated aspirations was the idea of a representative regional parliament for the Australian Capital Region (Carnell 2000b, 15–16).

Carnell convened the National Capital Futures Conference in September 1997, at which various controversial suggestions were made by speakers who included the Minister for Territories and Local Government, Warwick Smith. This led to the joint ACT–Commonwealth Working Party on the Review of the Governance of the ACT, independently chaired by Professor Philip Pettit of the Australian

National University (Pettit 1998).

Pettit reported in April 1998 after the Carnell government had been re-elected. The report reached favourable conclusions: 'Broadly sketched, the view reached by the Working Party was that the structure works quite well and that it has been evolving steadily, and for the good, over the decade it has been in existence' (Pettit 1998, 10).

Among its recommendations was one for a larger assembly (twenty-one seats rather than seventeen) and a larger executive (five ministers rather than four). The former was on the grounds that the ACT population was under-represented, while the latter was on the grounds of efficiency. Shortly afterwards, Carnell expanded her ministry with the addition of the independent, Michael Moore. Under an arrangement discussed in the Pettit report and called a 'loose coalition', Moore took office as Health Minister under a set of guidelines for the circumstances under which he would maintain his independence and those under which he would be bound by cabinet solidarity (Wettenhall 1998b, 88–90). The arrangement survived under considerable strain.

At about the same time, mid-May 1998, the ACT's second chief minister, Trevor Kaine, resigned from the Liberals to become first an independent then the sole member of a new United Canberra Party. Kaine had been a minister in the first Carnell government but had made way after the 1998 elections for the new member of the Legislative Assembly, Brendan Smyth. The Assembly's operations became even more fluid as a consequence.

The 'minoritarian' character (Moon 1995) of ACT governments has meant an important role for the Assembly, especially Assembly committees. The standing and select committees have played an 'active and influential role' in performing 'advisory-cum-investigatory' functions (Pettit 1998, 21–2; also Halligan and Wettenhall 2000a, 29). Carnell proposed after the 1998 elections that the executive and the cross-benches should be linked more closely by three executive committees, chaired by non-government members who would have a vote in cabinet on some items (Wettenhall 1998b, 87). The idea was rejected and Pettit's recommendation of an 'agency tracking' committee system that mirrored the distribution of portfolios was adopted instead (Pettit 1998, 50).

The general policy style of ACT government has been liberal. From 1995 to 2000 Carnell was the dominant figure and she traded on her popularity to locate the government closer to the centre of the political spectrum than the majority of her otherwise conservative party room would wish. She emphasized diversification of the ACT economy, in the face of Commonwealth public service cuts, and tourism-centred economic development. As part of the latter strategy, she committed expenditure to major sporting facilities, such as Bruce Stadium, in a somewhat secretive style that ultimately contributed to her political undoing in October 2000 (Harris 2000; Bennett 2000b). At the turn of the century, as Carnell's replacement as chief minister, Gary Humphries, held office with the support of socially conservative independent members of the Legislative Assembly, this liberal policy tradition was in the balance.

Conclusion

The ACT ended the twentieth century with a number of governance issues unresolved. The range of ACT government functions is likely to extend to include responsibility for a prison and an autonomous police force. There have been negotiations about the former and pressure to separate the police from the Australian Federal Police. Such a further extension of functions may assist to consolidate popular respect for the ACT government, which still lacks legitimacy in the eyes of important figures in the Canberra community. Popular visibility would be assisted if members of the Legislative Assembly were provided with offices in their electorate in addition to those in the Assembly building in central Canberra. This orthodox arrangement was recommended by the Pettit report (Pettit 1998, 58), and adopted by Labor leader, Stanhope, prior to the 2001 election.

The governance situation is fluid. Some of these issues, several of which remain the concern of Philip Pettit (Pettit 2000), relate to questions of ACT structure and process narrowly defined. Among these concerns is the problem of popular access to government in the ACT. ACT citizens are under-represented by a 17-person Assembly. The ratio of members to electors is about 1:14 000 compared to the Australian average of about 1:2250. Yet the politics of the size of the Assembly is unlikely to lead to a larger assembly because it is difficult to argue for more politicians in the present climate of opinion (Armitage 2000; *Canberra Times* 2000; Kirschbaum 2000). However, ACT Greens' MLA, Kerrie Tucker, did so in February 2000.

A second issue relates to the place of the ACT in its region. Carnell was particularly committed to Capital regionalism, implemented through the Regional Leaders Forum (Carnell 2000a). It is unclear whether future leadership will share her enthusiasm, but external relations will continue to develop with experience (Wettenhall 1998c). The ACT population will continue to overflow its boundaries. Reconsideration of those boundaries by the Commonwealth and New South Wales should be on the agenda for the twenty-first century.

A third issue relates to the evolution of local government structures within the ACT, initially perhaps through community councils but ultimately in the form of fully fledged local government. Such an eventuality would alter the functions of the Assembly.

The final issue relates to the characteristic ACT styles of governance. 'Coalition building, minority government and plural decision-making', Wettenhall speculates, 'come naturally' (Wettenhall 1998a, 14). Such speculation depends on the view that it is not just the proportional representation electoral system but something inherent in the ACT community that has produced minority government. That will only be tested by time as five elections is too small a sample on which to reach conclusions with any certainty. A majority government is not impossible in the ACT. But it would depend on the two major parties developing stronger party organization and becoming more substantial forces within the ACT community. To do this, they need to attract more highly regarded members of the community to their ranks in the Assembly. Should this occur, then the consensus and coalition-building behaviour evident to date within the Assembly would, in all likelihood, change.

Northern Territory

Dean Jaensch

The process of the constitutional development of the Northern Territory as a separate political entity began in 1863, when the Colonial Office of Great Britain vested control of the Northern Territory in the government of South Australia. In 1888 the South Australian government constituted the territory as a single, two-member electoral district for the South Australia House of Assembly, and with representation in the Legislative Council. By 1902 the South Australian government felt that the territory was too great a drain on the finances of the state and, after nine years of negotiation, the Commonwealth took over the administration of the Northern Territory.

For the next thirty-six years, from 1911 to 1947, the Northern Territory was governed directly by the Commonwealth, under the control of the Minister for External Affairs – a situation which did not please Territorians. Local authority was exercised by an administrator who acted on instructions from the Commonwealth. Territorians had no representative participation in their own affairs. In 1931 the Scullin Labor government introduced a bill for an ordinance-making Legislative Council for the territory, equivalent to the Councils in the colonies in the period 1850 to 1857. But even this minor reform was rejected by the Liberal–Country majority in the Senate, partly because the only political organization in the territory at the time was Labor.

In 1947 the Chifley Labor government passed an Act to establish a Legislative Council in the Territory 'to confer a measure of self-government on the residents of the Northern Territory'. But the 'measure' was limited in three important ways: it was a hybrid Council of seven

appointed members and six elected members, hence government dominated; its legislative authority was limited to a power to pass ordinances
which were then subject to the veto of the Commonwealth; and the
administrator of the territory had both a deliberative and a casting vote
in the Council. The reason for the qualifications established by the
Commonwealth was that 'the Northern Territory is not self-supporting
financially, and the greater part of the expenditure on its development
must be provided by the Commonwealth' (Walker 1986, 2–3). The
territory certainly was a small polity in 1947. At the first elections for
the Council, the total enrolment was only 4443 adult (white) citizens.
These reasons continued through the next half-century (Heatley 1979)
as the constitutional position and development of the territory
continued to be a burning issue for Territorians, coming to a head in the
debates about statehood from the early 1970s.

In 1968 the elected membership of the Council became a majority,
and this increased the pressures from territory residents for further
constitutional reform. In 1973 the Whitlam Labor government established a joint committee of the federal parliament to plan for a setting
up of a legislative assembly in 1974. But, in a style which Territorians
would claim has been a consistent pattern, the Commonwealth
Committee reported after the new assembly had been designed,
confirmed and elected. The Legislative Assembly of nineteen members
had all of the structures and processes of a representative parliament,
but its powers remained the same as those of the previous Legislative
Council. In 1978, however, after protracted negotiations with the
Fraser Liberal government, the territory was granted self-government
(Heatley 1990).

The structure of government

This new self-government was, however, one of a severely limited form
of self-government. At federation, the states which comprise the
Australian federation retained authority on a wide range of matters, but
the Northern Territory's powers were much more restricted. The
transfer of state-like functions excluded three policy areas which the
Northern Territory dearly wanted to control: Aboriginal affairs,
national parks, and uranium mining and treatment. In addition, the
Assembly's powers were restricted by the oversight and, if desired,
the veto of the Commonwealth. The transfer of powers under territory
self-government also did not restrict the Commonwealth from enacting
laws to cover the territory on any issue, including those which were
transferred to the territory government. A recent example was the

territory's legislation on voluntary euthanasia which was over-ridden by the Commonwealth parliament. And the Northern Territory Constitution remains an Act of the Commonwealth parliament, and can only be amended by the Commonwealth.

It was not surprising, then, that statehood was high on the agenda of the territory. But this remained linked to the question of capacity – the question of the ability of the territory government to fund expenditure from its own revenues. In 1975 caretaker Prime Minister Fraser seemed to pre-empt the issue when he told Territorians during the federal election campaign that he was committed to grant statehood in five years. Nothing eventuated. By the mid-1980s the pressure for statehood increased with bipartisan support and, at the 1998 federal election, the territory voted in a referendum for a Constitution. Despite years of planning and drafting by an Assembly Committee, the Country Liberal Party (CLP) government led by Shane Stone put its own radically different draft to the people, with the result that the referendum was narrowly defeated. In 2002 the Northern Territory remained in a constitutional limbo; self-government, but not statehood.

The territory's constitutional structure in 2002 included all of the components of the federal and state systems. Formal executive authority rests with an administrator, whose powers are equivalent to a state governor, with one important difference. Under the 1978 Act granting self-government, the administrator can reserve any proposed law passed by the Legislative Assembly 'for the Governor-General's pleasure', that is, for the consideration of the federal government.

The operation of the territory cabinet, public service and other government agencies is similar to the states. Before 1974 the Northern Territory public service was essentially an arm of the federal service. Secondment to the territory from elsewhere in Australia was the normal procedure for recruitment, resulting in rapid turnover of personnel and a service which reflected the views of the Commonwealth. After the inauguration of the Assembly, and especially after self-government in 1978, the public service has become very much territorian in personnel and in focus. Local government has been established in the major urban centres.

Given that about one quarter of the population of the Northern Territory is Aboriginal, much of the political debate concerns Aboriginal policy and, in this, Aboriginal groups play a major role. Aboriginal Land Councils claim to represent and speak for the broad Aboriginal population on matters concerning government policy. But there is often disagreement between the land councils, and the CLP government in power until 2001, while supporting the development of quasi-local government structures in Aboriginal areas in the form of community councils, did not bring Aboriginal groups into the formal structure of government. This may have been due to the tendency for Aboriginal groups to be closer to the Australian Labor Party (ALP) than the CLP.

Representation, parties and the electoral system

The issue of representation has been a matter of deep concern and impassioned debate in the Northern Territory for over a hundred years. It remains a contentious issue within the debates about statehood. The citizens of the territory first received some representation in 1890 when adult males, and, after 1893, adults, voted for two representatives in the South Australian House of Assembly. In 1901 Territorians also received a Commonwealth franchise, incorporated in the electorate of Grey. With the transfer of the territory to the Commonwealth in 1911, all parliamentary franchises were revoked. In 1922 the territory was allowed one member in the House of Representatives but, for fourteen years, with no speaking or voting rights. In 1936 this was extended to a right to speak and, in the limited area of motions to disallow regulations concerning the territory, to vote. In 1947 the formation of the Legislative Council provided some representation but this did little to reduce the sense that Territorians were, as the independent member of the House of Representatives for the territory described it, like 'the inhabitants of Siberian Russia or the inmates of a gaol'.

The inauguration of the Northern Territory Legislative Assembly in 1974 with a membership of only nineteen produced the smallest legislature and the least populous electoral districts in Australia. At the 1974 election the mean enrolment was only 2054. Following self-government in 1978 the Assembly was increased to twenty-five members.

Parties

In 2002 the Territory Assembly resembles other parliaments in Australia: governments and oppositions are formed by political parties; most bills and debates in the Assembly have their genesis in party policies and programs; and parties dominate the electoral processes. But this is a recent development. Where political parties became dominant in state and federal politics by the end of the first decade of federation, this was not the case in the territory.

In the period 1890 to 1911 the differences of opinion, interests and ideology which elsewhere were being shaped into political parties had little significance or impact in the territory. Its economy was rudimentary, its population was small and dispersed, and it was not self-administering. From 1922, when some representation was restored, the sole representative in Canberra, Harold Nelson, was a member of the ALP, but the party had no established organization in the territory. His successor, Adair Blain (1934–49), was an independent.

For the first twenty years of the Legislative Council, the only party involvement came from the labour movement, and even there, the idiosyncrasy of the territory came to the fore. Where Labor elsewhere had, from the beginning, been the disciplined political wing of the union movement, the party in the territory from 1947 to 1968 was divided between various components of labour. Elections saw separate candidates from the Labor Party, from independent Labor candidates, and from the North Australia Workers Union (see Jaensch 1990). But, despite its deep and bitter internal divisions, Labor was the only organized political force.

This party monopoly was tested in 1951 when the Country Party nominated one candidate, and in 1965 when a short-lived North Australia Party nominated candidates. In 1966 the first move towards a competitive party system came when the Country Party nominated Sam Calder to contest the federal election. This sparked the Liberal Party to form a local branch, but with little success. From 1966 to 1974 the competition between Labor and Country parties dominated territory politics, with the latter dominant. In the run-up to the first election for the Assembly, the Liberal Party re-formed, but with little welcome from the Country Party, which spoke of the impossibility of having two free-enterprise parties in the territory. On the eve of the election the two parties united to form a unique Country Liberal Party (CLP), which dominated Northern Territory elections until 2001. In 1987, with the support of Joh Bjelke-Petersen, the National Party attempted to break into the increasingly dominant two-party system, but won only one seat.

There have been some attempts by other parties to intervene. In the 1977 election the Progress Party eroded CLP support and won 10 per cent of the votes, but then disappeared. The Australian Democrats regularly contest territory elections; Green parties, Christian Democrats, Marijuana Party, Communist Party, Democratic Socialists and other mini-parties have attempted to intervene, but with little success. Independents, however, have won at least one seat at seven of the nine elections since 1974.

By 1994 the two major parties, CLP and Labor, dominated the votes, the seats and the Assembly, to the point where the 1997 election

Figure 10.1 Northern Territory Legislative Assembly, general elections
1974–2001: vote share of ALP, Country Liberal Party, National Party, and
minor parties (% of first preference vote)

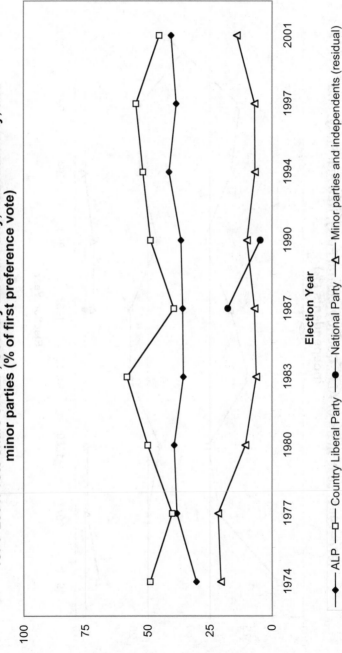

Source: calculated from the Australian Government and Politics Project database, University of Western Australia.

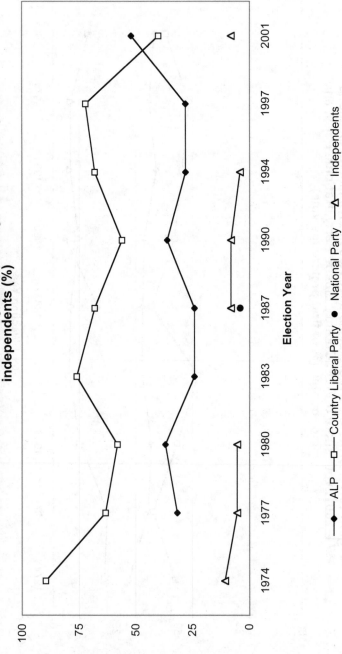

Figure 10.2 Northern Territory Legislative Assembly, general elections 1974–2001: seat share of ALP, Country Liberal Party, National Party, and independents (%)

Source: calculated from the Australian Government and Politics Project database, University of Western Australia.

saw the major parties win over 93 per cent of the votes, and win all of the seats for the first time. But the unique context of the territory still contained elements which could produce volatility, even a return to the situation in the 1970s and early 1980s when independents had strong support. The small population of the electoral districts, the resultant close contact between candidates and voters, the high proportions of Aborigines in a significant number of outback electorates, and the (to date unsuccessful) attempts to form Aboriginal parties, have the potential to undermine a party duopoly of representation.

This happened in the 2001 election. For a quarter of a century, the CLP had dominated the Northern Territory, in government, elections and policies. It had been the government since the first election in 1974. It was virtually unbeatable in elections, consistently winning a large majority of votes and seats in the urban centres – thus achieving a majority of seats in the Assembly – and it won one or two seats in each election in the Aboriginal-dominated outback areas. The major economic and business interests and groups supported the CLP. The public service had never worked under any other party. As a result, the policies put into place in the territory were exclusively CLP policies until 2001.

One reason for the CLP domination of a clear majority of the electoral districts for twenty-five years was their small population and the consequent advantage to incumbent members. In 1997, even after major population growth in the territory, the mean enrolment was only 4075. There has been a corresponding low turnover of seats, especially in the urban areas, since the first two elections in 1974 and 1977.

A more important reason for the CLP hegemony from 1974 to 2001 was the unique political division in the territory. Elsewhere in Australia the urban areas are essentially contests between the Labor and Liberal parties, and the rural areas are strongly non-Labor. In the territory, with the outback electorates containing a large proportion of Aboriginal voters, this pattern is reversed. The Aboriginal vote is far from a bloc vote for Labor, but the party has won a majority of the outback seats in all elections since 1974. The urban and some of the mixed outback–urban electoral districts were the stronghold of the CLP. The issue of race is a powerful component of territory politics, and of territory elections, and the CLP is consistently accused of playing the race card in its campaigns. The *Northern Territory News*, not noted for a pro-Labor position, commented at the 1997 election that:

> The CLP brings complex native title and land rights issues down to the lowest common denominator. Simply put, the CLP's translation is: 'Aborigines want your parks, your beaches, your fishing

spots, your homes'. History shows this tack is successful. Labor must distance itself from the land councils and their ambit claims. (1 September 1997)

Until the 2001 election, tensions within the Labor Party over Aboriginal policy were one of the major factors limiting the ability of the party to win government.

Electoral system

For the first two elections for the Assembly, the electoral structures and processes were set by the Commonwealth government. In 1978, with self-government, the territory won control of its election system. In 1974 the Commonwealth Parliamentary Joint Committee had debated election systems at length, especially one proposal that the territory would be best served by a multimember system of proportional representation allowing for representation of both urban and outback, and offering an improved opportunity for Aboriginal candidates. This was rejected as it would be 'too complicated', and that tribal and language barriers 'would create greater difficulties for Aboriginals voting for Aboriginal candidates' (Commonwealth Parliament, Joint Committee 1974, 15). From the beginning, then, the electoral system has been based on single-member electoral districts which, the committee believed, would 'better represent the scattered population centres that typify the Territory, and the diverse interests of these centres', and on compulsory preferential voting (the alternative vote).

Aborigines were granted full voting rights from the first election for the Assembly in 1974, at first with voluntary enrolment and voluntary voting; from 1983 compulsory enrolment and voting applied. To provide equal electoral opportunity for Aboriginal communities and for all citizens of the sparsely-settled outback, the territory was in the forefront in the use of mobile polling booths at both federal and territory elections after 1980.

Granting a full franchise to Aborigines, especially with compulsory voting, established an obligation on government for the provision of an electoral education program which would offer Aborigines the opportunity to obtain information on elections and voting. The Aboriginal Electoral Information Programme had been established in 1979 and, under its current name of Aboriginal Electoral Information Service, plays a major role in territory elections.

Establishing the electoral geography for the Territory's first election required facing up to a number of difficulties. There was a lack of an accurate census of Aboriginal communities, and a very mobile population in both urban and outback areas. The initial distribution established eleven of the nineteen electorates as urban, with nine in Darwin and two in Alice Springs. Eight electorates covered the remainder of the territory. Four had substantial urban components: Stuart (part Alice Springs), Nhulunbuy, Elsey (Katherine), and Barkly (Tennant Creek). Since then, the rapid population growth in the territory, and better means of dealing with the mobile population, has resulted in a number of redistributions, all of which have retained the basic division of urban, mixed and outback electoral districts. Given the nature of the first election, it is not surprising that the turnout was relatively low; 75 per cent for the territory overall, and 63 per cent in the rural areas. By 1997 the turnout was 79 per cent and 71 per cent respectively.

In the run-up to the 1974 election there had been some suggestion that Aboriginal voters would be unable to vote correctly, and hence there would be a high informal vote in the outback. In the event, the mean informal vote was 5.1 per cent, with the highest levels in both the rural electoral district of Arnhem (overwhelmingly Aboriginal) and Gillen (overwhelmingly non-Aboriginal). In succeeding elections, the levels of informal voting have not been significantly different from elsewhere in Australia, although it was still almost 8 per cent in the outback electoral districts in 1997.

Government and parliament

The unbroken hold of the CLP on government over twenty-eight years was approaching the record term of thirty-three years set by the Liberal Party in South Australia (from 1932 to 1965). From 1974 to 1978 the title of the leader of government was majority leader; since then the title has been chief minister, and in the period since 1974 seven men and one woman have filled the position. One, Goff Letts, lost his seat in the 1977 election. Two – Ian Tuxworth (1983–86) and Steve Hatton (1986–98) – had their terms shortened as a result of party divisions within the CLP. Shane Stone (1995–99) resigned following the defeat of the 1998 referendum on his draft of a constitution for statehood for the territory.

The number of ministers varied between a low of five in the first Everingham ministry to a high of nine. Given that the tasks which face the territory ministry are equivalent to a ministry in a state, the workloads carried by a small number of Territory ministers would be high. As Weller and Sanders (1982, 5) put it:

> The Territory government ... is in reality a state government in the
> Australian federation even if it is a small one. Small, in this situa-
> tion, may create heavier demands on ministers rather than alle-
> viate them ... The small size of the parliament and ministry may
> therefore increase rather than decrease the workload of ministers.

Because of the relatively small cabinet, portfolio responsibilities are
broader than in most states, but generally equivalent to Tasmania
which also has only twenty-five members in its lower house. A typical
ministry of eight ministers might have the following portfolio responsibilities: chief minister; treasurer; attorney-general; mines and energy;
correctional services; community development; education; health;
youth; sports; recreation; ethnic affairs; industry; small business;
tourism; primary production; conservation; ports; fisheries; lands;
transport; works; housing.

The hegemony of the CLP in the electorate over nearly thirty years
developed an attitude of confidence in the government which brought
allegations of arrogance and contempt for the parliamentary process,
not only from the opposition, but from the local media, which could
not be described as a friend of Labor. For example, the *Northern
Territory News* of 26 March 1986 stated: 'The NT [CLP] government
has made a mockery of Parliament and a travesty of democratic
convention ... That may be convenient and comfortable, but it is not
democracy'. In 1981 Gordon Reid presented a paper to a 'Small is
Beautiful' conference on territory politics in which he made the
following predictions (1981, 74):

> The power of the Territory's Legislative Assembly to participate
> in the making of legislation ... will be allowed to atrophy through
> disuse ... Backbench members of the Assembly will be dissuaded
> ... from introducing proposed laws and amendments to execu-
> tive-initiated proposed laws. The idea of standing committees to
> scrutinise proposed legislation will be unacceptable to the execu-
> tive ministers ... The elected Assembly will meet infrequently on
> the grounds that the minister must get on with the responsibili-
> ties of governing. The elected Assembly will be dissuaded from
> participating in matters of revenue raising and expenditure on the
> grounds that these are ministerial prerogatives.

All of these predictions proved correct. In a similar fashion,
Heatley's comment in 1980 (Heatley 1979, 17) is equally applicable
twenty years later:

> The scrutiny of ... legislation was often inadequate, not only because it was rushed through, but also because of the small membership of the Assembly, the omnibus responsibilities of ministers and their opposition counterparts ... the limited time for debate, the use of parliamentary devices ... to curtail consideration, and the inadequacy of research and support services. Consequently, the role of bureaucratic and ministerial advisers and legislative draftsmen in policy-making has been higher than elsewhere in Australia. It is no secret that some of the Darwin legal fraternity and several senior bureaucrats hold the legislative competence of the Assembly in small regard.

Some examples show the extent to which the Assembly's role in the governing process was downgraded in the territory under the CLP. Question time has been truncated over time, to the point where a three-day sitting in the early years of the Assembly saw an average of eighty questions, by the mid-1990s the number had fallen to thirty-four. And the CLP government increasingly used the tactic of putting questions on notice. As Bob Collins, the most effective leader of the opposition the Labor Party has produced, put it, 'Mr Speaker, you would qualify for your old-age pension waiting for answers to come back to questions on notice that the government does not want answered because it simply ignores them' (cited in Jaensch and Wade-Marshall 1994, 155). The Northern Territory Assembly has the least number of sitting days per year of any Australian parliament. A comparison in 1990 showed the New South Wales Legislative Council with the greatest number, seventy-two days, and an average of fifty-seven days for all federal and state houses. The territory Assembly sat for twenty-six days (Jaensch and Wade-Marshall 1994, 177). During its time in office CLP government rejected every demand for any semblance of a freedom of information Act for the territory.

Like any parliament in Australia, much of the time of members in the Assembly is involved in meetings of committees. The range of these in the territory is similar to other parliaments, and this means a high workload for such a small parliamentary membership. But there was one notable difference until 1988. The CLP government resisted the formation of a public accounts committee (PAC). From the beginning of its representation in the Assembly in 1977, the Labor opposition argued for the establishment of a PAC, and for a range of other auditing processes. The CLP responded that the functions of a PAC in a small parliament would be better carried out by the debate on the budget, a better use of question time, and other avenues. It was not until 1988, after strong political pressures from a range of sources including the clerk of the Assembly (Thompson 1980, 31), that the CLP finally acceded to the establishment of a PAC.

Whether this style of government will change with the advent of a Labor government in 2001 is hard to tell. It may be that the political colour of the government is less important than the logic of a small unicameral parliament in which strong party discipline guarantees government majority control of the Assembly.

The change of government in 2001

The election victory by the Labor Party in the 2001 Northern Territory election surprised almost every observer, including even the territory Labor Party. The leader of the party, Clare Martin, was as 'stunned as anyone else by the result' (*Sydney Morning Herald,* 20 August 2001). Labor had done what most observers thought was impossible; it had won a majority of seats and formed a government. Clare Martin had become the first woman to have led a party from opposition to government at any election in Australia.

To hope to win government, Labor had to pick up urban, and especially Darwin, seats, shore up its support in the outback, and take advantage of the internal cracks appearing in the CLP and the increasingly tarnished public image of the CLP government. In the event, the party increased its vote share by only 2 per cent over the previous election in 1997 to 40.6 per cent of the first preference vote, but the party had won the additional votes where it mattered. It gained thirteen of the twenty-five seats to the CLP's ten (with 45.4 per cent of the first preference vote). The CLP had suffered a 9.3 per cent swing against it, much of it going to some twenty independent candidates, two of whom gained seats.

Labor held all of its seven seats from the 1997 election, and won six from the CLP, all in Darwin's northern suburbs, the area which had formerly been the heartland of the CLP. The CLP was reduced from eighteen to ten seats in the election – in Northern Territory terms, a landslide. And the two independents were rewarded by the new Labor-controlled Assembly with the positions of speaker and deputy speaker, consolidating the party's hold on the legislature.

Most commentators focused on three explanations for the change in voting: the feeling in the electorate that it was time for a change; the positive campaign run by Labor and its new leader, Clare Martin; and a combination of arrogance within the CLP and a poor and negative campaign. But the key aspect was that Labor had finally realized that to have a chance of winning it needed to reform itself. The first important change was a new leader. With a public profile established as a long-time ABC television journalist, Clare Martin brought a new style and a new approach to Labor politics in the territory. From her election as leader of Territory Labor in 1998, the party changed its approach. The CLP was a target for criticism, but the party's approach emphasized the benefits that Labor would bring to government. Over a period of two years the party worked on its policies and image: pro-development, but through proper processes; tough on crime, but opposed to mandatory sentencing; open and receptive government; and, above all, an emphasis on middle-class policies, especially health and education, which was directed to the Darwin northern suburbs electoral districts held by the CLP. Further, the Labor Party had preselected its candidates well for a multi-ethnic electorate. Its team included five Aboriginal people, one Greek-born and one Malaysian-born candidate.

The new patterns of party support, especially in the crucial electoral districts in the northern suburbs of Darwin, may not be stable. If they swung once in response to a refurbished Labor Party and dissatisfaction with the incumbent CLP, they may swing back if the CLP revitalises itself and the Labor Party loses its way. It is not clear whether the territory has moved from one party dominance to competitive party politics or whether, if a party is to regain dominance, the beneficiary will be the ALP or the CLP.

Continuity and change

The description which can best be applied to the policy stance of both CLP and Labor is 'territorialism'. The Labor Party calls itself Territory Labor; the CLP uses symbols of the territory as widely as possible, and stresses that the CLP is separate and distinct from both the Liberal and National parties elsewhere.

The driving concern of the long-term CLP government was territory development, above all other considerations. This goal was to be achieved by methods which might occasionally look incompatible with a right of centre party. The CLP government had annoyed some of its supporters by its willingness to be pragmatic, even to the point where it had been accused of being quasi-socialist (Heatley 1979, 25).

Over the years of the territory self-government, the emphasis in legislative activity has changed significantly. In the first parliament, 1974 to 1977, there was a concentration on constitutional matters, a focus which was repeated in the second parliament as the implications of self-government were worked through. The structures of government had to be established, then modified, a local government system was introduced, and a host of administrative agencies and processes had to be designed. The result was frenzied legislative activity in these areas. A similar flurry occurred in 1998 over the question of statehood.

Beyond these periods, however, the emphasis of government legislation has varied little from the patterns in other states. An analysis of territory legislation based on the comparative work by Helen Nelson for the states (Nelson 1988) suggests that in only two areas – the relations between individuals and the state and individuals and groups – was the territory more active than the average.

The election policy emphases of the new Labor government included a stronger commitment than was ever offered by the CLP to issues of social policy – education, health, social services, and Aboriginal affairs. The widespread concern with the provision of these services – and their under-provision by successive CLP governments – are part of the explanation of the 2001 election result. But two key policy concerns will be retained by Labor – the economic development of the Northern Territory and the achievement of statehood for the territory. The Labor Party in government is as committed to these as was the CLP. There has been a change of party in government, but no change in the essential focus of government activity.

Chapter

11

One System or Nine?

Campbell Sharman and Jeremy Moon

A theme of this collection is the way in which a common institutional inheritance has been shaped to suit the preferences of nine political communities. The experience of British imperial and colonial government provided the source for almost all Australian governmental institutions. But this common heritage of British style parliamentary government was substantially modified by each of the Australian colonies during the nineteenth century. It has been further adapted to accommodate federation and the demands put on each political system over the course of the twentieth century. These modifications and the distinctive politics of each political community – Commonwealth, state and territory – have been the concern of the preceding chapters. While common elements have been noted, idiosyncrasy has been the prime focus.

This chapter looks at variations in some of the key components of representative government in the nine political communities which comprise the Australian political system. The goal is both to trace the extent and significance of differences and to stress the common elements which run through all systems This is a task which S.R. Davis addressed in his magisterial essay on state government and politics in 1960 (Davis 1960). He opened his comparative essay with a long quotation from Alfred Deakin in 1903 about the rise of national self-consciousness as the 'six little streams of public affairs' become one (Davis 1960, 559–60). But Davis argued persuasively that the states continued to express the differing political preferences of their client communities. The states remained the prime agencies for shaping key components of Australian political life and played a critical role in the

239

governmental process. Similar, if less forcefully articulated, views can be found in the studies of state politics published since the mid-1980s (Bennett 1992; Birrell 1987; Galligan 1986, 1988) and in the publications of the Evatt Foundation on the political economy of the states.

To claim that the states are an important part of the political process, however, is not the same thing as to argue that Australian society is strongly regionalized. Significant variations in the institutional structure of political communities – and in the political processes which occur within them – can exist even if there are only small variations in the social and economic characteristics of the states and territories. It is conceded that such a statement raises issues about the nature of politics and its relation to social activity but, unless it is argued that politics is only an epiphenomenon of social structure, it must be accepted that there is a realm for politics which involves choice on the part of citizens and governments. This choice and the vagaries of time, place and circumstance mean that the same set of political institutions may evolve in different ways in different communities independently of social structure. And these differences may be enhanced by such small socioeconomic variations as exist in each political community.

From this perspective, the study of the components of the Australian federation provides an opportunity to see how a broadly similar set of political institutions has responded to the opportunity to evolve in seven, and now nine, different political forums; each system is a variation on a common institutional theme. This means that charting the idiosyncrasies of each governmental stem is not only important for analysing the politics of a particular political community but as a means of understanding the logic and operation of political institutions as a set of rules and relationships. Australia's varied experience with preferential voting, for example, provides a wealth of analysis and information on the nature and consequences of this voting system and related electoral rules (Sharman et al. 2002).

This makes the comparative study of Australian state politics valuable both because it can address broad questions about the operation of parliamentary democracy and because it fosters a better appreciation of the common themes which run through Australian politics (Sharman 1988). The issue is not how much one system differs from another but what the variations between the Commonwealth, the states and territories indicate about the nature of Australian politics and the institutional rules which govern its operation.

In this concluding chapter, we examine two elements which are central to the understanding of any representative democracy: the nature of party competition and the shape of parliamentary government. We use data on elections, representation and periods in office over the last century to compare the experience of state and commonwealth political communities as a way of explaining characteristics of Australian politics. In this respect, Australia is both one and nine political systems.

Party, the party system and the competition for votes

All the previous chapters stress the importance of political parties as agencies for shaping the electoral process and for giving coherence to parliamentary government. Similarly, all point to the importance of the Australian Labor Party (ALP) as the first mass party in Australia and as a party which has been a major player in electoral and governmental politics. Both of these characteristics – the ALP's organization and its electoral success – have had a profound effect on representative democracy in Australia. The organizational structure of the ALP as a mass party required that its parliamentary representatives vote as a disciplined bloc in parliament, transforming the parliamentary process (Bongiorno 2001). The electoral success of the ALP in becoming the largest party around 1910 induced anti-Labor parties across Australia to coalesce into a single party, the Liberal Party, and to create the basis of the current party system (Loveday et al. 1977). It also started the process for the Liberal Party and its successors to begin to adopt a mass party structure similar to that of the ALP (Hancock 2000; Nethercote 2001). In addition to prompting the creation of a single large, right-of-centre party to rival the ALP in 1910, the existence of the ALP has continued to force insurgent anti-Labor groups and parties to regroup into a single party or semi-permanent coalition. The restructuring of the Liberal Party as the Nationalist Party around 1917, the creation of the United Australia Party in 1931 (Nethercote 2001), and the reformation of the Liberal Party in 1944 (Hancock 2000) are all examples of this process. The longstanding coalition arrangements with the National (Country) Party, first negotiated with the emergence of the Country Party around the end of the first world war, have continued to be important for Commonwealth elections and for those in New South Wales, Queensland, and Western Australia (Costar and Woodward 1985; Jaensch 1994).

The dominance of the ALP in terms of vote share has persisted since 1910, with the party being the largest party at most state and Commonwealth elections.[1] This has not meant that the ALP has been as dominant in terms of holding office – the party has been the largest party but has rarely gained a majority of the vote – but the large component of the vote won by the ALP at most elections since 1910 has had a profound effect on the party system.

The extent of this influence can be seen in figure 11.1 which shows the mean vote share of the ALP at state and Commonwealth elections from 1910 to 2001 and the range of this support over the same period. With the exception of Victoria, the average vote share for the ALP has been in a narrow band between 43.3 to 46.4 per cent for all state and Commonwealth general elections since 1910. Victoria's low average ALP vote share of 40.1 per cent reflects problems of party organization and electoral appeal, documented in chapter 7 of this book. As with all long-term averages, the mean hides significant variations. The range for all states and the Commonwealth, again with the exception of Victoria, is well in excess of 20 per cent and, in the case of Tasmania, 30 per cent; the details of these variations can be seen in the chapters dealing with each system. ALP support has also varied between state and Commonwealth elections in the same state, sometimes markedly (Sharman and Sayers 1998). In broad terms, however, the ALP has usually gained a vote share in the 40 per cent range at state and Commonwealth elections since 1910.

With a single left-of-centre party consistently gaining such a large share of the vote and being well placed to win government, it would be expected to have a strongly dichotomising effect on the party system in two respects. The first is an ideological one: the left-of-centre policies of the ALP would induce a right-of-centre party grouping. This left–right view of the party system has been a continuing theme in Australian politics and has coloured views of the Australian party system since before 1910. The second effect is to force an amalgamation of parties opposing the ALP to form a single right-of-centre party. These two effects are often run together so that Australia is seen to have essentially a two party system with the struggle for government being between the ALP and a rival 'coalition' which is synonymous with the Liberal Party (or its predecessors) on its own or in combination with the National (Country) Party (Costar 1994).

In broad terms, this is a useful way of analysing the dynamics of the party system in Australia since 1910 – it is used as one of the indicators of party competition in charts in all the previous chapters – but it masks significant variations between political systems and over time. It also overstates the degree to which the competition for votes is between only two parties. To sort out the competitiveness of the party system and the extent of variation between systems, a more subtle approach is needed. This can be provided by using Rae's index of fractionalization (Rae 1971) which, either in its original form or its derivative (the effective

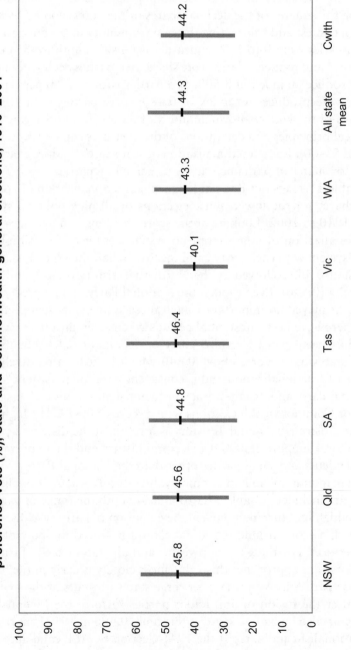

Figure 11.1 Average and range of support for the ALP by share of first preference vote (%), state and Commonwealth general elections, 1910–2001

Source: calculated from the Australian Government and Politics Project database, University of Western Australia.

number of parties – Laakso and Taagepera 1979), is commonly used in comparative politics. The fractionalization of the vote share (F_e) is a measure of the degree to which competitive electoral strength is concentrated in one party or is divided among several. It is calculated by adding the squares of the decimal shares of the votes won by parties in a given contest and subtracting the sum from unity to produce an index which varies from 0 to 1. The measure is sensitive both to the number of parties and to their relative vote share: two parties each with half the vote produce an index of 0.500; two parties with a 60/40 per cent split of the vote produces an index of 0.480; three parties with 40/30/30 division of the vote results in an index of 0.660. The underlying mathematical principles and derivations of the measures can be found in Rae (1971, 53–60). Rae's fractionalization of seat share (F_p) does exactly the same for shares of parliamentary seats gained by parties.

Table 11.1 sets out Rae's index for the fractionalization of vote and seat shares for the lower house elections of all nine political systems from 1910 to 2002. Looking at the scores for long-run averages of the fractionalization of vote shares, no system conforms to a simple two party system with each party gaining close to half the vote. Tasmania is closest at 0.569 followed by the Northern Territory (0.580) and South Australia (0.596). Even though the National Party and its predecessors have not played an important role in these systems, its score indicates that there have been substantial periods when a significant share of the vote has been won by a third party or groups of independents. The other states have scores above 0.640 which indicate a relatively high degree of fractionalization and is consistent with the persistence of the National Party and its important role in anti-Labor politics. This is also true for Commonwealth elections with a score of 0.639. The high score for the Australian Capital Territory is a result of the dispersed pattern of electoral support in its short electoral history and the importance of independents and small parties other than the National Party.

The minimum and maximum values for Rae's fractionalization index are included in table 11.1 to indicate both the range of variation and to highlight turning points in the evolution of party systems. At the low end, a score around 0.500 indicates a balanced duopoly of party competition. For the Commonwealth and all states except Tasmania, the score that approaches this value most closely is early in the history of mass parties in Australia – for three states it occurs at the first election after the fusion of anti-Labor parties to form the Liberal Party. Tasmania also had a low score at this time (0.496 in 1912) but the rout of Nationalist candidates at the 1941 election by ALP candidates with over 62 per cent of the vote produced an even lower index of 0.474.

Table 11.1 Rae's index of fractionalization for vote and seat shares, Commonwealth, State and Territory general elections, 1910–2002

Lower House	Rae's Index for vote share (F_e)						Rae's Index for seat share (F_p)					
	Mean	Standard deviation	Min	Year of min	Max	Year of max	Mean	Standard deviation	Min	Year of min	Max	Year of max
State assembly												
NSW (1910 to 1999: 31 elections)	0.648	0.040	0.578	1910	0.713	1999	0.605	0.047	0.474	1981	0.679	1988
Qld (1912 to 2001: 32 elections)	0.645	0.063	0.513	1918	0.747	1957	0.572	0.090	0.383	1935	0.739	1957
SA (1910 to 2002: 31 elections)	0.596	0.045	0.513	1910	0.671	1997/2002	0.534	0.052	0.335	1993	0.651	1938
Tas (1912 to 2002: 29 elections)	0.569	0.048	0.474	1941	0.671	1922	0.535	0.046	0.444	1941	0.651	1922
Vic (1911 to 1999: 32 elections)	0.644	0.050	0.518	1914	0.726	1943	0.601	0.067	0.448	1914	0.702	1937
WA (1911 to 2001: 29 elections)	0.641	0.055	0.523	1911	0.735	1917	0.608	0.059	0.410	1911	0.757	1921
Mean (State assembly)	0.624	0.050	0.520	na	0.711	na	0.576	0.060	0.416	na	0.697	na
Commonwealth House of Reps												
(1910 to 2001: 37 elections)	0.639	0.052	0.513	1917	0.738	1934	0.593	0.053	0.415	1917	0.691	1934
Territory assembly												
ACT (1989 to 2001: 5 elections)	0.682	0.029	0.643	1989	0.723	1992	0.631	0.021	0.595	2001	0.651	1995/ 1998
NT (1974 to 2001: 9 elections)	0.580	0.039	0.532	1983	0.637	1977	0.453	0.113	0.188	1974	0.563	2001

Source: calculated from the Australian Government and Politics Project database, University of Western Australia.

That such scores at the low end of the range occurred very early in the life of the current party system shows that Australian party systems have been tracking away from simple two party competition for most of their history.

At the other extreme, fractionalization scores around 0.700 indicate that one or both of the major party groupings has fallen apart or suffered substantial loss of votes to an insurgent party. For Tasmania (1922) and Western Australia (1917), their highest scores occurred when both major parties suffered from the insurgence of the Country Party and, in the case of Western Australia, compounded by a major split in ALP support. The highest fractionalization score for Victoria in 1943 corresponded with the low point in the dissolution of the United Australia Party and the dispersal of its vote among other parties and independents. For the Commonwealth, the highest score in 1934 results from the split in the ALP between the Federal Labor Party and the Lang Labor Party based in New South Wales. The split in the Queensland ALP in 1957 led to the highest fractionalization score for any party system in Australia (0.747) with support divided fairly evenly between the ALP, the Queensland Labor Party, the Liberal Party and the Country Party.

For New South Wales and South Australia, the highest fractionalization scores occur much more recently. In New South Wales, it corresponds with the slashing of the Liberal Party vote in 1999 and the proliferation of independents and minor parties, chief among them Pauline Hanson's One Nation Party. In South Australia, the highest score occurred in both 1997 and 2002 reflecting the continuing dissatisfaction with the largest two parties by a quarter of the electorate in a state which has not had a pattern of such dispersed support for most of the period since the 1930s.

If high fractionalization scores for vote shares indicate turmoil in the party system, both these states appear to be currently in transition from one party system to another or, rather, the realignment of non-Labor interests to form a strong rival to the ALP. High fractionalization scores are unlikely to persist in the Australian context for the same reason as scores below 0.500 are rare – the stabilizing effect of the ALP on the party system. Even when reduced to a third of the vote, the ALP represents a base from which a left-of-centre, trade union supported party can reassert itself. The party has won at least a substantial minority of votes at every election in every political forum across Australia since 1910. As such, its continued organizational existence makes it the beneficiary of electoral dissatisfaction with non-Labor governments and works to produce the dichotomous style of parliamentary politics to which Australians have become accustomed.

At the other extreme, high fractionalization scores represent either the temporary eclipse of the ALP as a consequence of intra-party disputes or the dispersal of non-Labor electoral support among several parties or groups of independents. Again, the existence of the ALP encourages non-Labor parties to coalesce or at least to form coalitions. The paradox of the ALP in electoral politics is that its majoritarian political stance and resilience as a left-of-centre party has worked to encourage the creation and persistence of strong anti-Labor parties which have been marginally more successful in gaining office than the ALP; this has been markedly so for competition at Commonwealth elections.

The party system and representation

In addition to showing fractionalization for party vote shares, table 11.1 also shows the fractionalization for seat shares. Rae (1971) argues that one of the effects of an electoral system is to defractionalize the party system; that is, that there will be fewer parliamentary parties than the number of parties which contest elections, and that the electoral system will lead to disproportionality in favour of large parties. Both these factors imply that seat fractionalization will be less than that for votes. This is clearly the case for the nine parliamentary lower houses in Australia when the average score for vote share and seat share indices are compared. The difference between these two average scores is smaller than might be expected given the prevalence of single-member district electoral systems, the under-representation of most small parties and the malapportionment which has been a characteristic of most Australian electoral systems until recently (Rydon 1968; 1976; and note Hughes 1977, appendix 1). Malapportionment can, however, work to increase seat share fractionalization if it over-represents small parties, as has often been the case with the National Party and its predecessors.

Very low seat fractionalization scores correspond with the collapse of representation of all but one large party so that one party dominates. The most dramatic since 1910 was the 37 to 10 seat margin won by the Liberals in South Australia in 1993. At the other end of the scale where seats are shared between a number of middle-sized parties, the fifty-seat West Australian Legislative Assembly elected in 1921 had party groupings with seventeen, sixteen, ten, four and three members. Most of these extreme events – both low and high scores – for the states and the Commonwealth occurred before 1960; the increasing vote share won by minor parties and independents since 1990 in all jurisdictions has

Table 11.2 Share of government, number and average length of period in office,* ALP and non-ALP governments, 1910†–2001**

Government System	ALP governments			Non-ALP governments		
	Share of government, 1910–2001 %	Number of periods in office n	Average length of period in office days	Share of government, 1910–2001 %	Number of periods in office n	Average length of period in office days
State						
New South Wales	59.7	15	1326	40.3	14	959
Queensland	53.7	11	1621	46.3	11	1397
South Australia	36.5	15	815	63.5	16	1327
Tasmania	64.3	18	1169	35.7	14	834
Victoria	23.9	10	788	76.1	26	963
Western Australia	49.1	12	1364	50.9	12	1415
Mean (State)	47.9	13.5	1180	52.1	15.5	1149
Commonwealth	34.5	11	1049	65.5	20	1097
Territory						
ACT (From 11 May 1989)	35.3	3	543	64.7	4	747
NT (From 20 Nov 1974)	1.4	1	135	98.6	7	1395

* See text for definition of 'period in office'.

† First period in office commencing after 1 January 1910.

** To 31 December 2001; includes incomplete terms of governments in office at 31 December 2001.

Source: calculated from the Australian Government and Politics project database, University of Western Australia.

had little effect on seat shares. For the purpose of this essay, seat fractionalization is important for confirming the general effect of lower house electoral systems in giving representation to a smaller number of parties than those which contest elections, in over-representing large parties, and in discriminating against the representation of minor parties and independents excepting those whose support is geographically concentrated.

The principal goal of parties is to win representation and, for large parties in a parliamentary system, to win enough seats to form a government. Table 11.2 shows the relative success of the ALP and its rival non-Labor parties in capturing government since the current party system emerged in 1910. Two of the terms in table 11.2 need clarification. Share of government refers to the length of time in government of the ALP or a non-Labor party or coalition. A period in office is defined by the time a particular premier (or prime minister or chief minister) holds that office. Such a period in office is terminated by the change of premier or, occasionally, by a change in the parliamentary support for a premier marked by a shift from single-party government to coalition government, from minority government to majority government, or any combination of these. The aim of this definition is to have a period of government specified by a combination of the time a premier holds office with a given pattern of parliamentary support (see Appendix).

The first point to note is the wide variation in the success of the ALP in winning government. The party has held office for almost two-thirds of the period since 1910 in Tasmania and close to 60 per cent of the time in New South Wales, but less than a quarter of the period in Victoria and only a little more than a third of the time for South Australian and Commonwealth governments. Excluding the territories, the long-term ALP share of office for all governments is just under 50 per cent. The ALP's success in usually being the largest single party in terms of vote share at elections since 1910 has not been translated into an equivalent success in winning government. The explanation for this lack of parliamentary dominance can be found in a combination of factors; the ALP has rarely won a majority of the vote, its electoral support has often been concentrated in safe seats and, as described in a number of chapters in this book, it has suffered from periods of malapportionment which discriminated in favour of its partisan opponents.

In addition to the total time in government enjoyed by the ALP and non-Labor parties, table 11.2 also shows the number of periods in office within this total.[2] As mentioned above, a period in office is the length of time during which a premier (or prime minister or chief minister) holds office with majority, coalition, or minority parliamentary support. A change in premier or a change between one of the categories of parliamentary support ends a period of office. Since 1910 the number of periods in office has varied from a high of thirty-six for Victoria (ten ALP periods in office and twenty-six non-Labor) to a low of twenty-one for Queensland (eleven ALP periods in office and eleven non-Labor). This measure compares the volatility of parliamentary politics both between and within parties. The source of this volatility can be found, as in Victoria, in the vagaries of party politics (see chapter 7) or, in the case of Tasmania, in the challenge of forming governments in a small Assembly with an even number of members (from 1909 until 1956) where the members are chosen by proportional representation (see chapter 6; and note Sharman et al. 1991).

The small number of periods in office in Queensland reflects the settled politics of partisan dominance which has characterized much of the state's history (see chapter 4); the ALP was in government (with only one break) from 1915 to 1957, and National (Country) Party, with or without the Liberal Party in coalition, was in power from 1957 until 1989. There is a consistent relationship between the proportion of time a party has been in government and its share of periods in office; for each governmental system, the larger the proportion of time in government won by a party, the longer the average period in office. But there are significant variations within this pattern. There are wide discrepancies between the length of average ALP and non-ALP periods in office in New South Wales and South Australia, but much smaller differences between these averages for Victoria and Western Australia, and especially for the Commonwealth. Periods in office for the Commonwealth are of similar average length for both major party groupings even though the non-Labor parties have been in office twice as often as the ALP.

Another, and more familiar, measure of competitiveness is the rate of alternation between parties in government, (see table 11.3). Party in government has been dichotomized between ALP and non-ALP; changes of government between non-Labor parties and alternations in parliamentary support have been ignored. With the exception of Queensland, the states and the Commonwealth have had between eleven and seventeen alternations of party in government with average periods from five to eight years between alternations (1887 days in Victoria to 2864 days in Tasmania). Queensland is anomalous among the states because of its small number of alternations and its long average period between changes of party in government of 12.5 years (4558 days).

The average period of alternation is only half the picture. Table 11.3 shows that three states have had very long periods without a

Table 11.3 Alternation, number and average length of continuous periods in government, ALP and non-ALP governments, 1910*–2001†

Government System	Number of alternations between periods of ALP and non-ALP government _n_	Average number of days between alternations of ALP and non-ALP government _days_	Longest single continuous period in government _days_	_party_
State				
New South Wales	14	2,205	8,763	ALP
Queensland	7	4,558	11,830	Non-ALP
South Australia	13	2,347	11,649	Non-ALP
Tasmania	11	2,864	12,757	ALP
Victoria	17	1,887	9,043	Non-ALP
Western Australia	13	2,540	5,090	ALP
Mean (State)	12.5	2,734	9,855	na
Commonwealth	11	2,850	9,093	Non-ALP
Territory				
ACT (From 11 May 1989)	4	1,142	2,440	Non-ALP
NT (From 20 Nov 1974)	1	9,768	9,768	Non-ALP

* The first period in government counted is the first government to take office after 1 January 1910. The first alternation is the first change in party government which follows the first period in government. Note that changes of periods in office between non-ALP parties are not included.

† To last alternation in party government before 31 December 2001.

Source: calculated from the Australian Government and Politics project database, University of Western Australia. For a list of the periods of office for the Commonwealth, the states and the territories over the last century, see the Appendix.

change in the party in government, periods well in excess of thirty years (Tasmania thirty-five years, Queensland more than thirty-two years, and South Australia almost thirty-two years). New South Wales, Victoria and the Commonwealth have all had unbroken periods in government by a single-party grouping of twenty-four years. Only in Western Australia is the ratio of the longest period in government to the average period as low as two, and the longest period in government by a single party being less than fourteen years.

The lack of alternation in government in a parliamentary system is, on the face of it, an indicator of the lack of competitiveness of the party system. It may also be a comment on the institutional structure of the parliament, on the electoral system, on the nature of the parties contesting elections or on the dynamics of the party system itself (Lusztig et al. 1997). But, as table 11.2 shows, the fact that one party is in government for a long period does not mean that there are no changes in the personnel in office or that there are no competitive pressures in the political system. Queensland may have had only seven alternations of party in government, but has had twenty-two different periods of office.

In addition, the rotation of members through parliament and shifts in parliamentary support may enhance the responsiveness of governments even though the party in government remains undefeated at elections, a characteristic of Tasmanian politics (Sharman et al. 1991). Nonetheless, the failure to 'throw the rascals out' after a number of years indicates the existence of some anti-competitive forces at work muting the struggle for the control of government which characterizes partisan politics in representative democracies. Very long periods in government may not be a feature of the twenty-first century; the increasing volatility of the electorate, the proliferation of candidates and parties running for election, and a trend for the vote share of the largest two parties to decline all make for a more competitive style of politics. No party in government in mid-2002 had been in office for more than seven years and only one (the Commonwealth) had won more than two consecutive elections.

Little reference has yet been made of the experience of the territories, yet the short period of self-government of these two political communities has put them at the extremes of the Australian experience of parliamentary government. In terms of the information displayed in table 11.3, the Australian Capital Territory has had four alternations of government between 1989 and 2001, the shortest average period of a party in government, and the lowest maximum period for a party in government (less than seven years). On the other hand, the Northern Territory had the same governing party from the date of self-government in 1974 until the election of August 2001. This gives it the longest average period of alternation: over twenty-six years. These figures may change with a longer period of self-government, but the current pattern is consistent with the very different electoral systems and patterns of party competition in each of the territories (see chapters 9 and 10).

Government and parliamentary support

Thus far, party and government have been examined in the context of partisan differences between ALP and non-Labor parties. Table 11.4 sets out information on parliamentary support for governments since 1910, whether single party or coalition, majority support or minority government. The calculations are based on the periods in office used for table 11.2 (and note Appendix). The table shows that, overall, the great majority of governments have had majority support in parliament since 1910 (column G). This is an unsurprising finding; indeed, it is now taken as axiomatic that, since the rise of the mass party, parliamentary government requires the government to have a majority in the lower house of parliament. The surprise might be the proportion of governments in Australia which have been minority governments (column H). Among the states, minority government accounts for an average of 19.5 per cent of the period, ranging from a low of 3.3 per cent for Queensland to a high of 37.7 per cent for Tasmania. Such minority status usually results from the governing party or coalition being kept in office by one or more independent or minor party members of parliament who are not willing to become part of the government but will support the government in a vote of confidence, often on condition that certain policies or parliamentary reforms are implemented (Moon 1995, and note Haward and Larmour 1993).

Most of the periods of minority government have been before 1950 reflecting the turbulence of party alignments in the first half of the century, but all states have had the experience of minority government during the 1990s, and all as a result of the balance of power in the assembly being held by minor party or independent members of parliament. This explanation fits the creation of most minority governments but two exceptions can be noted. The first is the stance of the ALP in Victoria in supporting the minority United Country Party government of Albert Dunstan from 1935 to 1943. The second is the propensity for the Tasmanian House of Assembly to produce minority governments over the period from 1909 to 1956 because of an even-numbered Assembly coupled with proportional representation (Howatt 1958; Townsley 1976).

Table 11.4 Single-party, coalition and minority governments: parliamentary support of governments, 1910*–2001†

Government System	Single party governments			Coalition governments			All govts with majority support in parlt %	All minority govts %
	with majority support in parlt %	minority govts %	all single-party govts %	with majority support in parlt %	minority govts %	all coalition govts %		
Share of period	A	B	C (A+B)	D	E	F (D+E)	G (A+D)	H (B+E)
State								
New South Wales	57.5	2.2	59.7	33.7	6.6	40.3	91.2	8.8
Queensland	68.1	0.7	68.8	28.6	2.5	31.2	96.7	3.3
South Australia	73.4	20.5	93.8	6.2	0.0	6.2	79.5	20.5
Tasmania	57.9	37.7	95.6	4.4	0.0	4.4	62.3	37.7
Victoria	50.7	31.6	82.3	15.4	2.3	17.7	66.1	33.9
Western Australia	48.2	3.0	51.3	39.0	9.7	48.7	87.2	12.8
Mean (State)	59.3	16.0	75.3	21.2	3.5	24.7	80.5	19.5
Commonwealth	37.3	9.9	47.2	51.6	1.2	52.8	88.8	11.2
Territory								
ACT (from 11 May 1989)	0.0	60.1	60.1	0.0	39.9	39.9	0.0	100.0
NT (from 20 Nov 1974)	100.0	0.0	100.0	0.0	0.0	0.0	100.0	0.0

* First period in office commencing after 1 January 1910 (see text for explanation of terms).

† To 31 December 2001; includes incomplete terms of governments in office at 31 December 2001.

Source: calculated from the Australian Government and Politics project database, University of Western Australia.

The experience of the territories, albeit over a short time period, is again of interest. Every government in the Australian Capital Territory since self-government has been a minority government. This has had all the consequences for the style of parliamentary government predicted for minority government (Moon 1995); the executive is highly responsive to the legislature both as to its legislative program and to its accountability for executive activity (see chapter 9). The opposite extreme can be found in the Northern Territory where parliamentary politics has been highly constrained by consistent majority government by a single party until 2001 (see chapter 10).

With the exception of the Northern Territory, minority government has been a small but significant component of the experience of parliamentary government across Australia. In a party system which has a tendency to multipartism and the frequent presence of minor party and independent candidates at general elections, minority government should not be seen as an aberration but as a version of parliamentary government in which the usual roles of government and opposition party groupings in the assembly are reversed, if only for a single period in office; the business of the assembly operates under the veto of the opposition rather than the government. While this may cause frustration to those on the government front benches and to interests in the community who favour executive dominance of the parliamentary process, periods of minority government are a timely reminder that parliamentary systems were designed to make the legislature an effective check on the executive. The experience of minority government in Australian legislatures – in some cases lasting for an extended period – provides a rich source for studies of its consequences on the dynamics of the parliamentary process (Moon 1995).

The other distinction between categories of parliamentary support for government shown in table 11.4 is that between single-party governments and coalition governments. In this context, a coalition government is one in which ministers are chosen from two or more political parties. For New South Wales, Queensland, Western Australia and the Commonwealth government, this distinction corresponds closely with the difference between ALP and non-ALP governments since the emergence of the Country Party about 1920. The presence of the National (Country) Party in these states, and its importance for the formation of non-Labor governments in coalition with the Liberal Party and its predecessors, has meant that the term 'coalition government' has become almost synonymous with 'non-Labor government'. The greater the success of non-Labor coalitions in winning office, the higher the proportion of coalition government.

This explains the high scores for coalition government for the Commonwealth (52.8 per cent), Western Australia (48.7 per cent) and New South Wales (40.3 per cent). The lower score for Queensland (31.2 per cent) is the result of both substantial periods of ALP rule and two period of single-party government by non-Labor parties since 1920. Tasmania and South Australia are at the other end of the scale with single-party governments predominating; the failure of the Country Party to establish a substantial presence in these states has left non-Labor governments dominated by the Liberal Party and its predecessors. Victoria is in the middle range reflecting the turbulent nature of non-Labor politics in this state until the late 1950s and the long period of single-party government under the Liberals from 1950 until 1982 (see chapter 7).

Yet again, the experience of the territories is instructive, particularly that of the Australian Capital Territory. All governments in the Australian Capital Territory have been minority governments, and 40 per cent of them have also been coalition governments. The importance of this mode of government in the Australian Capital Territory reflects the diversity of its party system and the operation of proportional representation (see chapter 9).

The conclusions to be drawn from the pattern of support for governments is a little at odds with the conventional picture of Australian government. Just as the dichotomizing effect of the ALP on voting at Australian elections can be overstated, the effect of the ALP on parliamentary politics is not what might be expected (note Sayers 2002). While the control of government is clearly split between ALP and non-Labor, the nature of parliamentary support on the non-Labor side is divided between coalition and single-party government. For two systems, the Commonwealth and Western Australia, coalition government represents close to half the experience of government since 1910, a figure which declines among the states to 6 per cent for South Australia. To say that this variation reflects differences in the configuration of non-Labor support in each system begs the question as to why this should be important in some systems and not others. As a national government, coalition may be expected for Commonwealth governments to accommodate a regionally dispersed set of non-Labor interests, but the divergence between, say, New South Wales (40.3 per cent) and Victoria (17.7 per cent) is harder to explain. Such extensive and variable experience of coalition government is unusual in comparable British-derived parliamentary systems. It is hard to know whether the existence of coalition government in Australia is caused by the ALP or persists in spite of it. While the existence of the ALP can explain the formation of non-ALP coalitions, why has not the domination of the ALP on the left of politics forced the continuing fusion of non-Labor interests as it did in 1910?

The same question might be asked about the frequency of minority government, but here the answer is clearer. The dichotomizing effect of the ALP in the context of a small but persistent share of the vote won by minor party and independent candidates will occasionally lead to minority government, an occurrence which may increase if the vote share of the largest two parties continues to decline as it has been doing for the last decade of the twentieth century. Again, the variability in the popularity of the major parties since 1910 raises broad issues about social change and the role of political parties. While the ALP is a major force in Australian politics and has shaped much of what makes Australian electoral and parliamentary politics distinctive, there are characteristics of the political process for which the existence of the ALP does not provide an explanation.

Federalism

Thus far, little mention has been made of the federal nature of Australian politics and government. Federalism has two aspects; the first is the dispersed nature of Australian settlement, the freezing of these regional communities into largely autonomous political entities by the middle of the nineteenth century and their entrenchment as states of a federal union in 1901. In this respect, federalism does no more than reflect the highly regionalized nature of Australian politics, accentuated by the dominance of large urban concentrations in the capitals of each of the states. It is this aspect of Australian federalism which is the focus of most of the essays in this book; the states – now joined by the territories – as semi-autonomous political communities, each with its own set of governmental institutions and political traditions.

The other aspect of federalism is the interaction of state and national governments and the generation of complex constitutional, economic, governmental and political relationships. This is a major field of study on its own and one which falls outside the ambit of this book. Fortunately, Australia has been well served by scholars who have investigated federal relationships. Galligan, in particular, both on his own (Galligan 1995) and in conjunction with other scholars (Galligan 1989; Galligan et al. 1991) has provided authoritative surveys of the nature of Australian federalism. This has been augmented by more detailed examinations of aspects of the federal process, notably Painter's (1998) analysis of the changing nature of intergovernmental relations.

To the extent that federalism requires citizens to be members of both state and national political communities, there is the question of the extent to which state politics is harmonized with national politics. A method of analysing the relationship between these two spheres of politics is to look at the way parties respond to the opportunity of competing in two forums. On the face of it, the fact that the ALP is a major player in all political forums in Australia should mean that there should be strong regularities between state political contests and those for national elections. In broad terms this is true, certainly in comparison with party competition in Canada (Sayers 2002; Stewart 1994). But there are several caveats. The first is that support for parties with the same name varies within states between state and national lower house elections, even for the ALP, and sometimes to a significant extent (Sharman and Sayers 1998). Secondly, political parties must adjust to Australia's federal structure. This can entail considerable organizational autonomy for state branches of a party (note Hancock 2000). In spite of its being a party which has been augmenting national level control of its organization, the centre of gravity of political activity of the ALP remains in the state branches (Parkin and Marshall 1994; Warhurst and Parkin 2000).

The final caveat is the variability of partisan control of governments in the federal system shown in figure 11.2. The chart shows the number of states with governments of the same partisan colour as the Commonwealth government, dichotomized between ALP and non-ALP. The date for counting the number of governments with the same partisanship is 30 June in each year from 1910 to 2002.[3] It is clear that states do not replicate the results of national elections over the period. But figure 11.2 raises another issue. The pattern of support appears to have followed a sequence of rises and falls, at least since 1930. Quite apart from the effect that this pattern may have on the dynamics of intergovernmental relations (Sharman 1994b), there is the question of what is the driver for the waves of partisan similarity with the national government which appear to move across Australia. And, once established, does a high level of partisan similarity between Commonwealth and state governments (a score of five or more in figure 11.2) induce a decline in partisan support of the party in power in Canberra? The evidence is mixed, but the pattern indicates that, while bound together in a federal system, the partisan complexion of each governmental component is determined as much by factors within each system as it is from national factors. Again, Australia operates as both one system and nine.

Figure 11.2 Number of state governments with the same partisan colour as the Commonwealth government at 30 June 1910–2001

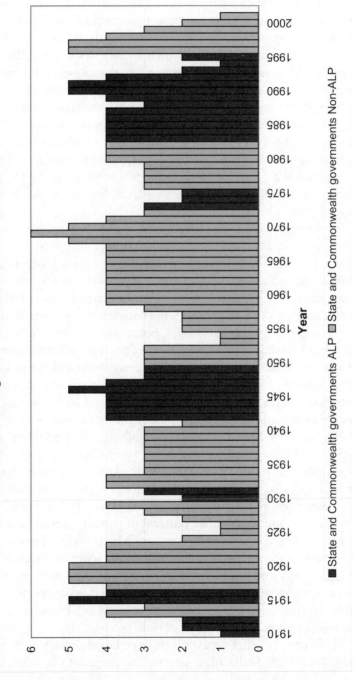

■ State and Commonwealth governments ALP ■ State and Commonwealth governments Non-ALP

Source: calculated from the Australian Government and Politics Project database, University of Western Australia.

Continuing themes

This chapter has surveyed the nature and variability of party competition and the shape of parliamentary government across Australia. We have chosen to concentrate on these areas because we believe that they are central components of representative democracy in Australia, because they are both elements which figure extensively in the previous chapters, and because we can bring to their analysis comparative data not previously used for their study. But we would not wish to leave the reader with the impression that the elements we have examined are the only sources of similarity and variation in Australian political institutions or that there are no other perspectives from which these topics can be examined. Information on the variety of approaches to Australian politics and the range of topics studied are surveyed in the political science section of *The Cambridge Handbook of Social Sciences in Australia* (McAllister et al. 2003).

In addition to the topics touched on in this chapter, there are several aspects of Australian state politics which have benefited from systematic comparative study since the groundbreaking work of S.R. Davis in 1960. Three of these should be noted. The pioneering work of Nelson in comparing the legislative outputs of the states (Nelson 1985; 1988) shows that legislative activity differed between the states with the larger states tending to be the innovators. Secondly, as several of the chapters in this book have shown, strong, elective parliamentary bicameralism is a characteristic of the Commonwealth government and five of the states. The evolution of state upper houses and the place of bicameralism in Australian liberal democracy has been surveyed by Stone (2002) who examines the transformation of these institutions over the last century. Finally, work by Moon and Sayers, building on a previous study by Hughes (1984), has used the analysis of ministerial portfolios to examine the growth of government activity over the last century in both state and national spheres, and to chart alterations in the focus and scope of government action over time (Moon and Sayers 1999). They have also used this technique to examine patterns of partisanship and convergence between state governments (Sayers and Moon 2002). They argue that states have all shown a general increase in the scope of government over the last century and broadly similar changes in the categories of activity and profile of government. Yet these very general changes mask considerable diversity. They conclude that there is no evidence of general convergence in the overall scope of state governments.

There are yet other areas which have largely escaped comparative study. These include the administration of justice in the states, differing patterns of interest group activity, and many aspects of the operation of state parties, campaigning, and the operation of state parliaments. There is much to learn about the comparative analysis of state and territory politics and government both for the benefit of understanding the Australian governmental process, and as an opportunity for comparative political analysis.

The encouragement of further study of the Australian states and territories has been one of the reasons for starting on the project which has led to the production of this book. As we set out in the introduction, the Australian federation remains a vigorous set of political communities – national, state, and territory – each with its own governmental institutions and political style. The centenary of federation has provided both an opportunity to celebrate the continuing existence of a lively federal system and to focus attention on its constituent components. We trust that readers of this book will accept the challenge of thinking about Australia not as a single undifferentiated system of government but as a network of nine overlapping elements in a system which, barring the occasional hiccup, works well to fulfil the expectations embodied in the ideas of representative democracy and parliamentary government.

Note on Sources and Links to The Web

The chapters in this collection provide a great deal of information about the politics and government of the component parts of the Australian federation – the Commonwealth, the states and the self-governing territories. Access to further information is provided in the references to books and articles listed in the Reference list. Apart from the Introduction, each chapter and the Appendix contains charts and tables summarizing particular aspects of representation and government. With only a few exceptions, the source for the information on which the charts and tables are based is the Australian Government and Politics project at the University of Western Australia.

One of the purposes of the Australian Government and Politics project has been to make information on Australian parties, elections, representation and governments available in machine-readable form both for the general public and for those who want to undertake research. Much of this information is available on the Australian Government and Politics website (http://elections.uwa.edu.au). Readers are invited to consult this website for further information on particular elections, on the votes and seats won by parties at Commonwealth state and territory elections, and on the periods in office of premiers and prime ministers. The website also contains a glossary of terms which can be used to supplement information in this volume. A description of the website, the database on which it is based, and details of the information it contains can be found in Sharman (2002).

The creation of the database and website have been heavily dependent on the work of Colin Hughes and his associates at the Australian National University in the 1960s in building a record of elections, representation and government in the Commonwealth and the states. This led to the publication of *A Handbook of Australian Government and Politics 1890–1964* compiled by Colin Hughes and B. D. Graham (Hughes and Graham 1968) which, together with its supplements, has provided core information for the Australian Government and Politics project at the University of Western Australia. The editors of this volume, however, are responsible for the updating and modification of much of the information and for the design and operation of the Australian Government and Politics database on which the charts and tables in this volume are based.

Notes

Chapter 2

1 For details of constitutional referendums, see Commonwealth of Australia 1999.

2 Since 1975 four senators represent the Australian Capital Territory and the Northern Territory but these senators are not counted in the number for calculating the size of the House of Representatives.

Chapter 3

1 The semi-permanent parliamentary coalition between the Liberal Party and the National Party has led to the combination of these two anti-Labor parties being referred to as 'the coalition'. Note that both parties have contested elections over the last century under a variety of names, and that the relationship between the parties has varied over time; see the section on the parties and the party system, below.

2 From 7 to 11 March 1994, for example, the *Daily Telegraph Mirror* ran a series of front-page stories, editorials and commentary criticizing the Council as a part-time chamber and 'colonial relic' and calling for its abolition.

3 An occasion where this did not happen and which led to the resignation of Premier Greiner in 1992 is well covered in Gleeson et al. (1992); R. Smith (1995); Chaples and Page (1995).

4 After the close 1976 election, public speculation that Independent MLA John Hatton might become speaker ended when Labor won a slim majority (Bennett 2001, 138). After the 1991 election, Liberal Premier Nick Greiner, leading a minority government, offered Hatton the speaker's role. Hatton declined the post (R. Smith 1995, 25).

5 Termed more loosely 'popularism' by some commentators (see Markey 1988).

6 The party has been called the Progressive, Country, United Country, National Country and National Party over its life. 'National' is used here unless the context makes the use of one of the party's earlier titles appropriate.

Chapter 4

1 In 1995 the National Party led by Rob Borbidge undertook to examine a proposal for the reintroduction of an upper house in return for Green preferences in four key seats. On becoming premier in 1996, the Borbidge government did not honour its

commitment; Premier Borbidge simply stated that he had other priorities.

2 Note the brief and temporary exception of the Liberal Party–Country Party coalition government of Gordon Chalk which lasted for eight days in August 1968 while the Country Party chose a new leader to succeed Premier Pizzey who had died in office.

Chapter 5

1 South Australia remains the only state never to have supplied an Australian prime minister, and Alexander Downer's brief period as Liberal Party leader in 1994–95 represents the only instance of a South Australian ever being the national opposition leader. The Australian Democrats are unusual in having developed a recent penchant for South Australian-based national party leadership.

2 The significance of the 'Torrens title' and its diffusion from South Australia to the rest of Australia, New Zealand, Canada, the United States, Africa and Asia is described in Stein and Stone (1991).

3 *South Australia v Victoria* (1911) 12 CLR 667.

4 The Methodism of some early Labor Party leaders is notable. The biographer of John Verran (Premier 1910–12) notes how he drew on his Methodist upbringing: 'His parliamentary speeches were replete with Biblical allusions and stories were repeated for years about his idiosyncratic sermons' (Hunt 1990, 323). His predecessor, Tom Price (Premier 1905–09) 'remained an active Methodist' and sponsored a number of bills intended to suppress gambling, drunkenness and other vices (Weeks 1988, 288).

5 These phrases from Pike's book title and preface have been particularly influential (see, for example, Stretton 1975, 133; Hutchings and Bunker 1986). The book itself ends up being somewhat more dismissive about those South Australians who succeeded the foundational generation.

6 Except where the parliament has chosen to bind itself and its successors otherwise. An example is the provision entrenched in 1975 which requires the approval of a referendum for any change to the principles of electoral distribution for the House of Assembly as now embodied in a separate *Electoral Act*.

7 One of these independent Liberals subsequently rejoined the Liberal Party upon securing party preselection for the next state election.

8 See, for example, the analysis by Mitchell (1962) of the role of J. W. Wainwright in the pre-war period and the analysis by Stretton (1978) of A. M. Ramsay's work in the post-war period.

9 The South Australian 'Karmel Report' is the report of the

Committee of Enquiry into Education in South Australia (1971). The Commonwealth 'Karmel Report' is the report of the Interim Committee for the Australian Schools Commission (1973).

Chapter 6

1 Ironically, O'Rourke's exemplar of this kind of economy is Tanzania, periodically confused with Tasmania by mail sorting clerks the world over.

2 In the Bacon ALP government elected in 1998, the treasurer, David Crean, sits in the Legislative Council.

Chapter 7

1 Candidates first ran for election under the name of the Liberal Party for the 1908 state election. In 1917 they regrouped as the National Party (Nationalists) until a change to the United Australia Party (UAP) at the 1932 state election. The current Liberal Party emerged in 1945 (see below).

Chapter 8

1 The Liberal Party became the Nationalist Party (Nationalists) in 1917 until the 1946 election when it reverted to the name 'Liberal' although, between 1950 and 1968, it called itself the Liberal and Country League. It contested several of the federal elections in Western Australia between 1931 and 1943 under the name of the United Australia Party.

2 As with the Liberal Party, the Country Party has contested state elections under various other names including the National Country Party, the Country and Democratic League and, since the party's reorganization for the 1986 election, as the National Party.

Chapter 9

1 Rebecca Fredericks assisted with the research for this chapter and Scott Bennett and Roger Wettenhall made very helpful comments on a draft of this chapter.

Chapter 11

1 This dominance has not extended to territory elections; the ALP has never won the largest vote share in the Northern Territory (see chapter 10, figure 10.1) and, depending on how minor parties and independents are treated, the ALP has won the largest vote share at less than half the elections in the Australian Capital Territory (see chapter 9, figure 9.1).

2 See the appendix for a list of periods of office over the last century for the Commonwealth, the states and the territories.

3 The choice is arbitrary but there is little difference in the pattern if any other date is chosen.

Appendix

Commonwealth, state and territory governments, periods in office by prime minister, premier or first minister, and by category of parliamentary support, 1890–2001

Commonwealth government, periods in office and parliamentary support, 1901–2001

Prime minister	Date of start of period in office*	Date of end of period in office*	Party of prime minister	Parliamentary support		Event leading to a change in parliamentary support affecting period in office*
				Majority or Coalition	Minority	
1 Edmund Barton	1 January 1901	24 September 1903	Protectionists		Minority	
2 Alfred Deakin	24 September 1903	27 April 1904	Protectionists		Minority	
3 John Christian Watson	27 April 1904	18 August 1904	Australian Labor Party		Minority	
4 George Houstoun Reid	18 August 1904	5 July 1905	Free Trade	Coalition		
5 Alfred Deakin	5 July 1905	13 November 1908	Protectionists		Minority	
6 Andrew Fisher	13 November 1908	2 June 1909	Australian Labor Party		Minority	
7 Alfred Deakin	2 June 1909	29 April 1910	Fusion	Coalition		
8 Andrew Fisher	29 April 1910	24 June 1913	Australian Labor Party	Majority		
9 Joseph Cook	24 June 1913	17 September 1914	Liberal Party	Majority		
10 Andrew Fisher	17 September 1914	27 October 1915	Australian Labor Party	Majority		
11 William Morris Hughes	27 October 1915	14 November 1916	Australian Labor Party	Majority		
12 William Morris Hughes	14 November 1916	17 February 1917	National Labor Party		Minority	
13 William Morris Hughes	17 February 1917	13 December 1919	Nationalist Party	Majority		
14 *William Morris Hughes*	*13 December 1919*	*13 December 1919*	*Nationalist Party*		*Minority*	*Election*
15 Stanley Melbourne Bruce	9 February 1923	9 February 1923	Nationalist Party	Coalition		
16 James Henry Scullin	22 October 1929	22 October 1929	Australian Labor Party	Majority		
17 Joseph Aloysius Lyons	6 January 1932	6 January 1932	United Australia Party		Minority	
18 Joseph Aloysius Lyons	9 November 1934	9 November 1934	United Australia Party	Coalition		

No.	Prime Minister			Party	Government	Minority	Election
19	Earle Christmas Grafton Page	7 April 1939	26 April 1939	Country Party	Coalition	Minority	
20	Robert Gordon Menzies	26 April 1939	14 March 1940	United Australia Party	Coalition		
21	Robert Gordon Menzies	14 March 1940	21 September 1940	United Australia Party	Coalition		
22	*Robert Gordon Menzies*	*21 September 1940*	*29 August 1941*	*United Australia Party*	*Coalition*	*Minority*	*Election*
23	Arthur William Fadden	29 August 1941	7 October 1941	Country Party	Coalition	Minority	
24	John Curtin	7 October 1941	12 August 1943	Australian Labor Party	Majority	Minority	
25	*John Curtin*	*12 August 1943*	6 July 1945	*Australian Labor Party*	*Majority*		*Election*
26	Francis Michael Forde	6 July 1945	13 July 1945	Australian Labor Party	Majority		
27	Joseph Benedict Chifley	13 July 1945	19 December 1949	Australian Labor Party	Majority		
28	Robert Gordon Menzies	19 December 1949	26 January 1966	Liberal Party	Coalition		
29	Harold Edward Holt	26 January 1966	19 December 1967	Liberal Party	Coalition		
30	John McEwen	19 December 1967	10 January 1968	Country Party	Coalition		
31	John Grey Gorton	10 January 1968	10 March 1971	Liberal Party	Coalition		
32	William McMahon	10 March 1971	19 December 1972	Liberal Party	Coalition		
33	Edward Gough Whitlam	19 December 1972	11 November 1975	Australian Labor Party	Majority		
34	John Malcolm Fraser	11 November 1975	13 December 1975	Liberal Party	Coalition	Minority	
35	*John Malcolm Fraser*	*13 December 1975*	11 March 1983	*Liberal Party*	*Coalition*		
36	Robert James Lee Hawke	11 March 1983	2 January 1992	Australian Labor Party	Majority		Election
37	Paul John Keating	2 January 1992	2 March 1996	Australian Labor Party	Majority		
38	John Winston Howard	2 March 1996		Liberal Party	Coalition		

* These dates should be treated with caution. They are usually the date the commission to form a government was granted to a prime minister which does not necessarily correspond with the date of an election. Dates and entries in italics show a change in parliamentary support during the government of a prime minister leading to a new 'period in office' for that prime minister. See chapter 11 for discussion of the definition of 'period in office', and the Glossary entry for 'period in office' in the Australian Government and Politics website (http://elections.uwa.edu.au).

Source: Australian Government and Politics Project, University of Western Australia; more information can be found at the Project's website (http://elections.uwa.edu.au) under 'Government' and 'Glossary'.

New South Wales, periods in office and parliamentary support, 1889–2001

Premier	Date of start of period in office*	Date of end of period in office*	Party of premier	Majority or Coalition	Minority	Event leading to a change in parliamentary support affecting period in office*
1 Henry Parkes	8 March 1889	23 October 1891	Free Trade		Minority	
2 George Richard Dibbs	23 October 1891	3 August 1894	Protectionist		Minority	
3 George Houstoun Reid	3 August 1894	14 September 1899	Free Trade		Minority	
4 William John Lyne	14 September 1899	28 March 1901	Protectionist		Minority	
5 John See	28 March 1901	15 June 1904	Protectionist		Minority	
6 Thomas Waddell	15 June 1904	30 August 1904	Protectionist		Minority	
7 Joseph Hector Carruthers	30 August 1904	2 October 1907	Liberal - Reform		Minority	
8 Charles Gregory Wade	2 October 1907	21 October 1910	Liberal - Reform		Minority	
9 James Sinclair T McGowen	21 October 1910	30 June 1913	Australian Labor Party	Majority		
10 William Arthur Holman	30 June 1913	15 November 1916	Australian Labor Party	Majority		
11 William Arthur Holman	15 November 1916	13 April 1920	Nationalists	Coalition		
12 John Storey	13 April 1920	6 October 1921	Australian Labor Party		Minority	
13 James Dooley	6 October 1921	20 December 1921	Australian Labor Party		Minority	
14 George Warburton Fuller	20 December 1921	20 December 1921	Nationalists	Coalition		
15 James Dooley	20 December 1921	13 April 1922	Australian Labor Party		Minority	
16 George Warburton Fuller	13 April 1922	17 June 1925	Nationalists	Coalition		
17 John Thomas Lang	17 June 1925	18 October 1927	Australian Labor Party	Majority		
18 Thomas Rainsford Bavin	18 October 1927	4 November 1930	Nationalists	Coalition		
19 John Thomas Lang	4 November 1930	13 May 1932	Australian Labor Party	Majority		
20 Bertram Sydney B Stevens	13 May 1932	11 June 1932	United Australia Party	Coalition	Minority	
21 *Bertram Sydney B Stevens*	*11 June 1932*	5 August 1939	*United Australia Party*	*Coalition*		*Election*
22 Alexander Mair	5 August 1939	16 May 1941	United Australia Party	Coalition		
23 William John McKell	16 May 1941	6 February 1947	Australian Labor Party	Majority		
24 James McGirr	6 February 1947	3 April 1952	Australian Labor Party	Majority		

25	John Joseph Cahill	3 April 1952	28 October 1959	Australian Labor Party	Majority		
26	Robert James Heffron	28 October 1959	30 April 1964	Australian Labor Party	Majority		
27	John Brophy Renshaw	30 April 1964	13 May 1965	Australian Labor Party	Majority		
28	Robin William Askin	13 May 1965	*6 May 1967*	Liberal Party	Coalition	Minority	
29	*Robin William Askin*	*6 May 1967*	3 January 1975	*Liberal Party*	*Coalition*		*Gain at by-election*
30	Thomas Lancelot Lewis	3 January 1975	23 January 1976	Liberal Party	Coalition		
31	Eric Archibald Willis	23 January 1976	14 May 1976	Liberal Party	Coalition		
32	Neville Kenneth Wran	14 May 1976	4 July 1986	Australian Labor Party	Majority		
33	Barrie John Unsworth	4 July 1986	25 March 1988	Australian Labor Party	Majority		
34	Nicholas Frank Hugo Greiner	25 March 1988	*25 May 1991*	Liberal Party	Coalition		
35	*Nicholas Frank Hugo Greiner*	*25 May 1991*	25 June 1992	*Liberal Party*	*Coalition*	*Minority*	*Election*
36	John Joseph Fahey	25 June 1992	2 May 1995	Liberal Party	Coalition	Minority	
37	Robert John Carr	2 May 1995		Australian Labor Party	Majority		

* These dates should be treated with caution. They are usually the date the commission to form a government was granted to a premier which does not necessarily correspond with the date of an election. Dates and entries in italics show a change in parliamentary support during the government of a premier leading to a new 'period in office' for that premier. See chapter 11 for discussion of the definition of 'period in office', and the Glossary entry for 'period in office' in the Australian Government and Politics website (http://elections.uwa.edu.au).

Source: Australian Government and Politics Project, University of Western Australia; more information can be found at the Project's website (http://elections.uwa.edu.au) under 'Government' and 'Glossary'.

Queensland, periods in office and parliamentary support, 1888–2001

Premier	Date of start of period in office*	Date of end of period in office*	Party of premier	Parliamentary support — Majority or Coalition	Parliamentary support — Minority	Event leading to a change in parliamentary support affecting period in office*
1 Boyd Dunlop Morehead	30 November 1888	12 August 1890	Ministerialist	Majority		
2 Samuel Walter Griffith	12 August 1890	27 March 1893	Ministerialist	Majority		
3 Thomas McIlwraith	27 March 1893	27 October 1893	Ministerialist	Majority		
4 Hugh Muir Nelson	27 October 1893	13 April 1898	Ministerialist	Majority		
5 Thomas Joseph Byrnes	13 April 1898	1 October 1898	Ministerialist	Majority		
6 James Robert Dickson	1 October 1898	11 March 1899	Ministerialist		Minority	
7 James Robert Dickson	11 March 1899	1 December 1899	Ministerialist	Majority		Election
8 Anderson Dawson	1 December 1899	7 December 1899	Australian Labor Party	Majority		
9 Robert Philp	7 December 1899	11 March 1902	Ministerialist		Minority	
10 Robert Philp	11 March 1902	17 September 1903	Ministerialist	Majority		Election
11 Arthur Morgan	17 September 1903	19 January 1906	Ministerialist	Coalition		
12 William Kidston	19 January 1906	18 May 1907	Ministerialist	Coalition	Minority	
13 William Kidston	18 May 1907	19 November 1907	Ministerialist	Coalition		Election
14 Robert Philp	19 November 1907	18 February 1908	Ministerialist	Coalition	Minority	
15 William Kidston	18 February 1908	29 October 1908	Ministerialist	Coalition	Minority	
16 William Kidston	29 October 1908	2 October 1909	Ministerialist	Coalition		Gain in parliamentary support
17 William Kidston	2 October 1909	7 February 1911	Ministerialist*	Coalition		Election
18 Digby Frank Denham	7 February 1911	1 June 1915	Liberal Party	Majority		
19 Thomas Joseph Ryan	1 June 1915	22 October 1919	Australian Labor Party	Majority		
20 Edward Granville Theodore	22 October 1919	26 February 1925	Australian Labor Party	Majority		
21 William Neal Gillies	26 February 1925	22 October 1925	Australian Labor Party	Majority		
22 William McCormack	22 October 1925	21 May 1929	Australian Labor Party	Majority		

No	Name	From	To	Party	Government	Notes
23	Arthur Edward Moore	21 May 1929	17 June 1932	Country & Prog. Nat. Party	Majority	
24	William Forgan Smith	17 June 1932	16 September 1942	Australian Labor Party	Majority	
25	Frank Arthur Cooper	16 September 1942	7 March 1946	Australian Labor Party	Majority	
26	Edward Michael Hanlon	7 March 1946	17 January 1952	Australian Labor Party	Majority	
27	Vincent Clair Gair	17 January 1952	12 August 1957	Australian Labor Party	Majority	
28	George Francis R Nicklin	12 August 1957	17 January 1968	Country Party	Coalition	
29	Jack Charles Allan Pizzey	17 January 1968	1 August 1968	Country Party	Coalition	
30	Gordon William W Chalk	1 August 1968	8 August 1968	Liberal Party	Coalition	
31	Johannes Bjelke-Peterson	8 August 1968	19 August 1983	Country Party	Coalition	
32	Johannes Bjelke-Petersen	19 August 1983	22 October 1983	National Party		Minority
33	*Johannes Bjelke-Petersen*	*22 October 1983*	1 December 1987	*National Party*	*Majority*	*Election*
34	Michael John Ahern	1 December 1987	25 September 1989	National Party	Majority	
35	Theo Russell Cooper	25 September 1989	1 January 1990	National Party	Majority	
36	Wayne Keith Goss	1 January 1990	20 February 1996	Australian Labor Party	Majority	
37	Robert Edward Borbridge	20 February 1996	13 June 1998	National Party	Coalition	Minority
38	Peter Douglas Beattie	13 June 1998	5 December 1998	Australian Labor Party	Minority	
39	Peter Douglas Beattie	*5 December 1998*		*Australian Labor Party*	*Majority*	*Gain at by-election*

* These dates should be treated with caution. They are usually the date the commission to form a government was granted to a premier which does not necessarily correspond with the date of an election. Dates and entries in italics show a change in parliamentary support during the government of a premier leading to a new 'period in office' for that premier. See chapter 11 for discussion of the definition of 'period in office', and the Glossary entry for 'period in office' in the Australian Government and Politics website (http://elections.uwa.edu.au).

Source: Australian Government and Politics Project, University of Western Australia; more information can be found at the Project's website (http://elections.uwa.edu.au) under 'Government' and 'Glossary'.

South Australia, periods in office and parliamentary support, 1889–2001

	Premier	Date of start of period in office*	Date of end of period in office*	Party of premier	Parliamentary support		Event leading to a change in parliamentary support affecting period in office*
					Majority or Coalition	Minority	
1	John Alexander Cockburn	27 June 1889	19 August 1890	Ministerialist		Minority	
2	Thomas Playford	19 August 1890	21 June 1892	Ministerialist		Minority	
3	Frederick William Holder	21 June 1892	15 October 1892	Ministerialist		Minority	
4	John William Downer	15 October 1892	16 June 1893	Liberal Party		Minority	
5	Charles Cameron Kingston	16 June 1893	1 December 1899	Liberal Party		Minority	
6	Vaiben Louis Solomon	1 December 1899	8 December 1899	Conservative Party		Minority	
7	Frederick William Holder	8 December 1899	15 May 1901	Liberal Party		Minority	
8	John Greeley Jenkins	15 May 1901	3 May 1902	Liberal Party	Coalition		
9	*John Greeley Jenkins*	*3 May 1902*	*4 July 1904*	*Liberal Party*		*Minority*	*Election*
10	*John Greeley Jenkins*	*4 July 1904*	1 March 1905	Liberal Party	Coalition		
11	Richard Butler	1 March 1905	26 July 1905	Conservative Party	Coalition		
12	Thomas Price	26 July 1905	5 June 1909	Australian Labor Party	Coalition		
13	*Archibald Henry Peake*	5 June 1909	*22 December 1909*	Liberal Party		Minority	
14	*Archibald Henry Peake*	*22 December 1909*	3 June 1910	*Liberal Party*	*Majority*		*Gain in parliamentary support*
15	John Verran	3 June 1910	17 February 1912	Australian Labor Party	Majority		
16	Archibald Henry Peake	17 February 1912	3 April 1915	Liberal Party	Majority		
17	Crawford Vaughan	3 April 1915	14 July 1917	Australian Labor Party	Majority		
18	Archibald Henry Peake	14 July 1917	27 August 1917	Liberal Party		Minority	
19	Archibald Henry Peake	27 August 1917	8 April 1920	Liberal Party	Coalition		
20	Henry Newman Barwell	8 April 1920	16 April 1924	Liberal Party	Majority		
21	John Gunn	16 April 1924	28 August 1926	Australian Labor Party	Majority		
22	Lionel Laughton Hill	28 August 1926	8 April 1927	Australian Labor Party	Majority		

No.	Premier			Party			
23	Richard Layton Butler	8 April 1927	17 April 1930	Liberal Party	Coalition		
24	Lionel Laughton Hill	17 April 1930	13 February 1933	Australian Labor Party	Majority		
25	Robert Stanley Richards	13 February 1933	18 April 1933	Australian Labor Party	Majority		
26	Richard Layton Butler	18 April 1933	*19 March 1938*	Liberal Country League	Majority		
27	*Richard Layton Butler*	*19 March 1938*	5 November 1938	*Liberal Country League*		*Minority*	*Election*
28	Thomas Playford jun	5 November 1938	*29 March 1941*	Liberal Country League		Minority	
29	*Thomas Playford jun*	*29 March 1941*	*3 March 1962*	*Liberal Country League*	*Majority*		*Election*
30	*Thomas Playford jun*	*3 March 1962*	10 March 1965	*Liberal Country League*		Minority	*Election*
31	Francis Henry Walsh	10 March 1965	1 June 1967	Australian Labor Party	Majority		
32	Donald Allan Dunstan	1 June 1967	17 April 1968	Australian Labor Party	Majority		
33	Raymond Steele Hall	17 April 1968	2 June 1970	Liberal Country League	Majority		
34	Donald Allan Dunstan	2 June 1970	*12 July 1975*	Australian Labor Party	Majority		
35	*Donald Allan Dunstan*	*12 July 1975*	*17 September 1977*	*Australian Labor Party*	*Majority*	*Minority*	*Election*
36	*Donald Allan Dunstan*	*17 September 1977*	15 February 1979	*Australian Labor Party*	*Majority*		*Election*
37	James Desmond Corcoran	15 February 1979	18 September 1979	Australian Labor Party	Majority		
38	David Oliver Tonkin	18 September 1979	10 November 1982	Liberal Party	Majority		
39	John Charles Bannon	10 November 1982	*25 November 1989*	Australian Labor Party	Majority		*Election*
40	*John Charles Bannon*	*25 November 1989*	4 September 1992	*Australian Labor Party*	*Majority*	*Minority*	
41	Lynn Maurice F Arnold	4 September 1992	11 December 1993	Australian Labor Party	Majority	Minority	
42	Dean Craig Brown	11 December 1993	28 November 1996	Liberal Party	Majority		
43	John Wayne Olsen	28 November 1996	*11 October 1997*	Liberal Party	Majority		
44	*John Wayne Olsen*	*11 October 1997*	22 October 2001	Liberal Party	*Majority*	*Minority*	*Election*
45	Robert Gerard Kerin	22 October 2001		Liberal Party	Majority	Minority	*Election*

* These dates should be treated with caution. They are usually the date the commission to form a government was granted to a premier which does not necessarily correspond with the date of an election. Dates and entries in italics show a change in parliamentary support during the government of a premier leading to a new 'period in office' for that premier. See chapter 11 for discussion of the definition of 'period in office', and the Glossary entry for 'period in office' in the Australian Government and Politics website (http://elections.uwa.edu.au).

Source: Australian Government and Politics Project, University of Western Australia; more information can be found at the Project's website (http://elections.uwa.edu.au) under 'Government' and 'Glossary'.

Tasmania, periods in office and parliamentary support, 1887–2001

Premier	Date of start of period in office*	Date of end of period in office*	Party of premier	Majority or Coalition	Minority	Event leading to a change in parliamentary support affecting period in office*
1 Philip Oakley Fysh	30 March 1887	17 August 1892	Liberal Party		Minority	
2 Henry Dobson	17 August 1892	14 April 1894	Conservative		Minority	
3 Edward Nicholas C Braddon	14 April 1894	20 January 1897	Liberal Party		Minority	
4 *Edward Nicholas C Braddon*	*20 January 1897*	*12 October 1899*	*Liberal Party*	*Majority*		*Election*
5 Neil Elliott Lewis	12 October 1899	9 April 1903	Conservative	Majority		
6 William Bispham Propsting	9 April 1903	12 July 1904	Liberal Democrats		Minority	
7 John William Evans	12 July 1904	30 April 1909	Liberal Party	Majority		
8 *John William Evans*	*30 April 1909*	*30 April 1909*	*Liberal Party*	*Majority*		*Election*
9 Neil Elliot Lewis	19 June 1909	19 June 1909	Liberal Party	Majority	Minority	
10 John Earle	20 October 1909	20 October 1909	Australian Labor Party		Minority	
11 Neil Elliot Lewis	27 October 1909	27 October 1909	Liberal Party	Majority		
12 Albert Edgar Solomon	14 June 1912	14 June 1912	Liberal Party	Majority		
13 *Albert Edgar Solomon*	*10 January 1914*	*10 January 1914*	*Liberal Party*		*Minority*	*Loss of by-election*
14 John Earle	6 April 1914	15 April 1916	Australian Labor Party		Minority	
15 Walter Henry Lee	15 April 1916	31 May 1919	Liberal Party		Minority	
16 *Walter Henry Lee*	*31 May 1919*	*10 June 1922*	*Liberal Party*	*Majority*		*Election*
17 *Walter Henry Lee*	*10 June 1922*	*12 August 1922*	*Liberal Party*		*Minority*	*Election*
18 John Blyth Hayes	12 August 1922	14 August 1923	Nationalists	Coalition	Minority	
19 Walter Henry Lee	14 August 1923	25 October 1923	Nationalists		Minority	
20 Joseph Aloysius Lyons	25 October 1923	3 June 1925	Australian Labor Party		Minority	
21 *Joseph Aloysius Lyons*	*3 June 1925*	15 June 1928	*Australian Labor Party*	*Majority*		*Election*
22 John Cameron McPhee	15 June 1928	*9 May 1931*	Nationalists		Minority	
23 *John Cameron McPhee*	*9 May 1931*	15 March 1934	*Nationalists*	*Majority*		*Election*

24	Walter Henry Lee	15 March 1934	Nationalists	Majority		
25	Albert George Ogilvie	22 June 1934	Australian Labor Party	Majority	Minority	
26	*Albert George Ogilvie*	*20 February 1937*	*Australian Labor Party*	*Majority*		*Election*
27	Edmund Dwyer-Gray	11 June 1939	Australian Labor Party	Majority		
28	Robert Cosgrove	18 December 1939	Australian Labor Party	Majority		
29	Edward Brooker	19 December 1947	Australian Labor Party	Majority		
30	Robert Cosgrove	25 February 1948	Australian Labor Party	Majority		
31	*Robert Cosgrove*	*21 August 1948*	*Australian Labor Party*	*Majority*	*Minority*	*Election*
32	Eric Elliot Reece	26 August 1958	Australian Labor Party	Majority	Minority	
33	*Eric Elliot Reece*	*2 May 1964*	*Australian Labor Party*	*Majority*		*Election*
34	Walter Angus Bethune	26 May 1969	Liberal Party	Coalition		
35	Eric Elliot Reece	3 May 1972	Australian Labor Party	Majority		
36	William Arthur Neilson	31 March 1975	Australian Labor Party	Majority		
37	Douglas Ackley Lowe	1 December 1977	Australian Labor Party	Majority		
38	Harold Norman Holgate	11 November 1981	Australian Labor Party	Majority		
39	Robin Trevor Gray	27 May 1982	Liberal Party	Majority		
40	Michael Walter Field	29 June 1989	Australian Labor Party	Majority	Minority	
41	Raymond John Groom	17 February 1992	Liberal Party	Majority		
42	Anthony Maxwell Rundle	18 March 1996	Liberal Party	Majority	Minority	
43	James Alexander Bacon	14 September 1998	Australian Labor Party	Majority		

* These dates should be treated with caution. They are usually the date the commission to form a government was granted to a premier which does not necessarily correspond with the date of an election. Dates and entries in italics show a change in parliamentary support during the government of a premier leading to a new 'period in office' for that premier. See chapter 11 for discussion of the definition of 'period in office', and the Glossary entry for 'period in office' in the Australian Government and Politics website (http://elections.uwa.edu.au).

Source: Australian Government and Politics Project, University of Western Australia; more information can be found at the Project's website (http://elections.uwa.edu.au) under 'Government' and 'Glossary'.

Victoria, periods in office and parliamentary support, 1886–2001

Premier	Date of start of period in office*	Date of end of period in office*	Party of premier	Parliamentary support		Event leading to a change in parliamentary support affecting period in office*
				Majority or Coalition	Minority	
1 Duncan Gillies	18 February 1886	5 November 1890	Conservative Party	Coalition	Minority	
2 James Munroe	5 November 1890	16 February 1892	Liberal Party		Minority	
3 William Shiels	16 February 1892	23 January 1893	Liberal Party	Majority		
4 James Brown Patterson	23 January 1893	27 September 1894	Conservative Party			
5 George Turner	27 September 1894	14 October 1897	Liberal Party		Minority	
6 *George Turner*	*14 October 1897*	*5 December 1899*	*Liberal Party*	*Majority*		*Election*
7 Allan McLean	5 December 1899	19 November 1900	Liberal Party	Majority		
8 George Turner	19 November 1900	12 February 1901	Liberal Party		Minority	
9 Alexander James Peacock	12 February 1901	10 June 1902	Liberal Party		Minority	
10 William Hill Irvine	10 June 1902	16 February 1904	Reform		Minority	
11 Thomas Bent	16 February 1904	1 June 1904	Reform		Minority	
12 *Thomas Bent*	*1 June 1904*	*1 June 1904*	*Reform*	*Majority*		*Election*
13 John Murray	8 January 1909	8 January 1909	Liberal Party	Coalition		
14 *John Murray*	*16 November 1911*	*16 November 1911*	*Liberal Party*	*Majority*		*Election*
15 William Alexander Watt	18 May 1912	18 May 1912	Liberal Party	Minority		
16 George Alexander Elmslie	9 December 1913	9 December 1913	Australian Labor Party	Minority		
17 William Alexander Watt	22 December 1913	22 December 1913	Liberal Party	Majority		
18 Alexander James Peacock	18 June 1914	18 June 1914	Liberal Party	Majority		
19 John Bowser	29 November 1917	29 November 1917	Nationalists	Majority		
20 Harry Sutherland W Lawson	21 March 1918	21 March 1918	Nationalists	Majority		
21 *Harry Sutherland W Lawson*	*21 October 1920*	*21 October 1920*	*Nationalists*		*Minority*	*Election*
22 Harry Sutherland W Lawson	7 September 1923	7 September 1923	Nationalists	Coalition		
23 Harry Sutherland W Lawson	19 March 1924	19 March 1924	Nationalists		Minority	
24 Alexander James Peacock	28 April 1924	18 July 1924	Nationalists		Minority	

#	Name			Party	Coalition	Majority	Minority	Election
25	George Michael Prendergast	18 July 1924	18 November 1924	Australian Labor Party			Minority	
26	John Allan	18 November 1924	20 May 1927	Country Party	Coalition			
27	Edmond John Hogan	20 May 1927	22 November 1928	Australian Labor Party			Minority	
28	William M McPherson	22 November 1928	12 December 1929	Nationalists			Minority	
29	Edmond John Hogan	12 December 1929	19 May 1932	Australian Labor Party			Minority	
30	Stanley Seymour Argyle	19 May 1932	2 April 1935	United Australia Party	Coalition			
31	Albert Arthur Dunstan	2 April 1935	14 September 1943	Country Party				
32	John Cain Sr	14 September 1943	18 September 1943	Australian Labor Party			Minority	
33	Albert Arthur Dunstan	18 September 1943	2 October 1945	Country Party	Coalition			
34	Ian Macfarlan	2 October 1945	21 November 1945	Liberal Party			Minority	
35	John Cain	21 November 1945	20 November 1947	Australian Labor Party			Minority	
36	Thomas Tuke Hollway	20 November 1947	3 December 1948	Liberal Party	Coalition			
37	Thomas Tuke Hollway	3 December 1948	27 June 1950	Liberal Party			Minority	
38	John Gladstone B McDonald	27 June 1950	28 October 1952	Country Party			Minority	
39	Thomas Tuke Hollway	28 October 1952	31 October 1952	Electoral Reform League			Minority	
40	John Gladstone B McDonald	31 October 1952	17 December 1952	Country Party			Minority	
41	John Cain Sr	17 December 1952	7 June 1955	Australian Labor Party		Majority		
42	Henry Edward Bolte	7 June 1955	31 May 1958	Liberal and Country Party			Minority	
43	*Henry Edward Bolte*	*31 May 1958*	*31 May 1958*	*Liberal and Country Party*		*Majority*		*Election*
44	Rupert James Hamer	23 August 1972	23 August 1972	Liberal Party		Majority		
45	Lindsay Hamilton S Thompson	5 June 1981	5 June 1981	Liberal Party		Majority		
46	John Cain Jr	8 April 1982	8 April 1982	Australian Labor Party		Majority		
47	Joan Elizabeth Kirner	10 August 1990	10 August 1990	Australian Labor Party		Majority		
48	Jeffrey Gibb Kennett	6 October 1992	6 October 1992	Liberal Party	Coalition			
49	Stephen Phillip Bracks	18 September 1999	18 September 1999	Australian Labor Party			Minority	

* These dates should be treated with caution. They are usually the date the commission to form a government was granted to a premier which does not necessarily correspond with the date of an election. Dates and entries in italics show a change in parliamentary support during the government of a premier leading to a new 'period in office' for that premier. See chapter 11 for discussion of the definition of 'period in office', and the Glossary entry for 'period in office' in the Australian Government and Politics website (http://elections.uwa.edu.au).

Source: Australian Government and Politics Project, University of Western Australia; more information can be found at the Project's website (http://elections.uwa.edu.au) under 'Government' and 'Glossary'.

Western Australia, periods in office and parliamentary support, 1890–2001

	Premier	Date of start of period in office*	Date of end of period in office*	Party of premier	Parliamentary support — Majority or Coalition	Parliamentary support — Minority	Event leading to a change in parliamentary support affecting period in office*
1	John Forrest	29 December 1890	15 February 1901	Conservative		Minority	
2	George Throssell	15 February 1901	27 May 1901	Conservative		Minority	
3	George Leake	27 May 1901	21 November 1901	Liberal Party		Minority	
4	Alfred Edward Morgans	21 November 1901	23 December 1901	Conservative		Minority	
5	George Leake	23 December 1901	1 July 1902	Liberal Party		Minority	
6	Walter Hartwell James	1 July 1902	10 August 1904	Liberal Party		Minority	
7	Henry Daglish	10 August 1904	25 August 1905	Australian Labor Party		Minority	
8	Cornthwaite Hector Rason	25 August 1905	27 October 1905	Liberal Party		Minority	
9	*Cornthwaite Hector Rason*	*27 October 1905*	*27 October 1905*	*Liberal Party*	*Majority*		*Election*
10	Newton James Moore	7 May 1906	7 May 1906	Liberal Party	Majority		
11	Frank Wilson	16 September 1910	16 September 1910	Liberal Party	Majority		
12	John Scaddan	7 October 1911	7 October 1911	Australian Labor Party	Majority		
13	Frank Wilson	27 July 1916	27 July 1916	Liberal Party		Minority	
14	Henry Bruce Lefroy	28 June 1917	28 June 1917	National Coalition	Coalition		
15	Hal Pateshall Colebatch	17 April 1919	17 April 1919	National Coalition	Coalition		
16	James Mitchell	17 May 1919	17 May 1919	National Coalition	Coalition		
17	Philip Collier	16 April 1924	16 April 1924	Australian Labor Party	Majority		
18	James Mitchell	24 April 1930	24 April 1930	Nationalist	Coalition		
19	Philip Collier	24 April 1933	24 April 1933	Australian Labor Party	Majority		
20	John Collings Willcock	20 August 1936	20 August 1936	Australian Labor Party	Majority		
21	Frank Joseph Scott Wise	31 July 1945	31 July 1945	Australian Labor Party	Majority		
22	Duncan Ross McLarty	1 April 1947	1 April 1947	Liberal Party	Coalition		
23	Albert Redvers G Hawke	23 February 1953	23 February 1953	Australian Labor Party	Majority	Minority	
24	David Brand	2 April 1959	*31 March 1962*	Liberal Party	Coalition	Minority	

25	*David Brand*	*31 March 1962*	3 March 1971	*Liberal Party*	*Coalition*	*Election*
26	John Trezise Tonkin	3 March 1971	8 April 1974	Australian Labor Party	Majority	
27	Charles Walter Michael Court	8 April 1974	25 January 1982	Liberal Party	Coalition	
28	Raymond James O'Connor	25 January 1982	25 February 1983	Liberal Party	Coalition	
29	Brian Thomas Burke	25 February 1983	26 February 1988	Australian Labor Party	Majority	
30	Peter M'Callum Dowding	26 February 1988	13 March 1990	Australian Labor Party	Majority	
31	Carmen Mary Lawrence	13 March 1990	*13 April 1991*	Australian Labor Party	Majority	
32	*Carmen Mary Lawrence*	*13 April 1991*	16 February 1993	*Australian Labor Party*	*Minority*	*Defection of party members*
33	Richard Fairfax Court	16 February 1993	16 February 2001	Liberal Party	Coalition	
34	Geoffrey Ian Gallop	16 February 2001		Australian Labor Party	Majority	

* These dates should be treated with caution. They are usually the date the commission to form a government was granted to a premier which does not necessarily correspond with the date of an election. Dates and entries in italics show a change in parliamentary support during the government of a premier leading to a new 'period in office' for that premier. See chapter 11 for discussion of the definition of 'period in office', and the Glossary entry for 'period in office' in the Australian Government and Politics website (http://elections.uwa.edu.au).

Source: Australian Government and Politics Project, University of Western Australia; more information can be found at the Project's website (http://elections.uwa.edu.au) under 'Government' and 'Glossary'.

Australian Capital Territory, periods in office and parliamentary support, 1989–2001

Chief Minister	Date of start of period in office*	Date of end of period in office*	Party of chief minister	Parliamentary support	
				Majority or Coalition	Minority
1 Rosemary Follett	11 May 1989	5 December 1989	Australian Labor Party		Minority
2 Trevor Thomas Kaine	5 December 1989	6 June 1991	Liberal	Coalition	Minority
3 Rosemary Follett	6 June 1991	9 March 1995	Australian Labor Party		Minority
4 Anne Katherine (Kate) Carnell	9 March 1995	27 April 1998	Liberal		Minority
5 Anne Katherine (Kate) Carnell	27 April 1998	18 October 2000	Liberal	Coalition	Minority
6 Gary John Joseph Humphreys	18 October 2000	12 November 2001	Liberal	Coalition	Minority
7 Jonathon Donald Stanhope	12 November 2001		Australian Labor Party		Minority

* These dates should be treated with caution. They are usually the date the commission to form a government was granted to the chief minister and do not necessarily correspond with election dates. See chapter 11 for discussion of the definition of 'period in office' and the Glossary entry for 'period in office' in the Australian Government and Politics website (http://elections.uwa.edu.au).

Source: Australian Government and Politics Project, University of Western Australia; more information can be found at the Project's website (http://elections.uwa.edu.au) under 'Government' and 'Glossary'.

Northern Territory, periods in office and parliamentary support, 1974–2001

Chief Minister*	Date of start of period in office †	Date of end of period in office †	Party of chief minister	Parliamentary support	
				Majority or Coalition	Minority
1 Godfrey Alan Letts	20 November 1974	21 September 1977	Country Liberal Party	Majority	
2 Paul Edward Anthony Everingham	21 September 1977	17 October 1984	Country Liberal Party	Majority	
3 Ian Lindsay Tuxworth	17 October 1984	15 May 1986	Country Liberal Party	Majority	
4 Stephen Paul Hatton	15 May 1986	14 July 1988	Country Liberal Party	Majority	
5 Marshal Bruce Perron	14 July 1988	1 July 1995	Country Liberal Party	Majority	
6 Shane Leslie Stone	1 July 1995	8 February 1999	Country Liberal Party	Majority	
7 Denis Gabriel Burke	8 February 1999	18 August 2001	Country Liberal Party	Majority	
8 Clare Majella Martin	18 August 2001		Australian Labor Party	Majority	

* Known as Majority Leader until 1 July 1978.

† These dates should be treated with caution. They are usually the date the commission to form a government was granted to the chief minister and do not necessarily correspond with election dates. See chapter 11 for discussion of the definition of 'period in office' and the Glossary entry for 'period in office' in the Australian Government and Politics website (http://elections.uwa.edu.au).

Source: Australian Government and Politics Project, University of Western Australia; more information can be found at the Project's website (http://elections.uwa.edu.au) under 'Government' and 'Glossary'.

References

Aimer, Peter. 1974. *Politics, Power and Persuasion: the Liberals in Victoria*, Melbourne: James Bennett.

Aitkin, Don. 1969. *The Colonel: A Political Biography of Sir Michael Bruxner*, Canberra: Australian National University Press.

Aitkin, Don. 1972. *The Country Party in New South Wales: A Study of Organisation and Survival*, Canberra: Australian National University Press.

Alaba, Richard. 1994. *Inside Bureaucratic Power: The Wilenski Review of NSW Government*, Sydney: Hale and Iremonger.

Alford, John & Deirdre O'Neil. 1994. *The Contract State: Public Management and the Kennett Government*, Geelong, Vic.: Centre for Applied Social Research, Deakin University.

Amos, Keith. 1976. *The New Guard Movement 1931–1935*, Carlton: Melbourne University Press.

Arklay, Tracey. 2000. Reinterpreting Electoral Relations between the Queensland Coalition Parties, Brisbane: unpublished BCom (Hons) thesis, Griffith University.

Armitage, Liz. 2000. 'More MLAs: Good Idea but Bad Politics', *Canberra Times*, 19 August.

Armstrong, Hugo. 1992. 'The Tricontinental Affair', in Mark Considine & Brian Costar (eds), *Trials in Power: Cain, Kirner and Victoria 1982–1992*, Carlton: Melbourne University Press.

Atkins, Ruth. 1978. *The Government of the Australian Capital Territory*, St Lucia: University of Queensland Press.

Australian Bureau of Statistics (ABS). 1999a. *1999 Year Book Australia, No. 81*, Canberra.

Australian Bureau of Statistics (ABS). 1999b. *South Australian Year Book No. 32: 1999*, Adelaide.

Australian Bureau of Statistics (ABS). 2000a. *Australian Capital Territory in Focus*, Canberra.

Australian Bureau of Statistics (ABS). 2000b. *Australian Social Trends 2000 Population – State Summary Tables*, Canberra.

Australian Bureau of Statistics (ABS). 2001a. *Australian National Accounts: State Accounts*, Canberra.

Australian Bureau of Statistics (ABS). 2001b. *Labour: Characteristics of Employment*, Canberra.

Australian Bureau of Statistics (ABS). 2001c. *Wage and Salary Earners, Australia*, Canberra.

Australian Bureau of Statistics (ABS). 2002. *Wage and Salary Earners Australia*, Canberra.

Bacchi, Carol. 1986. 'The Woman Question', in Eric Richards (ed.), *The Flinders History of South Australia*, vol. 1, *Social History*, Adelaide: Wakefield Press.

Badcock, Blair. 1989. 'The Role of Housing Expenditure in State Development;

South Australia, 1936–88', *International Journal of Urban and Regional Research*, 13: 438–61.

Bannon, John. 1994. *The Crucial Colony: South Australia's Role in Reviving Federation, 1891–97*, Canberra: Federalism Research Centre.

Barnett, David. 1999. 'Tasmania's Green Disease', *Institute of Public Affairs Review*, 51(1): 3–5.

Beilharz, Peter. 1994. *Transforming Labor: Labor Tradition and the Labor Decade in Australia*, Cambridge: Cambridge University Press.

Bennett, Scott. 1986. 'Tasmanian Labor under Attack 1947–1948', *Tasmanian Historical Research Association*, 33(1): 67–81.

Bennett, Scott. 1992. *Affairs of State: Politics in the Australian States and Territories*, North Sydney: Allen & Unwin.

Bennett, Scott. 1997. 'The Australian Capital Territory', in Clive Bean et al. (eds), *The Politics of Retribution: The 1996 Federal Election*, St Leonards, NSW: Allen & Unwin.

Bennett, Scott. 2000a. 'Government in the ACT: A Shift from "Westminster"?', Canberra: Commonwealth Parliamentary Library.

Bennett, Scott. 2000b. *The End of the Carnell Government in the ACT*, Canberra: Commonwealth Parliamentary Library.

Bennett, Scott. 2001. '1976', in Hogan & Clune 2001, vol. 3.

Bennett, Scott & Gerard Newman. 2001. *Queensland Election 2001*, Canberra: Commonwealth Parliamentary Library.

Besant, Christopher W. 1990. 'Two Nations, Two Destinies: A Reflection on the Significance of the Western Australian Secession Movement to Australia, Canada and the British Empire', *Western Australia Law Review*, 20(2) special issue, 209–310.

Birrell, Mark (ed.). 1987. *The Australian States: Towards a Renaissance*, Melbourne: Longman Cheshire.

Birtles, Terry. 2000. 'The Australian Capital Region: "Free Form" Operation or a Grass Roots Anomaly?', in Halligan & Wettenhall 2000.

Black, David. 1979. 'The Liberal Party and Its Predecessors', in Pervan & Sharman 1979, 191–232.

Black, David. 1991a. 'Factionalism and Stability, 1911–1947', in Black 1991b, 153–84.

Black, David (ed.). 1991b. *The House on the Hill: A History of the Parliament of Western Australia 1832–1990*, Perth: Parliament of Western Australia.

Blainey, Geoffrey. 1974. *The Tyranny of Distance: How Distance Shaped Australia's History*, Melbourne: Macmillan.

Blazey, Peter. 1990. *Bolte: A Political Biography*, new edn, Mandarin: Melbourne.

Blewett, Neal. 1973. 'Redistribution Procedures', in Henry Mayer & Helen Nelson (eds), *Australian Politics: A Third Reader*, Melbourne: Cheshire.

Blewett, Neal & Dean Jaensch. 1971. *Playford to Dunstan: The Politics of Transition*, Melbourne: Cheshire.

Bolton, Geoffrey. 1981. 'Black and White after 1897', in C T Stannage (ed.), *A New History of Western Australia*, Perth: University of Western Australia Press.

Bolton, Geoffrey. 1989. 'Perth: A Foundling City', in Statham 1989a.

Bolton, Geoffrey. 2000. *Edmund Barton*, St Leonards, NSW: Allen & Unwin.

Bongiorno, Frank. (2001) 'The Origins of Caucus 1856–1901', in John Faulkner & Stuart Macintyre (eds), *True Believers: The Story of the Federal Parliamentary Labor Party*, Sydney: Allen & Unwin, 3–16.

Boyce, Peter. 1991. 'Governor and Parliament', in Black 1991b.

Bulbeck, Chilla. 1987. 'The Hegemony of Queensland's Difference', *Journal of Australian Studies*, 21: 19–28.

Butler, David. 1968. 'The Electoral Advantage of Being in Power', *Politics*, 3(1): 16–20.

Buxton, Jeremy. 1979. 'Electoral Politics Past and Present in Western Australia', in Pervan & Sharman 1979.

Cain, John. 1995. *John Cain's Years: Power, Parties and Politics*, Carlton: Melbourne University Press.

Campbell, Eric. 1965. *The Rallying Point: My Story of the New Guard*, Carlton: Melbourne University Press.

Canberra Times. 2000. 'A Case for a Bigger Assembly', Editorial, 2 February.

Capling, Ann, Mark Considine & Michael Crozier. 1998. *Australian Politics in the Global Era*, Melbourne: Addison Wesley Longman.

Carnell, Kate. 1999. 'A Test of Maturity', in John Uhr (ed.), *The Australian Republic: The Case for Yes*, Leichhardt, NSW: Federation Press.

Carnell, Kate. 2000a. 'ACT Governance and the Australian Capital Region', in Halligan & Wettenhall 2000a.

Carnell, Kate. 2000b. 'Chief Minister's Oration', in Halligan and Wettenhall 2000a.

Centenera, Jeff. 2000 'Postponement of Heroin-injection Trial a "Sad Day" for Reform', *Canberra Times*, 11 July.

Chaples, Ernie & Barbara Page. 1995. 'The New South Wales Independent Commission Against Corruption', in Martin Laffin & Martin Painter (eds), *Reform and Reversal: Lessons from the Coalition Government in New South Wales 1988–1995*, Melbourne: Macmillan.

Chaples, Ernie, Helen Nelson & Ken Turner (eds). 1985. *The Wran Model: Electoral Politics in New South Wales, 1981 and 1984*, Melbourne: Oxford University Press.

Chapman, Ralph. 1985. 'From Quill to Keyboard: The Tasmanian Government Administration in Transition', in Australian Bureau of Statistics, Tasmanian Office, *Tasmanian Yearbook* 19: 77–96.

Chapman, Ralph, Graham Smith, James Warden and Bruce Davis. 1986. 'Tasmania' in Brian Galligan (ed.), *Australian State Politics*, Melbourne: Longman Cheshire.

Charlton, Peter. 1983. *State of Mind: Why Queensland is Different*, North Ryde, NSW: Methuen-Haynes.

Clack, Peter. 2000. 'Carnell's Threat to Call Poll', *Canberra Sunday Times*, 2 July.

Clune, David. 1992. 'The Legislative Assembly of New South Wales: 1941 to 1991', *Legislative Studies*, 7(1): 13–24.

Clune, David. 2001a. '1947', in Hogan & Clune 2001.

Clune, David. 2001b. '1953', in Hogan & Clune 2001.

Clune, David & Ken Turner. 2001. '1973', in Hogan & Clune 2001.

Coaldrake, Peter. 1989. *Working the System: The Government of Queensland*, St Lucia: University of Queensland Press.

Cockburn, Stewart. 1991. *Playford: Benevolent Despot*, Kent Town, SA: Axiom.

Collins, Peter. 2000. *The Bear Pit: A Life in Politics*, St Leonards, NSW: Allen & Unwin.

Committee of Enquiry into Education in South Australia. 1971. *Report: Education in South Australia*, Adelaide: Government Printer.

Commonwealth Bureau of Census and Statistics (CBCS). 1908. *Official Year Book of the Commonwealth of Australia 1901–1907*, Melbourne.

Commonwealth Grants Commission. 1995. *Equality in Diversity: History of the Commonwealth Grants Commission*, 2nd edn, Canberra: Australian Government Publishing Service.

Commonwealth of Australia (Parliamentary Handbook). 1999. *Parliamentary Handbook of the Commonwealth of Australia*, 28th edn, Canberra.

Commonwealth Parliament, Joint Committee. 1974. *Constitutional Development in the Northern Territory: Report from the Joint Committee on the Northern Territory*, Canberra: Australian Government Publishing Service.

Commonwealth Parliament, Senate Select Committee on South West Tasmania. 1982. *Report on Demand and Supply of Electricity for Tasmania and Other Matters*. Canberra: Australian Government Publishing Service.

Commonwealth Parliamentary Library. 1998. *Against the Odds: The 1998 ACT Election*, Canberra.

Connell, Robert & Florence Gould. 1967. *Politics of the Extreme Right: Warringah 1966*, Sydney: Sydney University Press.

Considine, Mark & Brian Costar (eds). 1992. *Trials in Power: Cain, Kirner and Victoria 1982–1992*, Carlton: Melbourne University Press.

Coper, Michael. 1983. *The Franklin Dam Case: Commentary and Full Text of the Decision in Commonwealth of Australia v State of Tasmania*. Sydney: Butterworths.

Cosgrove, Kevin. 2001. '1927', in Hogan & Clune 2001.

Costar, Brian. 1985a. 'National–Liberal Party Relations in Victoria', in Hay, Halligan & Warhurst 1985.

Costar, Brian. 1985b. 'Victoria', in Costar & Woodward 1985.

Costar, Brian. 1990. 'The Merger Idea and Australia's Non-Labor Parties, 1917–1990', in Brian Costar & Scott Prasser (eds), *Amalgamate or Perish? The Future of Non-Labor Parties in Australia*, Toowoomba, Qld: School of Management, University College of Southern Queensland.

Costar, Brian. 1992. 'Constitutional Change', in Considine & Costar 1992.

Costar, Brian (ed.). 1994. *For Better or for Worse: The Federal Coalition*, Carlton: Melbourne University Press.

Costar, Brian. 1999. 'Coalition Government: An Unequal Partnership', in Costar & Economou 1999.

Costar, Brian & Nicholas Economou. 1992a. 'The 1992 Victorian Election: Emphatically Ending the Labor Decade', *Current Affairs Bulletin* 69: 27–31.

Costar, Brian & Nicholas Economou. 1992b. 'Elections and electoral change', in Considine & Costar 1992.

Costar, Brian & Nicholas Economou (eds). 1999. *The Kennett Revolution: Victorian Politics in the 1990s*, Sydney: University of New South Wales Press.

Costar, Brian & Colin A Hughes (eds). 1983. *Labor to Office: The Victorian State Election, 1982*, Blackburn, Vic: Drummond.

Costar, Brian & Dennis Woodward (eds). 1985. *Country to National: Australian Rural Politics and Beyond*, Sydney: Allen & Unwin.

Crocker, Walter. 1983. *Sir Thomas Playford: A Portrait*, Carlton: Melbourne University Press.

Crowley, F K. 1960. *Australia's Western Third*, London: Macmillan.

Cumming, F. 1991. *Mates: Five Champions of the Labor Right*, St Leonards, NSW: Allen & Unwin.

Cunneen, Christopher. 2000. *William John McKell: Boilermaker, Premier, Governor-General*, Sydney: University of New South Wales Press.

Cunneen, Christopher. 2001. '1944', in Hogan & Clune 2001.

Dale, Brian. 1985. *Ascent to Power: Wran and the Media*, St Leonards, NSW: Allen & Unwin.

Davis, Bruce. 1986. 'Tasmania: the Political Economy of a Peripheral State', in Brian Head (ed.), *The Politics of Development In Australia*, Sydney: Allen & Unwin.

Davis, Glyn. 1997. 'Executive Government: Cabinet and the Prime Minister', in Dennis Woodward, Andrew Parkin & John Summers (eds), *Government, Politics, Power and Policy in Australia*, 6th edn. Melbourne: Addison Wesley Longman.

Davis, Richard. 1981. 'Tasmanian Labor and the Trade Union Movement', *Tasmanian Historical Research Association* 28(2): 85–104.

Davis, S R. 1960. 'Diversity in Unity', in S R Davis (ed.), *The Government of the Australian States*, London: Longmans.

de Garis, Brian. 1974. '1890–1900', in F K Crowley (ed.), *A New History of Australia*, Melbourne: Heinemann.

de Garis, Brian. 1977. 'Western Australia', in Loveday, Martin & Parker 1977.

de Garis, Brian. 1991. 'Self-government and the Emergence of Political Parties, 1890–1911', in Black 1991b, 63–95.

de Garis, Brian. 1999. 'Western Australia', in Helen Irving (ed.), *The Centenary Companion to Australian Federation*, Cambridge: Cambridge University Press, 285–325.

DeGaris, Renfrey. 1976. 'Reappraisal of the "Functional Gerrymander"', unpublished typescript, Adelaide.

Dempsey, Robert J. 2001. '1968', in Hogan & Clune 2001.

Denemark, David & Campbell Sharman. 1994. 'Political Efficacy, Involvement and Trust: Testing for Regional Political Culture in Australia', *Australian Journal of Political Science*, 29 special issue, *Election '93*: 81–102.

Dickson, E I. 1999. *General Election for Legislative Assembly (52nd Parliament) 27 March, 1999: Statistical Return*, Sydney: Parliament of New South Wales.

Domberger, Simon & Christine Hall. 1996. 'Contracting for Public Services: A Review of Antipodean Experience', *Public Administration*, 74(1): 129–47.

Dunstan, Don. 1981. *Felicia: The Political Memoirs of Don Dunstan*, South Melbourne: Macmillan.

Dunstan, Don. 1998. '1998 Whitlam Lecture', delivered at the Entertainment Centre, Adelaide, 21 April.

Dunstan, Keith. 1968. *Wowsers; Being an Account of the Prudery Exhibited by Certain Outstanding Men and Women in Such Matters as Drinking, Smoking, Prostitution, Censorship and Gambling*, Sydney: Angus & Robertson.

Economou, Nicholas & Brian Costar. 1999. 'The Electoral Contest And Coalition Dominance', in Costar & Economou 1999.

Edgar, Suzanne & R F I Smith. 1979. 'Butler, Sir Richard Layton', in Bede Nairn & Geoffrey Serle (eds), *Australian Dictionary of Biography*, vol. 7, 1891–1939, Carlton: Melbourne University Press.

Edwards, John. 1996. *Keating: The Inside Story*, Ringwood, Vic: Viking.

Electoral and Administrative Review Commission [Queensland] (EARC). 1993. *Report on Consolidation and Review of the Queensland Constitution*, Brisbane.

Electoral Commission Queensland (ECQ). 1995. *Queensland's Electoral History*, Brisbane.

Electoral Commission Queensland (ECQ). 2002. *Queensland Election 2001: Ballot Paper Survey* (Research report 1/2002), Brisbane.

Electoral Council of Australia. 2002. 'Electoral Systems: New South Wales', http://www.eca.gov.au/systems/australia/by_area/nsw.htm.

Ellis, Ulrich R. 1933. *New Australian States*, Sydney: Endeavour Press.

Evans, John. 1997. 'State of Play in the NSW Legislative Council: Minorities in Upper Houses', *Legislative Studies*, 11(2): 46–50.

Evatt Research Centre. 1989. *State of Siege: Renewal or Privatisation for Australian State Public Services?*, Leichhardt, NSW: Pluto Press.

Evatt, Herbert V. 1979. *William Holman: Australian Labour Leader*, Sydney: Angus & Robertson.

Faulkner, John & Stuart Macintyre. 2001. *True Believers: The Story of the Federal Parliamentary Labor Party*, Crows Nest, NSW: Allen & Unwin.

Felmingham, Bruce. 1993. 'Recession and Minorities: The Tough Times in Tasmania', *Canberra Bulletin of Public Administration*, 73: 99–104.

Fitzgerald, Ross. 1982. *From the Dreaming to 1915: A History of Queensland*, St Lucia: University of Queensland Press.

Fitzgerald, Ross. 1984. *From 1915 to the Early 1980s: A History of Queensland*, St Lucia: University of Queensland Press.

Fitzgerald, Ross & Harold Thornton. 1989. *Labor in Queensland: From the 1880s to 1988*, St Lucia: University of Queensland Press.

Follett, Rosemary. 1992, 'Commonwealth – Territory Relations from an ACT Perspective', *Australian Journal of Public Administration*, 5(4): 405–9.

Follett, Rosemary. 1997. 'Minority Government in the Australian Capital Territory: the ALP Experience', *Legislative Studies*, 11(2): 51–6.

Foster, S G. 1976. 'The Concession of Responsible Government to New South Wales', in Legislative Council, Parliament of New South Wales, *New South Wales: Autocracy to Parliament, 1824–1856*, Sydney.

Freudenberg, Graham. 1987. *A Certain Grandeur: Gough Whitlam in Politics*, Ringwood, Vic: Penguin.

Freudenberg, Graham. 1991. *Cause for Power: The Official History of the New South Wales Branch of the Australian Labor Party*, Leichhardt, NSW: Pluto Press.

Galligan, Brian (ed.). 1986. *Australian State Politics*, Melbourne: Longman Cheshire.

Galligan, Brian. 1987. *Politics of the High Court: A Study of The Judicial Branch of Government in Australia*, St Lucia: University of Queensland Press.

Galligan, Brian (ed.). 1988. *Comparative State Politics*, Melbourne: Longman Cheshire.

Galligan, Brian (ed.). 1989. *Australian Federalism*, Melbourne: Longman Cheshire.

Galligan, Brian. 1991. 'Australia', in David Butler & D A Low (eds), *Sovereigns and Surrogates: Constitutional Heads of State in the Commonwealth*, Basingstoke: Macmillan.

Galligan, Brian. 1995. *A Federal Republic: Australia's Constitutional System of Government*, Cambridge: Cambridge University Press.

Galligan, Brian, Owen Hughes & Cliff Walsh (eds). 1991. *Intergovernmental Relations and Public Policy*, Sydney: Allen & Unwin.

Gallop, Geoffrey. 1986. 'Western Australia', in Galligan 1986, 74–97.

Gallop, Geoffrey & Lenore Layman. 1985. 'Western Australia', in Costar & Woodward 1985.

Gellatly, Colin. 1994. 'Reinventing Government in New South Wales', *Canberra Bulletin of Public Administration*, 77: 49–54.

Gerritsen, Rolph. 1988. 'State Budgetary Outcomes and Typologies of the Australian States', in Galligan 1988.

Glass, Margaret. 1997. *Charles Cameron Kingston: Federation Father*, Carlton: Melbourne University Press.

Gleeson, Michael, Toni Allan & Michael Wilkins. 1992. *An Act of Corruption?*, Sydney: ABC Books.

Gollan, Robin. 1960. *Radical and Working Class Politics : A Study of Eastern Australia, 1850–1910*, Carlton: Melbourne University Press

Goot, Murray. 1986. *Electoral Redistribution in Australia: A Comparative Analysis*, Sydney: New South Wales Parliamentary Library.

Gorjanicyn, Kate. 1992. 'Legislating Social Reform: Guns, Grog and Prostitution', in Considine & Costar, 1992.

Graham, Bruce. 1966. *The Formation of the Australian Country Parties*, Canberra: Australian National University Press.

Green, Antony. 1993. *NSW Elections 1984 to 1991: A Comparative Analysis*, Sydney: New South Wales Parliamentary Library.

Green, Antony. 1997. *Where Do You Draw the Line? Prospects for the 1997 New South Wales Redistribution*, Sydney: New South Wales Parliamentary Library.

Green, Antony. 1998. *1997/98 New South Wales Redistribution: Analysis of Final Boundaries*, Sydney: New South Wales Parliamentary Library.

Green, Antony. 1999. *New South Wales Elections 1999*, Sydney: New South Wales Parliamentary Library.

Green, Antony. 2001. '1991', in Hogan & Clune 2001.

Green, Antony. 2002. 'Players Still Queue for NSW's Most Exclusive Club', *Sydney Morning Herald*, 16 January.

Grundy, Philip, Bill Oakes, Lynne Reeder and Roger Wettenhall 1996. *Reluctant Democrats: The Transition to Self-Government in the Australian Capital Territory*, Fyshwyck, ACT: Federal Capital Press.

Hagan, Jim & Craig Clothier. 2001. '1988', in Hogan & Clune 2001.

Hagan, Jim & Ken Turner. 1991. *A History of the Labor Party in New South Wales: 1891–1991*, Melbourne: Longman Cheshire.

Hallam, Jack. 1983. *The Untold Story: Labor in Rural NSW*, Sydney: George Allen & Unwin.

Halligan, John. 2000. 'The ACT Model: An Analysis', in Halligan & Wettenhall 2000a.

Halligan, Jack & John Power. 1992. *Political Management in the 1990s*, Melbourne: Oxford University Press.

Halligan, John & Roger Wettenhall (eds). 2000a. *A Decade of Self-Government in the Australian Capital Territory*, Canberra: Centre for Research in Public Sector Management, University of Canberra.

Halligan, John & Roger Wettenhall. 2000b. 'Ten Years of Self-Government: Editors' Introduction', in Halligan and Wettenhall 2000a.

Hamill, David & Paul Reynolds. 1983. *Three-Cornered Contests in South East Queensland State Seats*, St Lucia: Department of Government, University of Queensland.

Hancock, Ian. 2000. *National and Permanent: The Federal Organisation of the Liberal Party of Australia 1944–1965*, Carlton: Melbourne University Press.

Hancock, Ian. 2002. *John Gorton: He Did It His Way*, Sydney: Hodder Headline Australia.

Harkness, Alistair. 1999. 'The Victorian Parliament: An Institution in Decline?', in Costar & Economou 1999.

Harman, Elizabeth & Brian Head (eds). 1982. *State, Capital and Resources in the North and West of Australia*, Perth: University of Western Australia Press.

Harris, Tony. 2000. 'Due Process Eluded Carnell', *Australian Financial Review*, 24 October.

Harwin, Don. 2001. '1971', in Hogan & Clune 2001.

Haward, Marcus & Graham Smith. 1990. 'The 1989 Tasmanian Election: The Green Independents Consolidate', *Australian Journal of Political Science* 25: 196–217.

Haward, Marcus & Peter Larmour (eds). 1993. *The Tasmanian Parliamentary Accord and Public Policy 1989–92: Accommodating The New Politics?*, Canberra: Federalism Research Centre, Australian National University.

Hawker, Geoffrey. 1971. *The Parliament of New South Wales 1856–1965*, Ultimo, NSW: Government Printer.

Hay, Peter, Ian Ward & John Warhurst (eds). 1979. *Anatomy of an Election*, Melbourne: Hill of Content.

Hay, Peter, John Halligan & John Warhurst (eds). 1985. *Essays on Victorian Politics*, Warrnambool, Vic: Warrnambool Institute Press.

Head, Brian. 1986a. 'Queensland Political Culture' in *Social Alternatives*, 5(4): 45–7.

Head, Brian. 1986b. 'Western Australia: The Pursuit of Growth', in Brian Head (ed.), *The Politics of Development in Australia*, Sydney: Allen & Unwin, 163–81.

Hearn, Mark & Harry Knowles. 1996. *One Big Union: A History of the Australian Workers' Union 1886–1994*, Cambridge: Cambridge University Press.

Heatley, Alistair J. 1979. *The Government of the Northern Territory*, St. Lucia: University of Queensland Press.

Heatley, Alistair J. 1981. 'Constitutional, Legislative and Political Developments', in Dean Jaensch & Peter Loveday (eds.) *Under One Flag: The 1980 Northern Territory Election*, Sydney: Allen & Unwin.

Heatley, Alistair J. 1990 *Almost Australians: The Politics Of Northern Territory Self-Government*, Darwin: North Australia Research Unit, Australian National University.

Hede, Andrew, Scott Prasser & Mark Neylan (eds). 1992. *Keeping Them Honest: Democratic Reform in Queensland*, St Lucia: University of Queensland Press.

Henderson, Gerard. 1998. *Menzies' Child: The Liberal Party of Australia, 1944–1994*, St Leonards, NSW: Allen & Unwin.

Herr, Richard & W J Hemmings. 1975. 'Accountability and Proportional Representation: The Tasmanian Case', *Politics*, 10: 216–20.

Hickie, David. 1985. *The Prince and the Premier: The Story of Perce Galea, Bob Askin and the Others Who Gave Organised Crime Its Start In Australia*, Sydney: Angus & Robertson.

Hiller, Harry. 1987. 'Secession in Western Australia: A Continuing Phenomenon?', *Australian Quarterly* 59(2): 222–33.

Hiller, Harry. 1989. 'Resources and Regional Rebellion: Western Australia and Western Canada', in Bruce W Hodgins et al. (eds), *Federalism in Canada and Australia: Historial Perspectives 1920–88*, Peterborough, Ontario: Trent University Press.

Hirst, John. 1988. *The Strange Birth of Colonial Democracy: New South Wales 1848–1884*, Sydney: Allen & Unwin.

Hirst, John. 1998. 'New South Wales', in Graeme Davison, John Hirst & Stuart Macintyre (eds), *The Oxford Companion to Australian History*, Melbourne: Oxford University Press.

Hogan, Michael. 2001a. '1901', in Hogan & Clune 2001.

Hogan, Michael. 2001b. '1904', in Hogan & Clune 2001.

Hogan, Michael. 2001c. '1907', in Hogan & Clune 2001.

Hogan, Michael. 2001d. '1910', in Hogan & Clune 2001.

Hogan, Michael. 2001e. '1913', in Hogan & Clune 2001.

Hogan, Michael. 2001f. '1917', in Hogan & Clune 2001.

Hogan, Michael. 2001g. '1920', in Hogan & Clune 2001.

Hogan, Michael & David Clune (eds). 2001. *The People's Choice: Electoral Politics in 20th Century New South Wales*, vol. 1–3, Sydney: Parliament of New South Wales and University of Sydney.

Holmes, Jean. 1976. *The Government of Victoria*, St Lucia: University of Queensland Press.

Holmes, Jean & Campbell Sharman. 1977. *The Australian Federal System*, Sydney: George Allen & Unwin.

Holton, R J. 1986. 'Twentieth Century South Australia: From a Patrician to a Plebian View', in Eric Richards (ed.), *The Flinders History of South Australia*, vol. 1, *Social History*, Adelaide: Wakefield Press.

Homeshaw, Judith. 2001. 'Tasmania: The Model Arithmetocracy' in Sawer 2001.

Howatt, George. 1958. *Democratic Representation under the Hare–Clark System: The Need for Seven-member Electorates*, Hobart: Tasmanian Government Printer.

Howell, P A. 1986. 'Constitutional and Political Development, 1857–1890', in Dean Jaensch (ed.), *The Flinders History of South Australia*, vol. 2, *Political History*, Adelaide: Wakefield Press.

Howell, P A. 1996. 'South Australia, Federalism and the 1890s: The Making of a Federation', in Andrew Parkin (ed.), *South Australia, Federalism and Public Policy: Essays Exploring the Impact of the Australian Federal System on Government and Public Policy in South Australia*, Canberra: Federalism Research Centre, Australian National University.

Hudson, Graham. 2000. 'Victoria: Factional Battles, Realignments and Renewal', in Warhurst & Parkin 2000.

Hughes, Colin A. 1969. *Images and Issues: The Queensland State Elections of 1963 and 1966*, Canberra: Australian National University Press.

Hughes, Colin A. 1977. *A Handbook of Australian Government and Politics 1965–1974*, Canberra: Australian National University Press.

Hughes, Colin A. 1980. *The Government of Queensland*, St Lucia: University of Queensland Press.

Hughes, Colin A. 1984. 'The Proliferation of Portfolios', *Australian Journal of Public Administration*, 43(3): 257–74.

Hughes, Colin A & B D Graham. 1968. *A Handbook of Australian Government and Politics 1890–1964*, Canberra: Australian National University Press.

Hughes, David. 1998, 'Australian Capital Territory, January to June 1998', *Australian Journal of Politics and History*, 44(4): 623–9.

Hughes, Owen. 1998. *Australian Politics*, 3rd edn, Melbourne: Macmillan Education.

Hull, Crispin, 2000. 'If Budget is Defeated, First Task is to Elect New Chief Minister', *Canberra Times*, 29 June.

Hunt, Arnold D. 1990. 'Verran, John', in John Ritchie (ed.), *Australian Dictionary of Biography*, vol. 12, 1891–1939, Carlton: Melbourne University Press.

Hutchings, Alan & Raymond Bunker (eds). 1986. *With Conscious Purpose: A History of Town Planning in South Australia*, Netley, SA: Wakefield Press.

Interim Committee for the Australian Schools Commission. 1973. *Report: Schools in Australia*, Canberra: Australian Government Publishing Service.

Jackman, Simon. 1992. 'Split Parties Finish Last: Preferences, Pluralities and the 1957 Queensland Election', *Australian Journal of Political Science*, 27(3): 434–48.

Jaensch, Dean. 1971. 'Under-Representation and the "Gerrymander" in the Playford Era', *Australian Journal of Politics and History*, 17: 82–95.

Jaensch, Dean. 1977. *The Government of South Australia*, St Lucia: University of Queensland Press.

Jaensch, Dean. 1981. 'Electoral Reform', in Parkin & Patience 1981.

Jaensch, Dean. 1986. 'Parliament and Government', in Dean Jaensch (ed.), *The Flinders History of South Australia*, vol. 2, *Political History*, Adelaide: Wakefield Press.

Jaensch, Dean. 1994. *Power Politics: Australia's Party System*, 3rd edn, St Leonards, NSW: Allen & Unwin.

Jaensch, Dean. 1990. *The Legislative Council of the Northern Territory: An Electoral History 1947–74*, Darwin: North Australian Research Unit, Australian National University.

Jaensch, Dean & Deborah Wade-Marshall. 1994. *Point of Order: The Legislative Assembly of the Northern Territory, 1974–1994*, Darwin: Legislative Assembly of the Northern Territory and the North Australia Research Unit, Australian National University.

Johns, Gary. 1999. 'Party Democracy: An Audit of Australian Parties', *Australian Journal of Political Science*, 35: 401–25.

Johnston, Peter W. 1989. 'The Repeal of Section 70 of the Western Australian Constitution Act 1889: Aborigines and Governmental Breach of Trust', *University of Western Australia Law Review* 19: 318–51.

Joyce, R B. 1978. 'George Ferguson Bowen and Robert George Wyndham Herbert: the Imported Openers', in Denis Murphy & R B Joyce (eds),

Queensland Political Portraits: 1859–1952, St Lucia: University Queensland Press.

Juddery, Bruce. 1983. 'Australian Capital Territory: Social Democrats', in Parkin & Warhurst 1983.

Juddery, Bruce. 1989. 'Self-Government for the Australian Capital Territory', *Australian Journal of Public Administration,* 48(4): 411–21.

Jupp, James. 1983. 'Victoria: Left, Right and Centre', in Parkin & Warhurst 1983.

Keating, Michael & John Wanna. 2000. 'Remaking Federalism?', in Michael Keating, John Wanna & Patrick Weller (eds), *Institutions on the Edge?: Capacity For Governance,* St Leonards, NSW: Allen & Unwin.

Kelly, Paul. 1992. *The End of Certainty: The Story of the 1980s,* St Leonards, NSW: Allen & Unwin.

Kelly, Paul. 1995. *November 1975: The Inside Story of Australia's Greatest Political Crisis,* St Leonards, NSW: Allen & Unwin.

Kennedy, K H. 1978. *The Mungana Affair: State Mining and Political Corruption in the 1920s,* St Lucia: University of Queensland Press.

Kenny, Chris. 1993. *State of Denial,* Kent Town, SA: Wakefield Press.

Kerr, M J. 1993. 'The Role of Parliamentary Committees in Serving the Public Interest: The New South Wales Experience', *Legislative Studies,* 8(1): 20–3.

Killey, Ian D. 1991. 'Tasmania, a New Convention? Comment on whether the actions of the Governor of Tasmania, Sir Phillip Bennett, in dissolving the Tasmanian Parliament in 1989 and appointing the Field Government were in accordance with constitutional conventions and practice', *Public Law Review,* 2(4): 221–7.

Kirschbaum, Miko. 2000. 'We need more MLAs', *Canberra Times,* 12 August.

Laakso, Markku & Rein Taagepera. 1979. ' "Effective" Number of Parties: A Measure with Application to Western Europe', *Comparative Political Studies,* 12: 3–27.

La Nauze, J A. 1972. *The Making of the Australian Constitution,* Carlton: Melbourne University Press.

La Nauze, J A. 1979. *Alfred Deakin: A Biography,* Sydney: Angus & Robertson.

Lack, Clem. 1962. *Three Decades of Queensland Political History: 1929–1960,* Brisbane: Government Printer.

Laffin, Martin. 1995. 'The Public Service', in Martin Laffin & Martin Painter (eds), *Reform and Reversal: Lessons from the Coalition Government in New South Wales 1988–1995,* Melbourne: Macmillan.

Layman, Lenore. 1979. 'The Country Party: Rise and Decline', in Pervan & Sharman 1979.

Leigh, Andrew. 2000. 'Factions and Fractions: A Case Study of Power Politics in the Australian Labor Party', *Australian Journal of Political Science,* 35(3): 427–48.

Lindell, Geoffrey. 1992. 'The Arrangements for Self-government for the Australian Capital Territory: A Partial Road to Republicanism in the Seat of Government?', *Public Law Review,* 3(1): 5–32.

Lloyd, Clem. 1989. 'Honest Graft: Aspects of Queensland's Fitzgerald Report', *Politics*, 24(2): 125–33.

Loveday, Peter & Allan Martin. 1966. *Parliament, Factions and Parties: The First Thirty Years of Responsible Government in New South Wales, 1856–1889*, Carlton: Melbourne University Press.

Loveday, Peter, Allan Martin & Robert Parker (eds). 1977a. *The Emergence of the Australian Party System*, Sydney: Hale & Iremonger.

Loveday, Peter, Allan Martin & Patrick Weller. 1977b. 'New South Wales', in Loveday, Martin & Parker 1977a.

Lowi, Theodore. 1964. 'American Business, Public Policy, Case Studies and Political Theory', *World Politics*, 16: 677–715.

Lucy, Richard. 1985a. 'New South Wales', in Costar & Woodward 1985.

Lucy, Richard. 1985b. 'The National Country Party', in Chaples et al. 1985.

Lumb, R D. 1977. *The Constitutions of the Australian States*, 4th edn, St Lucia: University of Queensland Press.

Lunn, Hugh. 1987. *Joh: The Life and Political Adventures of Johannes Bjelke-Petersen*, 2nd edn, St Lucia: University of Queensland Press.

Lusztig, Michael, Patrick James & Jeremy Moon. 1997. 'Falling From Grace: Non-Established Brokerage Parties and the Weight of Predominance', *Publius*, 27: 59–82.

Mackerras, Malcolm. 1973. *New South Wales Elections*, Canberra: Department of Political Science, Research School of Social Sciences, Australian National University.

Mackerras, Malcolm. 1985. 'The 1981 Election and Referendum Results', in Chaples et al. 1985.

Mackerras, Malcolm. 1990. 'A Revisionist Interpretation of the Impact of Queensland's Electoral System', *Australian Journal of Political Science*, 25(2): 339–49.

Maddox, Graham. 1989. *The Hawke Government and Labor Tradition*, Ringwood, Vic: Penguin.

Main, James. 1986. 'The Foundation of South Australia', in Dean Jaensch (ed.), *The Flinders History of South Australia*, vol. 2, *Political History*, Adelaide: Wakefield Press.

Markey, Ray. 1988. *The Making of the Labor Party in New South Wales, 1891–1900*, Kensington, NSW: New South Wales University Press.

Marsh, Ian. 1995. *Beyond the Two Party System: Political Representation, Economic Competitiveness, and Australian Politics*, Cambridge: Cambridge University Press.

Marshall, Vern. 1992. 'The Labor Party', in Parkin & Patience 1992.

Mathews, Russell L and W R C Jay. 1972. *Federal Finance: Intergovernmental Financial Relations in Australia Since Federation*, Melbourne: Nelson.

McAllister, Ian, Steve Dowrick & Riaz Hassan (eds). 2003. *The Cambridge Handbook of Social Sciences in Australia*, Cambridge: Cambridge University Press.

McGill, Maryanne. 1979. 'Barwell, Sir Henry Newman', in Bede Nairn &

Geoffrey Serle (eds), *Australian Dictionary of Biography*, vol. 7, 1891–1935, Carlton: Melbourne University Press.

McQueen, Humphrey. 1975. 'Victoria', in Denis Murphy (ed.), *Labor in Politics: The State Labor Parties in Australia, 1880–1920*, St Lucia: University of Queensland Press.

McRae, M D. 1956. 'The Tasmanian Labor Party and the Trade Unions 1903–1923', *Tasmanian Historical Research Association*, 51: 4–13.

Mitchell, Douglas. 1983. 'Western Australia: The Struggle to Adapt', in Parkin & Warhurst 1993.

Mitchell, T J. 1962. 'J.W. Wainwright: The Industrialisation of South Australia 1935–40', *Australian Journal of Politics and History*, 8(1): 27–40.

Moon, Jeremy. 1995. 'Minority Government in the Australian States: From Ersatz Majoritarianism to Minoritarianism', *Australian Journal of Political Science*, 31, special issue, 142–63.

Moon, Jeremy & Christine Fletcher. 1988. 'New Government and Policy Change in Western Australia 1983–1988: Did Mr Burke Make a Difference?', *Politics* 23: 78–89.

Moon, Jeremy & Anthony Sayers. 1999. 'The Dynamics of Governmental Activity: A Long-Run Analysis of the Changing Scope and Profile of Australian Ministerial Portfolios', *Australian Journal of Political Science*, 34(2): 149–67.

Morrison, Allan. 1960. 'The Government of Queensland', in S R Davis (ed.), *The Government of the Australian States*, London: Longmans.

Muirden, Bruce. 1978. *When Power Went Public – A Study in Expediency: The Nationalisation of the Adelaide Electric Supply Company*, Adelaide: Australasian Political Studies Association.

Mulgan, Richard G. 1995. 'The Australian Senate as a "House of Review"', *Australian Journal of Political Science*, 31: 191–204.

Mullins, Patrick. 1986. 'Queensland: Populist Politics and Development', in Brian Head (ed.), *The Politics of Development in Australia*, Sydney: Allen & Unwin.

Murphy, Denis & R B Joyce. 1978. 'Introduction: The Politics of Queensland', in Denis Murphy & R B Joyce (eds), *Queensland Political Portraits: 1859–1952*, St Lucia: University Queensland Press.

Murray, Robert. 1972. *The Split: Australian Labor in the Fifties*, 2nd edn, Melbourne: Cheshire.

Murray, Robert & Kate White. 1992. *The Fall of the House of Cain*, Melbourne: Spectrum.

Nairn, Bede. 1986. *The 'Big Fella': Jack Lang and the Australian Labor Party 1891–1949*, Carlton: Melbourne University Press.

Nelson, Helen. 1977. 'Legislative Record, 1925–27. How Radical?', in Heather Radi & Peter Spearritt (eds), *Jack Lang*, Sydney: Hale & Iremonger.

Nelson, Helen. 1985. 'Policy Innovation in the Australian States', *Politics*, 20(2): 77–88.

Nelson, Helen. 1988. 'Legislative Outputs', in Galligan 1988.

Nethercote, J R. (ed.). 2001. *Liberalism and the Australian Federation Sydney*, Sydney: Federation Press, 287–302.

Newman, Gerard. 1998. A*gainst the Odds: The 1998 ACT Election*, Canberra: Commonwealth Parliamentary Library

Newman, Terry. 1985. 'Tasmania Rejects a Smaller Parliament: Notes on Constitutional and Political Matters', *Parliamentarian*, 66(2): 77–9.

Newman, Terry. 1992. *Hare–Clark in Tasmania: Representation of All Opinions*, Hobart: Joint Library Committee of the Parliament of Tasmania.

New South Wales Premier's Department. 2000. *NSW Public Sector Workforce Profile: Agency Staffing Levels*, Sydney.

New South Wales Treasury. 1999. *Golden Heritage*, Sydney: Office of Financial Management, New South Wales Treasury.

New South Wales Treasury. 2001. *2001–2002 Budget Papers*, Sydney.

Nile, Fred. 2001. *Fred Nile: An Autobiography*, Sydney: Strand Publishing.

Nixon, Peter. 1997. *Tasmania into the 21st century: Report to the Prime Minister of Australia and the Premier of Tasmania*, Hobart: Commonwealth State Inquiry into the Tasmanian Economy.

O'Rourke, P J. 1998. *Eat the Rich: A Treatise on Economics*, Chippendale, NSW: Picador.

Okely, Bruce. 1991. 'Parliament at Work', in Black 1991b, 19–34.

Orchard, Lionel. 1999. 'Housing Policy', in John Spoehr (ed.), *Beyond the Contract State: Ideas for Social and Economic Renewal in South Australia*, Kent Town: Wakefield Press.

Page, Barbara. 1990. *The Legislative Council of New South Wales: Past, Present and Future*, Sydney: New South Wales Parliamentary Library.

Page, Barbara. 1991. 'Developments in the Legislative Council of New South Wales Since 1978', *Legislative Studies*, 5(2): 23–31.

Painter, Martin. 1987. *Steering the Modern State: Changes in Central Coordination in Three Australian State Governments*, Sydney: University of Sydney Press.

Painter, Martin. 1995. 'Microeconomic Reform and the Public Sector', in Martin Laffin and Martin Painter (eds), *Reform and Reversal: Lessons from the Coalition Government in New South Wales 1988–1995*, Melbourne: Macmillan.

Painter, Martin. 1998. *Collaborative Federalism: Economic Reform in Australia in the 1990s*, Cambridge: Cambridge University Press.

Parker, Robert. 1978. *The Government of New South Wales*, St Lucia: University of Queensland Press.

Parker, Robert. 1981. 'Public Service Neutrality – A Moral Problem: The Creighton Case', in Sol Encel, Peter Wilenski & Bernard Schaffer (eds), *Decisions: Case Studies in Australian Public Policy*, Melbourne: Longman Cheshire.

Parkin, Andrew. 1981. 'The Dunstan Governments: A Political Synopsis', in Parkin & Patience 1981.

Parkin, Andrew. 1992. 'The Bannon Decade: Restraint with Integrity', in Parkin & Patience 1992.

Parkin, Andrew. 1996a. 'The Significance of Federalism: A South Australian Perspective', in Andrew Parkin (ed.), *South Australia, Federalism and Public Policy: Essays Exploring the Impact of the Australian Federal System on Government and Public Policy in South Australia*, Canberra: Federalism Research Centre, Australian National University.

Parkin, Andrew. 1996b. 'South Australia, Federalism and the 1990s: From Co-operative to Competitive Reform', in Andrew Parkin (ed.), *South Australia, Federalism and Public Policy: Essays Exploring the Impact of the Australian Federal System on Government and Public Policy in South Australia*, Canberra: Federalism Research Centre, Australian National University.

Parkin, Andrew. 1997. 'South Australia: July to December 1996', *Australian Journal of Politics and History*, 43(2): 239–44.

Parkin, Andrew & Allan Patience (eds). 1981. *The Dunstan Decade: Social Democracy at the State Level*, Melbourne: Longman Cheshire.

Parkin, Andrew & Allan Patience (eds). 1992. *The Bannon Decade: The Politics of Restraint in South Australia*, St Leonards, NSW: Allen & Unwin.

Parkin, Andrew & Cedric Pugh. 1981. 'Urban Policy and Metropolitan Adelaide', in Parkin & Patience 1981.

Parkin, Andrew & John Summers. 1996. 'The States, South Australia and the Australian Federal System', in Andrew Parkin (ed.), *South Australia, Federalism and Public Policy: Essays Exploring the Impact of the Australian Federal System on Government and Public Policy in South Australia*, Canberra: Federalism Research Centre, Australian National University.

Parkin, Andrew & John Warhurst (eds). 1983. *Machine Politics in the Australian Labor Party*, Sydney: George Allen & Unwin.

Parkin, Andrew & Vern Marshall. 1992. 'Federal Relations', in Parkin & Patience 1992.

Parkin, Andrew & Vern Marshall. 1994. 'Frustrated, Reconciled or Divided? The Australian Labor Party and Federalism', *Australian Journal of Political Science*, 29(1): 18–39.

Patapan, Haig. 2000. *Judging Democracy: The New Politics of the High Court of Australia*, Cambridge: Cambridge University Press.

Patience, Allan. 1992. 'The Bannon Decade: Preparation For What?', in Parkin & Patience 1992.

Pervan, Ralph & Douglas Mitchell. 1979. 'The Changing Nature of the Australian Labor Party', in Pervan & Sharman 1979.

Pervan, Ralph & Campbell Sharman (eds). 1979. *Essays on Western Australian Politics*, Perth: University of Western Australia Press.

Pettit, Philip. 1998. *Review of the Governance of the Australian Capital Territory*, Canberra: Publications and Public Communication for Chief Minister's Department.

Pettit, Philip. 2000. 'Three Problems with ACT Governance', in Halligan & Wettenhall 2000a.

Pike, Douglas. 1967. *Paradise of Dissent: South Australia 1829–1851*, 2nd edn, Cambridge: Cambridge University Press.

Playford, John. 1982. 'The "Playmander" Reassessed', *Quadrant*, vol. 26, 64–7.

Playford, John. 1986. 'The Adelaide Club and Politics', in Dean Jaensch (ed.), *The Flinders History of South Australia*, vol. 2, *Political History*, Adelaide: Wakefield Press.

Prasser, Scott, Rae Wear & J R Nethercote (eds). 1990. *Corruption and Reform: The Fitzgerald Vision*, St Lucia: University of Queensland Press.

Pugh's Almanac and Queensland Directory. 1859– . Brisbane.

Puplick, Christopher. 2001. '1965', in Hogan & Clune 2001.

Pusey, Michael. 1991. *Economic Rationalism in Canberra: A Nation-Building State Changes Its Mind*, Cambridge: Cambridge University Press.

Queensland Commission of Inquiry into Possible Illegal Activities and Associated Police Misconduct (Queensland Commission of Inquiry). 1989. *Report of a Commission of Inquiry pursuant to Orders in Council* [The Fitzgerald Report], Brisbane: Government Printer.

Radi, Heather. 1977. 'Lang's Legislative Councillors', in Heather Radi & Peter Spearritt (eds), *Jack Lang*, Sydney: Hale & Iremonger.

Rae, Douglas. 1971. *The Political Consequences of Electoral Laws*, New Haven: Yale University Press.

Rawson, D W. 1977. 'Victoria', in Loveday, Martin & Parker 1977a.

Reading, Geoffrey. 1989. *High Climbers: Askin and Others*, Sydney: John Ferguson.

Reid, Gordon S. 1979. 'Western Australia and the Federation', in Pervan & Sharman 1979.

Reid, Gordon S. 1981. 'Executive-Parliamentary Relationships', in Richard Herr & Peter Loveday (eds), *Small is Beautiful: Parliament in the Northern Territory*, Darwin: Australasian Study of Parliament Group and the North Australia Research Unit, Australian National University.

Reid, Gordon S & Martyn Forrest. 1989. *Australia's Commonwealth Parliament, 1901–1988: Ten Perspectives*, Carlton: Melbourne University Press.

Reid, R L, L C L Blair & K A F Sainsbury. 1960. 'The Government of South Australia', in S R Davis (ed.), *The Government of the Australian States*, London: Longmans.

Reynolds, Steven. 1998. 'Minority Government from the Other Side of the Fence: Policy Outcomes for the NSW Independents 1991–95 and the Tasmanian Greens 1989–1992', *Legislative Studies*, 13(1): 17–39.

Richards, Eric. 1986. 'South Australia Observed, 1836–1986', in Eric Richards (ed.), *The Flinders History of South Australia*, vol. 1, *Social History*, Adelaide: Wakefield Press.

Robinson, Geoffrey. 2001. '1932', in Hogan & Clune 2001.

Robson, Lloyd. 1983. *A History of Tasmania*, Melbourne: Oxford University Press.

Rose, Richard. 1976. 'On the Priorities of Government: A Developmental Analysis of Public Policies', *European Journal of Political Research*, 4: 247–89.

Rothwell, Nicholas. 1997. 'Lost Island: Tasmania is Struggling to Survive in the Face Of Shrinking Incomes, Population, Employment and Options', *The Australian*, 26–27 April, Weekend Review.

Rubenstein, Colin. 1999. 'Kennett's Multicultural Victoria', in Costar & Economou 1999.

Rydon, Joan. 1968. '"Malapportionment" Australian Style', *Politics*, 3(2): 133–47.

Rydon, Joan. 1976. 'The Electoral System', in Henry Mayer & Helen Nelson (eds), *Australian Politics: A Fourth Reader*, Melbourne: Longman Cheshire.

Santamaria, B A. 1997. *Santamaria: A Memoir*, rev. edn, Melbourne: Oxford University Press.

Sawer, Marian (ed.). 2001. *Elections Full, Free and Fair*, Sydney: Federation Press.

Sayers, Anthony. 2000. 'Western Australia: Picking up the Pieces', in Warhurst & Parkin 2000.

Sayers, Anthony. 2002. 'Regionalism, Political Parties and Parliamentary Politics in Canada and Australia', in Lisa Young & Keith Archer (eds), *Regionalism and Party Politics in Canada*, Don Mills, Ontario: Oxford University Press.

Sayers, Anthony & Jeremy Moon. 2002. 'State Government, Convergence and Partisanship: A Long-Run Analysis of Australian Ministerial Portfolios', *Canadian Journal of Political Science*, 35(3): 589–612.

Scott, Alistair & Stuart Young. 1994. *The Tasmanian Legislative Council as a House of Review: An Analysis of The Process of Review Of Legislation by the Legislative Council from July 1989 to December 1993*, Hobart: Department of the Premier and Cabinet.

Scott, Joanne, Ross Laurie, Bronwyn Stevens & Patrick Weller. 2001. *The Engine Room of Government: The Queensland Premier's Department 1859–2001*, St Lucia: University of Queensland Press.

Selway, Bradley. 1997. *The Constitution of South Australia*, Sydney: Federation Press.

Serle, Geoffrey. 1977. *The Golden Age: A History of the Colony of Victoria, 1851–1861*, Carlton: Melbourne University Press.

Sharman, Campbell. 1977a. 'Tasmania: the Politics of Brokerage', *Current Affairs Bulletin* 53: 15–23.

Sharman, Campbell. 1977b. 'The Australian Senate as a States House', *Politics* 12(2), 64–75.

Sharman, Campbell. 1988. 'The Study of the States', in Galligan 1988.

Sharman, Campbell. 1990. 'The Party Systems of the Australian States: Patterns of Partisan Competition', *Publius*, 20: 85–104.

Sharman, Campbell. 1991. 'The Constitution of Western Australia 1890 and 1990', in Black 1991b.

Sharman, Campbell (ed.). 1994a. *Parties and Federalism in Australia and*

Canada, Canberra: Federalism Research Centre, Australian National University.

Sharman, Campbell. 1994b. 'Discipline and Disharmony: Party and the Operation of the Australian Federal System', in Sharman 1994a.

Sharman, Campbell. 1997. 'Politics in the States', in Brian Galligan, Ian McAllister & John Ravenhill (eds), *New Developments in Australian Politics*, Melbourne: Macmillan.

Sharman, Campbell. 1999. 'The Representation of Small Parties and Independents in the Senate', *Australian Journal of Political Science*, 34: 353–61.

Sharman, Campbell. 2002. 'A Web-based Database on Australian Government and Politics (http://elections.uwa.edu.au)', *Australian Journal of Political Science*, 37(2): 347–51.

Sharman, Campbell & Narelle Miragliotta. 2000. 'Western Australia', in Simms & Warhurst 2000: 129–35.

Sharman, Campbell & Anthony Sayers. 1998. 'Swings and Roundabouts? Patterns of Voting for the Australian Labor Party at State and Commonwealth Lower House Elections, 1901–96', *Australian Journal of Political Science*, 33: 339–54.

Sharman, Campbell, Anthony Sayers & Narelle Miragliotta. 2002. 'Trading Party Preferences: The Australian Experience of Preferential Voting', *Electoral Studies*, 21(4): 543–60.

Sharman, Campbell, Graham Smith & Jeremy Moon. 1991. 'The Party System and Change of Regime: The Structure of Partisan Choice in Tasmania and Western Australia', *Australian Journal of Political Science*, 26: 409–28.

Sharman, Campbell & Jan Stuart. 1981. 'Patterns of State Voting in National Referendums', *Politics* 16: 261–70.

Simms, Marian. 2000. 'New South Wales: The Microcosm of a Nation', in Warhurst and Parkin 2000.

Simms, Marian & John Warhurst (eds). 2000. *Howard's Agenda: The 1998 Australian Election*, Brisbane: University of Queensland Press.

Smith, Graham. 1982. 'The 1982 Tasmanian Election', *Politics* 17: 121–7.

Smith, Graham, Richard Herr & Bruce Davis. 1980. 'Tasmanian Politics 1979: Elections, Factionalism and the Electoral Crisis', *Politics*, 18: 81–8.

Smith, Patricia. 1985. 'Queensland's Political Culture', in Allan Patience (ed.), *The Bejelke-Petersen Premiership 1968–1983: Issues in Public Policy*, Melbourne: Longman Cheshire.

Smith, Rodney. 1995. 'Parliament', in Martin Laffin & Martin Painter (eds), *Reform and Reversal: Lessons from the Coalition Government in New South Wales 1988–1995*, Melbourne: Macmillan.

Smith, Rodney. 1997 'The Australian Democrats in NSW Politics', in Warhurst 1997.

Smith, Rodney. 2001a. *Australian Political Culture*, Frenchs Forest, NSW: Pearson Education.

Smith, Rodney. 2001b. '1999', in Hogan & Clune 2001.

Smith, Tony. 2001. '1995', in Hogan & Clune 2001.

Spearritt, Peter. 1978. *Sydney Since the Twenties*, Sydney: Hale & Iremonger.

Statham, Pamela. 1989a. *The Origins of Australia's Capital Cities*, Cambridge: Cambridge University Press.

Statham, Pamela. 1989b. 'Patterns and Perspectives', in Statham 1989a.

Statham, Pamela. 1989c. 'Western Australia Becomes British', in Statham 1989a.

Stein, Robert & Margaret Stone. 1991. *Torrens Title*, Sydney: Butterworths.

Steketee, Mike. 1993. 'Party Interest versus Constituency Interest: The NSW Experience', *Legislative Studies*, 7(2): 28–32.

Steketee, Mike & Milton Cockburn. 1986. *Wran: An Unauthorised Biography*, Sydney: Allen & Unwin.

Stevens, Bron & John Wanna (eds). 1993. *The Goss Government: Promise and Performance of Labor in Queensland*, South Melbourne: Macmillan Education.

Stevenson, Garth. 1981. 'Western Alienation in Australia and Canada', in Larry Pratt & Garth Stevenson (eds), *Western Separatism: The Myths, Realities and Dangers*, Edmonton: Hurtig.

Stewart, David K. 1994. 'Comparing Party Systems in Canadian Provinces and Australian States', in Sharman 1994a.

Stock, Jenny T. 1991. 'The "Playmander" Revisited: The Significance of Cross-Voting in Estimating the Two-Party Vote in South Australia, 1943–1953', *Australian Journal of Political Science*, 26(2): 331–41.

Stock, Jenny T. 1992. 'The Australian Democrats', in Parkin & Patience 1992.

Stokes, Geoff. 1983. 'South Australia: Consensus Politics', in Parkin & Warhurst 1983.

Stokes, Geoff & Richard Cox. 1981. 'The Governing Party: The ALP and the Politics of Consensus', in Parkin & Patience 1981.

Stokes, Michael. 1996. 'A Tangled Web: Redistributing Electoral Boundaries For Tasmania's Legislative Council', *University of Tasmania Law Review*, 15(2): 143–95.

Stone, Bruce. 1993. 'Accountability Reform in Australia: The WA Inc Royal Commission in Context', *Australian Quarterly*, 65(2): 17–30.

Stone, Bruce, 1997. 'Taking "WA Inc" Seriously: An Analysis of the idea of its Application to West Australian Politics', *Australian Journal of Public Administration*, 56(1): 71–81.

Stone, Bruce. 1998. 'Size and Executive-Legislative Relations in Australian Parliaments', *Australian Journal of Political Science*, 33(1): 37–55.

Stone, Bruce. 2002. 'Bicameralism and Democracy: The Transformation of Australian State Upper Houses', *Australian Journal of Political Science*, 37(2): 267–81.

Stretton, Hugh. 1970. *Ideas for Australian Cities*, self-published, North Adelaide.

Stretton, Hugh. 1975. *Ideas for Australian Cities*, 2nd edn, Melbourne: Georgian House.

Stretton, Hugh. 1978. 'Obituary – A.M. Ramsay and the Conventional Wisdom', *Australian Quarterly*, 50(3): 90–100.

Summers, John. 1981. 'Aboriginal Policy', in Parkin & Patience 1981.

Summers, John & Andrew Parkin. 2000. 'South Australia: Declining Fortunes and a "New Machine"', in Warhurst & Parkin 2000.

Tasmania. 1984. *Report of the Advisory Committee on the Proposed Reduction in the Number of Members Elected to Both Houses of the Tasmanian Parliament to the Premier the Honourable Robin Trevor Gray, MHA*, Hobart: Government Printer.

Tasmania. 1994. *Report of the Board of Inquiry into the Size and Constitution of the Tasmanian Parliament* [The Morling Inquiry]. Hobart: Government Printer.

Thompson, Elaine. 1985. 'The New South Wales Parliament, 1978–81', in Chaples et al. 1985.

Thompson, F K M. 1980. 'Staffing a Small Legislature: The Legislative Assembly of the Northern Territory of Australia, *The Parliamentarian*, 61: 256–8.

Townsley, W A. 1956. 'The Parliament, House of Assembly, Legislative Council: Constitutional Conflicts between the Houses', in F C Green (ed.), *A Century of Responsible Government, 1856–1956*, Hobart: Government Printer.

Townsley, W A. 1976. *The Government of Tasmania*. St Lucia: University of Queensland Press.

Townsley, W A. 1991. *Tasmania: From Colony to Statehood 1803–1945*, Hobart: St David's Park Publishing.

Turner, Ken. 1969. *House of Review? The New South Wales Legislative Council, 1934–68*, Sydney: Sydney University Press.

Turner, Ken. 1985a. 'New South Wales: A Labor State?', in Chaples et al. 1985.

Turner, Ken. 1985b. 'The New Rules of the Game', in Chaples et al. 1985.

Turner, Ken. 1985c. 'Back to a Contest: 1981–84', in Chaples et al. 1985.

Turner, Ken. 2001a. '1981', in Hogan & Clune 2001.

Turner, Ken. 2001b. '1984', in Hogan & Clune 2001.

Victorian Parliament, Federal–State Relations Committee. 1998. *Report on Australian Federalism: The Role of the States*, Mebourne: Government Printer.

Walker, F W. 1986. *A Short History of the Legislative Council for the Northern Territory*, Darwin: Government Printer.

Wanna, John. 2001. 'A Conservative Debacle: the Electoral Rout in Queensland 2001', *Australian Parliamentary Review*, 16(1): 34–44.

Ward, John. 1976. 'The "Blended" Legislative Council in New South Wales', in Legislative Council, Parliament of New South Wales, *New South Wales – Autocracy to Parliament, 1824–1856*, Sydney.

Ward, John. 1977. 'The Dismissal', in Heather Radi & Peter Spearritt (eds), *Jack Lang*, Sydney: Hale & Iremonger.

Warhurst, John. 1997. *Keeping the Bastards Honest: The Australian Democrats' First Twenty Years*, St Leonards, NSW: Allen & Unwin.

Warhurst, John. 2000. 'Australian Capital Territory: Diminished Capital', in Warhurst & Parkin 2000.

Warhurst, John & Andrew Parkin (eds). 2000. *The Machine: Labor Confronts the Future*, St Leonards, NSW: Allen & Unwin.

Watson, Lex. 1979. 'The United Australia Party and Its Sponsors', in Cameron Hazlehurst (ed.), *Australian Conservatism: Essays in Twentieth Century Political History*, Canberra: Australian National University Press.

Webber, Michael & Mary Crooks (eds). 1996. *Putting the People Last: Government, Services and Rights in Victoria*, South Melbourne: Hyland House.

Weeks, Steven. 1988. 'Price, Thomas', in Geoffrey Serle (ed.), *Australian Dictionary of Biography*, volume 11, 1891–1939, Carlton: Melbourne University Press.

Weller, Patrick. 1977. 'Tasmania', in Loveday, Martin & Parker 1977a.

Weller, Patrick. 1989. *Malcolm Fraser, PM. A Study in Prime Ministerial Power*, Ringwood Vic: Penguin.

Weller, Patrick. 2001a. 'Ministerial Codes, Cabinet Rules, and the Power of Prime Ministers', in Jenny Fleming & Ian Holland (eds), *Motivating Ministers to Morality*, Aldershot, UK: Ashgate.

Weller, Patrick. 2001b. *Australia's Mandarins: The Frank and the Fearless?*, Crows Nest, NSW: Allen & Unwin.

Weller, Patrick & Will Sanders. 1982. *The Team at the Top: Ministers in the Northern Territory*, Darwin: North Australian Research Unit, Australian National University.

West, Katherine. 1965. *Power in the Liberal Party: A Study in Australian Politics*, Melbourne: Cheshire.

Western Australia, Royal Commission into Commercial Activities of Government and Other Matters (WA Inc Royal Commission). 1992. *Report*, Perth.

Western Australia, Royal Commission into Parliamentary Deadlocks (WARCPD). 1985. *Report*, Perth.

Western Australia. 1934. *The Case of the People of Western Australia in Support of their Desire to Withdraw from the Commonwealth of Australia ...*, Perth.

Western Australian Commission on Government (WACOG). 1995. *Report No.1*, Perth: Western Australian Commission on Government.

Western Australian Commission on Government (WACOG). 1996. *Report No.5*, Perth: Western Australian Commission on Government.

Western Australian Constitutional Committee (WACC). 1995. *The Report of the Western Australian Constitutional Committee*, Perth.

Wettenhall, Roger. 1998a. 'Governing the ACT as a Small Quasi-State', *Canberra Bulletin of Public Administration*, 87: 8–20.

Wettenhall, Roger. 1998b. 'Towards a Canberra Model: The Pettit Report and Government Change in the ACT', *Canberra Bulletin of Public Administration*, 90: 91.

Wettenhall, Roger. 1998c. 'The External Relations of a Small Quasi-State Within a Federal System: The Case of the Australian Capital Territory', *Public Administration and Development*, 18(2): 123–39.

Wheelwright, Ted. 1983. 'New South Wales: The Dominant Right', in Parkin & Warhurst 1983.

White, Kate. 1982. *John Cain and Victorian Labor, 1917–1957*, Sydney: Hale & Iremonger.

White, Paul. 1985. 'Wran: Our Do-Nothing Man?', in Chaples et al. 1985.

Williams, George & Geraldine Chin. 2000. 'The Failure of Citizens' Initiated Referenda Proposals in Australia: New Directions for Popular Participation?', *Australian Journal Of Political Science*, 35(1): 27–48.

Woodward, Dennis & Brian Costar. 2000. 'The Victorian Election of 18 September 1999: Another Case of Electoral Volatility?', *Australian Journal of Political Science*, 35(1), 125–34.

Wright, Raymond. 1992. *A People's Counsel : A History of the Parliament of Victoria, 1856–1990*, South Melbourne: Oxford University Press.

Young, Liz. 1999. 'Minor Parties and the Legislative Process in the Australian Senate: A Study of the 1993 Budget', *Australian Journal of Political Science*, 34(1): 7–27.

Young, Maxine. 1987. 'The British Administration of New South Wales, 1786–1812', in John J Eddy & J R Nethercote (eds), *From Colony to Coloniser: Studies in Australian Administrative History*, Sydney: Hale & Iremonger.

Index